NATURAL SCIENCES IN AMERICA

NATURAL SCIENCES IN AMERICA

Advisory Editor
KEIR B. STERLING

Editorial Board
EDWIN H. COLBERT
EDWARD GRUSON
ERNST MAYR
RICHARD G. VAN GELDER

FAUNA AMERICANA

Introduction by
Keir B. Sterling

ARNO PRESS
A New York Times Company
New York, N. Y. • 1974

Reprint Edition 1974 by Arno Press Inc.

Reprinted from copies in The American
Museum of Natural History and the
University of Illinois Libraries

NATURAL SCIENCES IN AMERICA
ISBN for complete set: 0-405-05700-8
See last pages of this volume for titles.

Manufactured in the United States of America

Publisher's Note: The articles in this
compilation have been reprinted from the
best available copies.

————————◆————————

Library of Congress Cataloging in Publication Data

Main entry under title:

Fauna Americana.

    (Natural sciences in America)
    CONTENTS: Harlan, R. Fauna Americana, being a
description of the mammiferous animals inhabiting
North America.--Godman, J. D. Natural history and
Remarks on an article in the North American review.--
Godman, J. D. Review of Fauna Americana. [etc.]
    . 1. Harlan, Richard, 1796-1843. II. Godman,
John Davidson, 1794-1830. III. Series.
QL715.F38   599'.09'7   73-17819
ISBN 0-405-05735-0

CONTENTS

INTRODUCTION

Richard Harlan (1796-1843), the author of *Fauna Americana,* and his bitter rival John Davidson Godman (1794-1830) were both physician naturalists and important members of the "Philadelphia School" of early 19th century American zoologists. Both were affiliated with the important scientific institutions of their day in that city, including Charles Willson Peale's famous Philadelphia Museum, the American Philosophical Society, and the Academy of Natural Sciences.

Born in Philadelphia, Harlan was a graduate of the University of Pennsylvania Medical School in 1818, and had already travelled to India as a ship's surgeon prior to completing his studies. He began practicing in his native city and by 1821 had been named Professor of Comparative Anatomy and Surgery at the Philadelphia Museum. Harlan was a facile writer whose main interests outside of comparative anatomy lay in the fields of zoology and vertebrate paleontology, and his accomplishments in this latter area were internationally recognized. His work with fossils was more extensive than that of anyone else working in America at the time or previously.

Harlan was instrumental in persuading his European colleagues of the validity of American research and conclusions on the subject. A devoted disciple. of Georges Cuvier, the French founder of comparative zoology and paleontology (though the two never met), Harlan simply expanded the quantity of known information on the subject, as George Gaylord Simpson has pointed out, on the basis of what Cuvier had "established and organized . . . Harlan's lifetime coincided with a sort of plateau in the rise of vertebrate paleontology." It was no fault of Harlan's that, despite his considerable efforts, several decades followed his death before sufficient information and material had been collected to permit further qualitative development of the subject. Nevertheless, Harlan's work was held in great respect by such European authorities as Richard Owen and Henry de Blainville, both before and after Cuvier's death in 1832.

When Harlan's *Fauna Americana,* dealing with both recent and fossil mammals, appeared in 1825, however, the reaction was less than enthusiastic among his American colleagues, notably John Godman, despite the fact that Harlan's was the first text by an American devoted exclusively to native mammals.[1]

John Godman, born in Wilmington, Delaware, and two years Harlan's senior, had lost both parents before he was five and his guardian, an aunt, before the age of six. Despite this and other adversities, he persevered, completing his medical studies at the University of Maryland in 1818, the same year as Harlan. He practiced briefly in several rural communities in Pennsylvania and Maryland before being made Professor of Surgery at the Medical College of Ohio in Cincinnati, a post he held for less than

---

(1) Samuel Latham Mitchill of New York has made a few additions to the first American edition of the *General History of Quadrupeds,* by the Englishman Thomas Bewick, in 1804. These were a "hamster," (pocket gopher), "wild sheep" (Bighorn), and the "Mammoth of New York." George Ord's "North American Zoology" appeared anonymously in the third edition of William Guthrie's *A new Geographical, Historical, and Commercial Grammar,* published in 1815. In twenty-three pages he discussed mammals, and birds, together with some reptiles, amphibians, fish and insects. He depended heavily upon Thomas Pennant, Turton's edition of Linnaeus' *Systema Naturae,* and the Lewis and Clark Expedition material in Peale's Museum.

a year. He resigned because of the institution's uncertain future, then founded and briefly edited the first medical journal published west of the Alleghanies, the *Western Quarterly Reporter*. His interests in natural history were already strong when he arrived in Philadelphia in 1822, and he began his researches in this area in earnest while lecturing in medicine there. Beginning in 1826, he also taught anatomy at Rutgers Medical College in New York City, but was already aware that he had an advanced case of consumption.

When Harlan's book appeared, Godman was himself at work on a treatise dealing with American mammals, his *American Natural History,* which appeared in three volumes in 1826-1828. Married to Angelica Peale, a granddaughter of the Philadelphia Museum's founder, he was drawing heavily upon the Museum's resources for his own work, and clearly felt jealous pangs when his younger colleague's book appeared first. He attacked the *Fauna Americana,* however, on the grounds that it had been largely plagiarized from the *Mammalogie* of Anselme Gaetan Desmarest (1784-1838), a professor at the Ecole Veternaire of Alfort, France, which had been published in several volumes between 1820 and 1822.

Godman's criticisms first appeared in the Philadelphia *Franklin Journal and American Mechanics Magazine* in January, 1826, though he may also have been responsible for another review of Harlan's book which appeared in the *North American Review* shortly beforehand. Harlan was quick to issue a private pamphlet in rebuttal, *Refutation of Certain Misrepresentations,* in which he denied Godman's charges and suggested that only Godman's "total incapacity" and "personal animosity" could have prompted him to write as he had. Harlan admitted that he had relied heavily on Desmarest, together with several other authors, and argued that Desmarest's biggest contribution lay in "improvment in the scientific arrangement (of mammals), and in endeavouring to restore order to a subject heretofore disfigured by confusion." Desmarest had, essentially, done an excellent job of compilation. Despite this fact, Harlan asked, "was this author's book considered not the less original, useful, and meritorious(?)."

His book, Harlan continued, bore "the same relation to the mammalia of the United States as does the work of Desmarest to the four quarters of the globe," except for the fact that he had added some new species. Though he also included other original material, dealing for example with the tooth structure in the assigning of names to particular species and genera, and corrected certain of Desmarest's errors of fact, he did rely upon that Frenchman and other writers, notably Cuvier, Thomas Say, the American naturalist, and two English authorities, Sir Edward Sabine and Sir John Richardson, for the majority of his descriptions, and his book stands "principally as a compilation (which) served a useful purpose for the time." Harlan's announced intention to revise the book, and to publish "a second edition, which is to include the description of all the Reptilia known to inhabit the United States," was never carried out, in part because of the seriousness with which Godman's renewed attack in a letter to the Editor of the *Franklin Journal* was taken by the scientific fraternity.

The two men were not finished with each other, however, for when Godman published an article in 1830 on a mastodon-like animal secured from a site in Orange County, N. Y., near the place where C. W. Peale had excavated one in 1801, Harlan was among those who found fault with his conclusions. Godman's specimen was an anomaly, with four tusks instead of two, and a somewhat longer jaw than was customary in the common mastodon with which Peale and others had worked. He therefore created a new genus for his specimen. Harlan and others refused to consider it as tenable, but Godman also had his supporters, and the battle between the two groups went on for years without decisive result. Godman emphasized "one or two characters over the whole," while the Harlan group "emphasized the whole over the part," foreshadowing the continuing debate between "splitters" and "lumpers" which was to divide the scientific community in the late 19th century. Godman died shortly thereafter of consumption at the age of 35, but the debate sputtered on for some time.

Godman's own work, the *American Natural History: Part I: Mastology,* which is included in this Arno Press series, was the first American study of mammals which was both comprehensive and based upon the author's own research and observations. It is considered the best work of its type since Pennant's *Arctic Zoology,* published half a century before. While his work also reflected dependence upon other authorities, Godman used a greater variety of sources, his descriptions were fuller and his original observations much more conspicuous than Harlan's. In general, what was known of the life history of each genus was given prominence, with known species described in considerable detail. Godman's volumes were illustrated with indifferent engravings based on drawings by Charles Le Sueur and others, based upon mounted specimens in Peale's Museum, whereas Harlan's single volume had no illustrations. Harlan's book, on the other hand, emphasized anatomical detail and other "essential characters" in more succinct form, with less detail given to life history material.

As for Harlan's later career, in 1832 he was a member of a commission sent by the Philadelphia Sanitary Board to New York and Canada to study cholera, a disease which had raged in Philadelphia a short time previously. In 1838, he made a trip to Europe, following which he lived in New Orleans until his death at the age of 47 in 1843. There is no biography available, but useful discussions of his work will be found in George Gaylord Simpson, "The Beginnings of Vertebrate Paleontology in America," *Proceedings of the American Philosophical Society,* vol. 86, no. 1, September, 1942, pp. 130-188, and Patsy A. Gerstner, "Vertebrate Paleontology, an Early Nineteenth Century Transatlantic Science," *Journal of the History of Biology,* vol. 3, no. 1, Spring, 1970, pp. 137-148. Godman's career is covered in Thomas Sewall's memoir in *The North American Review,* vol. 40, pp. 57-99, January, 1835, and an anonymous sketch included in the first edition of his *Rambles of a Naturalist* (Philadelphia, 1833), pp. 13-36.

Despite its limitations, the *Fauna Americana* served as a useful digest of what was known concerning American mammals at the close of the first quarter of the nineteenth century, and Harlan's contributions to Desmarest's material were not inconsiderable.

February, 1974   Keir B. Sterling
                                  Tarrytown, N. Y.

Fauna Americana:

BEING

A DESCRIPTION

OF THE

MAMMIFEROUS ANIMALS

INHABITING NORTH AMERICA.

BY RICHARD HARLAN, M. D.

PROFESSOR OF COMPARATIVE ANATOMY TO THE PHILADELPHIA MUSEUM ;
MEMBER OF THE AMERICAN PHILOSOPHICAL SOCIETY ; OF THE
ACADEMY OF NATURAL SCIENCES OF PHILADELPHIA;
CORRESPONDING MEMBER OF THE LYCEUM OF
NATURAL HISTORY OF NEW YORK,
&c. &c.

" The manor of living nature is so ample, that all may be allowed to sport on it freely;
the most jealous proprietor cannot entertain any apprehension that the game will be ex-
hausted, or even perceptibly thinned."

PHILADELPHIA:

PUBLISHED BY ANTHONY FINLEY.

J. HARDING, PRINTER.

1825

TO

JAMES E. DEKAY, M. D.

MEMBER OF THE LYCEUM OF NATURAL HISTORY OF NEW YORK ; OF THE
ROYAL MEDICAL SOCIETY OF EDINBURGH ; CORRESPONDING
MEMBER OF THE ACADEMY OF NATURAL SCIENCES
OF PHILADELPHIA, &c. &c.

THIS ATTEMPT

TO ILLUSTRATE THE NATURAL HISTORY

OF

NORTH AMERICA,

IS MOST RESPECTFULLY INSCRIBED

BY HIS MUCH OBLIGED FRIEND

THE AUTHOR.

INTRODUCTION.

I HAVE engaged in the present undertaking with a full conviction of its absolute necessity, and am very sensible of the difficulties attending the complete attainment of its aim.

A work having for its object the illustration of the natural history of our country, cannot fail to prove interesting, and has long been a desideratum to naturalists. However unqualified for the task, I have nevertheless found ample room for additions, alterations and improvements. On the *utility* of the undertaking it will be unnecessary to insist, when, on referring to the latest authorities who have treated of this subject, we are struck with the confusion, the errors and the deficiences which still prevail. In the very latest work, Desmarest's Mammalogie, published in the year 1820, which professes to describe all the species of Mammalia, hitherto known, the number inhabiting North America, is limited to one hundred *species.* Of these many are described as uncertain, and his accounts of the manners and habits of most of them, are at best deficient.

These remarks are not intended to imply any reflection on the author, whose work is really one of great merit. I have found his synonymes most generally correct, and his descriptions for the most part extremely minute and accurate. The errors are such as are necessarily connected with the nature of the research; the deficiency of materials :

the want of accurate information, &c.* Scarcely indeed, has
he had it in his power to quote a single American author,
who, inhabiting the same regions with the animals, which
are the objects of his research, would alone be capable of
obtaining precise information concerning them. We may
further remark, that since the publication of Mr. Desmarest's work, many discoveries have been made, and much
valuable information has been collected in this department
of natural history, the high rank and importance of which,
beginning to be perceived by a liberal public, individuals,
who have hitherto confined their investigations more particularly to other branches, have now turned their attention to
this. Urged by similar motives, our common guardians and
enlightened statesmen, have organized *exploring expeditions,* which under the command of a most judicious offi-
cer, accompanied by men of science, have made such discoveries in almost every department of natural history, as
confer an invaluable boon upon their country. The naturalists who accompanied Major Long's expedition to the
Rocky Mountains, have described *twelve* new species of
quadrupeds, besides fixing the characters, and detailing the
habits of many others hitherto imperfectly known.

To Mr. Sabine's appendix to Captain Parry's and Captain
Franklin's expeditions, we have been indebted for much
valuable information, as well as for the description of several new species.

* Mr. Desmarest, in his advertisement to the second part of his " Mammalogie," p. 7, limits the number of mammalia inhabiting North America,
to fifty-four species : as this statement does not in any degree correspond
with his descriptions, we presume he has permitted a typographical error, of great importance, to escape his notice. We have enumerated from
his work one hundred species, as inhabiting North America; the descriptions of about fifty of these having been found very accurate, are accordingly translated with very little alteration.

Mr. Rafinesque, professor in the Transylvania University, in the State of Kentucky, has described, or rather indicated, a great variety of animals; but his insulated situation, and almost utter ignorance of the labours of other naturalists, have seduced him into grievous errors, and occasioned much confusion in natural history. It is possible, that some of his animals may be new species, but from the looseness of his imperfect descriptions, we have been obliged to reject them in almost every instance.

I should commit an act of injustice towards the most valuable of friends, were I to pass *sub silentio*, the reiterated proofs of kindness I have received from Dr. Dekay of New York. The unusual interest he has displayed in the success of this work; the important references he has afforded, and the valuable hints he has suggested, entitle him to my warmest acknowledgments.

By collecting together all the detached observations published in various journals, aided by personal observation, when this was in our power, we have been able to distinguish with considerable accuracy, *one hundred and forty-seven species*, as inhabiting North America.* Of these,

---

* Commencing at the most southern boundary of the United States, and not including the animals of Mexico, many of which are as yet but imperfectly known. Hernandez and Clavigero in their account of the natural history of this country, have noticed a number of animals, some of which are no doubt fabulous. The following is a list of such as inhabit Mexico, according to Clavigero :—

" Wild cats; bears; wolves; foxes; stags; buck; wild goats; badgers; pole-cats; weasels; martins; squirrels; rabbits; hares; otters; rats; a species of apes, called *mono* by the Spaniards; peccari; zorillo; opossum; armadillo; techichi or alco; swizzero; saricovienne; tapir; cynocephala cercopitheca of Briss.; ant-eater; coyoto or cojotl and porcupine."

Of these animals, some are common to South America and Mexico :

several are entirely new, and not before described: *eleven* species are fossil, and no longer exist in a living state, in this, or any other country; many were imperfectly noticed, or erroneously described; others merely indicated. In several instances *species*, and in three or four cases, *genera*, have been confounded.

With regard to the distribution of the North American mammalia, they are thus divided—119 are Quadrupeds, 28 Cetacea.

To the order Primates belong,	- -	1 species.
Carnivora,	- - -	60
Glires,	- - - -	37
Edentata,	- - -	6
Pachydermata,	- -	2
Ruminantia,	- -	13
Cetacea,	- - - -	28
		147

Twenty-five species are *common* to both Continents, without including the cetaceous animals, viz:—

Of the Mole,	- - - - -	1 species
Shrew,	- - - - -	2
Bear,	- - - - -	1

others to Mexico and the United States, a few species only being peculiar to Mexico, viz:—Cebus apella; phyllostoma spectrum; potos caudivolvula; canis mexicanus; felis mitis; felis mexicanus; didelphis cancrivora; didelphis cayopollin. (Hernand.) If we add these to the number described in the following pages, it will afford a sum total of 155 species as inhabiting North America, a computation which no doubt falls far short of the actual number.

Glutton,	-	-	-	-	1
Otter,	-	-	-	-	1
Wolf,	-	-	-	-	2
Fox,	-	-	-	-	2
Seal,	-	-	-	-	2
Weasel,	-	-	-	-	2
Beaver,	-	-	-	-	1
Field Mouse,	-	-	-	-	1
Campagnol,	-	-	-	-	1
Squirrel,	-	-	-	-	1
Deer,	-	-	-	-	2
Sheep,	-	-	-	-	1
Fossil,	-	-	-	-	4

Total, - 25*

The present publication may be viewed rather as an outline, or foundation of one, in many respects more extensive and more perfect. Sensible of the imperfections of this, his first effort, the author has the consolation of knowing, that it is the only attempt of the kind which has been made by an American naturalist, and flatters himself, that he would be foremost to hail with pleasure, and to read with delight, a more successful production from any of his fellow labourers in this field of science. The manor is inexhaustible and opens to our view an immense intellectual horizon.

We enjoy the most pleasing prospect, in the present rapid progress towards a complete illustration of the natural

* Where any doubt exists, or further information is requested, concerning any species, the same is signified by being marked with an asterisk. *

2

history of our country.   The most zealous, able and inde-
fatigable naturalists, are at this moment engaged in and have
nearly perfected the departments of American *ornithology, conchology* and *entomology.*   An equal degree of attention bestowed on *herpetology* is alone requisite to complete the circle of American zoology.

FAUNA AMERICANA:

BEING

A DESCRIPTION

OF THE

MAMMIFEROUS ANIMALS

INHABITING NORTH AMERICA.

ORDER PRIMATES.

Characters. Four extremities, the inferior of which are proper for progression, the superior terminated by hands; fingers furnished with nails: three kinds of teeth; body organized for the vertical station, two pectoral mammæ.

*Genus....*1. HOMO.

CHARACTERS.

Dental formula.—Teeth 32.
{
superior 16. { Incisor 4. / Canine 2. / Molar 10.
inferior 16. { Incisor 4. / Canine 2. / Molar 10.
}

Teeth forming a regular, unbroken series; the line formed by the surface of the upper series

slightly convex; the line formed by the surface
of the lower series slightly concave. Incisors
proceed in a direction more or less vertical with
the maxillary bones; the two middle ones of the
upper jaw are broadest; inferior incisors nearly
equal, the two exterior rather broadest; canines
in either jaw, not projecting, with their summits
more or less obtusely triangular; the two first
molars in either jaw are the smallest, their crowns
furnished with two blunt tubercles, one internal,
the other external; the three remaining molars
nearly equal, those of the upper jaw have the
crowns furnished with three tubercles; two on
the outer, one on the inner side; the crowns of
the inferior, with generally four tubercles, two on
the outer, two on the inner side.

Superior extremities terminated by a hand; an
organ eminently prehensile, and susceptible from
its structure of a greater variety of motions than
that of any other animal; five-fingered; thumb
possessing the power of motion in all directions,
independent of the fingers; fore-arm shorter than
the arm.

Inferior extremities constructed for the upright
posture only ; the feet at right angles with the
legs ; five toes, with broad flat nails ; sole, more
or less arched, the weight of the body being supported chiefly by the *os calcis*, and extremities of
the tarsal bones, the posterior borders of the former resting firm and flat upon the ground.

Body for the most part naked, and defenceless, those parts being most hairy, which in animals are most bare, viz. the axillæ and pubes. Finally, *Man* is the only being that worships God, and anticipates immortality.

Species....1. Homo Sapiens.

Characters of the species, are those peculiar to the genus.

Inhabit all parts of the earth, omnivorous, disputing for territory; uniting together for the express purpose of destroying their own species.

Varieties....1. American Race.

Char. Face rather large, features well pronounced; nose sufficiently projecting, frequently aquiline; hair black, strong, glossy and dense on the head, rather flattened, a transverse section being rather more oval than a section of the hair of the Caucasian, seldom becomes gray; beard rather sparse by nature.

Facial angle rather oblique, averaging about 80: the lower jaw is large and robust; teeth very strong, with broad crowns; chin well formed; lips rather tumid; cheek bones prominent, but rounded; the expression of the countenance is austere, never vacant, sometimes ferocious. The orbits of the eyes are larger, and more nearly quadrangular than those of the Mongolian; the transverse diameter of the American is one inch six-tenths.

the vertical diameter one inch five-tenths; transverse diameter of the Mongolian, in a skull which I possess, from Kamtschatka, one inch sixtenths, vertical diameter of the same, one inch two-tenths. The feet, though exceedingly well formed, are wider immediately above the toes in the American, than in the Caucasian, which is due probably to the absence of pressure in the former.

By European authors, the aborigines of America have been placed as the *fourth* in number, in the series of the varieties of the human race; but in proportion as their history is investigated and their character more fully developed, we shall find them to rise in our estimation. In a physical or moral and intellectual point of view, if we take into consideration their limited means for improvement, I am convinced we shall find little to boast or to hope for on the score of superiority. Destitute of all the comforts and conveniences of civilized life, exposed to the severest endurance of cold, fatigue and hunger, the American savage has displayed energies of mind, and qualities of the heart, which would not derogate from the character of a Socrates or a Solon. The Indian by nature is hospitable, eloquent, noble, generous and brave; their utter contempt of danger and death, their perfect self-possession, has been too frequently construed by superficial observers, as apathy, coldness, or indifference. On the contrary, numerous examples testify, that they are not wanting in heroic sympathy; though the warrior seldom smiles, perhaps never laughs, there are occasions, when he thinks it not unmanly to shed a tear.

As far as my observations extend, I should be inclined to rank the *North American* native, as second to the *Caucasian* variety.

They inhabit all America, excepting probably the Esquimaux, which possess stronger affinities to the Mongolian than the others.

Order CARNIVORA.

Char. The incisors, canine, and molars, most generally adapted for animal food.

Four extremities, the anterior of which are never terminated by hands, or a thumb separate from the fingers, and opposable; mammæ varying in number.

Articulation of the lower jaw directed transversely, not admitting any lateral motion.

Orbits not separate from the temporal fossæ.

Stomach simple, membranous; intestines short.

Nourishment according to the species, flesh, fresh or corrupted, insects, eggs, and even vegetable substances. Inhabit all the earth, which is habitable for quadrupeds.

Family Cheiroptera.

Char. General form disposed for flight; incisors in very variable numbers; canines more or less strong; crowns of the molars sometimes tuberculated, sometimes grooved lengthwise; a fold of skin extended between the four extremities, and between the fore-fingers.

Two pectoral mammæ; penis of the male free; powerful clavicles, scapulæ broad; fore-arm not susceptible of pronation or supination.

Tribe, Vespertilio.

Char. Fore-fingers excessively elongated, and supporting a very fine membrane, with the thumb only separate, not opposable.

Incisors, canine, and molars easily distinguishable by their forms; membrane naked both above and below.

Genus.

Rhinopoma, *Geoff.*

Vespertilio, *Belon, Brunich.*

CHARACTERS.

Dental formula.—Teeth 28.
- superior 12.
  - Incisor 2.
  - Canine 2.
  - Molar 8.
- inferior 16.
  - Incisor 4.
  - Canine 2.
  - Molar 10.

Superior incisors separate from each other; nose long, conical, truncated at the extremity, and surmounted by a small membranous fold; nostrils narrow, transverse and operculated, broad and concave above; ears large, approximate and falling over the face; auriculum exterior: Interfemoral membrane narrow, and terminating in a square border; tail long, enveloped at its base.

HABIT. Feeding on insects, which they catch during the evening, on the wing.

Inhabit Egypt and the United States of America.

Species.

1. *Rhinopoma caroliniensis*, Geoff.

Colour of the hair brown; tail long and thick.

DIMENSIONS. Total length two inches; length of the tail one inch six lines; spread of the wings eight inches.

DESCRIPTION. Ears moderate, nearly triangular; the two superior incisors simple, directed inwards; the four inferior incisors bilobate, and crowded in between the canines, which are, nevertheless, not very strong, and are in contact only at their base; colour of the hair, brown; membranes obscure; interfemoral membrane envelops one half the tail. Inhabits South Carolina, (according to Geoff.)

Genus.

Vespertilio, Linn. Erxleb. Briss. Pall. Shreb. Cuv. Geoff. Illig.

Plecotus, Geoff.

3

CHARACTERS.

1. VESPERTILIO, *Linn.*

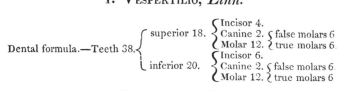

Dental formula.—Teeth 38. {
   superior 18. { Incisor 4. / Canine 2. / Molar 12. { false molars 6 / true molars 6
   inferior 20. { Incisor 6. / Canine 2. / Molar 12. { false molars 6 / true molars 6

2. VESPERTILIO, *Desm.*

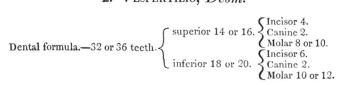

Dental formula.—32 or 36 teeth. {
   superior 14 or 16. { Incisor 4. / Canine 2. / Molar 8 or 10.
   inferior 18 or 20. { Incisor 6. / Canine 2. / Molar 10 or 12.

Superior incisors separated into pairs, cylindrical and pointed; inferior approximate with bilobate edges inclined and directed forwards.

Canines moderate, and not touching at base.

Anterior molars simply conical; the posterior with broad crowns and tuberculated points; the inferior grooved on the sides; the superior twice as large, having an oblique cutting crown.

Nose not foliated, nor grooved, nor wrinkled, nor operculated over the nostrils.

Lower lip simple; tongue smooth, not protractile.

Ears more or less large, with an auriculum.

Wing-membranes very extensive, and measuring in spread, four or five times the total length of the body.

Index finger having only one phalanx; middle finger three, annular and little finger two.

Tail entirely comprised in the interfemoral membrane, and very extensive; fur soft and thick.

Sebaceous glands beneath the skin of the face, affecting different forms and dimensions, according to the species.

HABIT. Nocturnal; hibernating in caves, suspending themselves from the sides of vaults, caverns, &c. by their hind legs, the head downwards, and the body enveloped by the wing membranes; feeding on insects which they catch during the crepusculum; producing generally only one young at a birth; flying easily and silently. The organ of hearing is acute, that of touch very perfect.

Inhabit the temperate regions of both continents.

Species.

1. *Vespertilio caroliniensis*, Geoff. Ann. Mus. d'hist. Nat. tom. 8. pl. 47.

Char. Essent. Ears oblong, of the size of the head, in part hairy; auriculum demi-cordiform; colour above chesnut brown, beneath yellow.

DESCRIPTION. Ears of moderate size, without folds at the internal border, their external surface furnished with fine hair on the first half; auriculum nearly cordiform; extreme point of the tail free; colour chesnut brown above, yellowish beneath, each hair being blackish-cinereous at base.

Inhabit the neighbourhood of Charleston, South Carolina.

1st *Division*, Vespertilio, *Geoff*.

CHARACTERS.

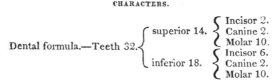

Dental formula.—Teeth 32.
{ superior 14. { Incisor 2.
  { Canine 2.
  { Molar 10.
{ inferior 18. { Incisor 6.
  { Canine 2.
  { Molar 10.

Superior incisors very separate from each other, and very near to each canine; four false molars, six true in each jaw; the anomalous false molar has a small tubercle placed at the internal border of the base of the canine. The species hitherto observed, are the Vespertilio *lasiure*, V. *noveboracencis*, V. *paradoxus*, and probably also the V. *pruinosus*.

Species.

1. *Vespertilio noveboracensis.* New-York bat. Penn. Syn. p. 367, *tab.* 31, *fig.* 2. Linn. Gmel.

Char. Essent. Ears short and broad, rounded; tail wholly enveloped in the interfemoral membrane.

Dimensions. Total length two inches five-tenths; tail nearly two inches; spread of the wings more than ten inches.

Description. Nose short, pointed; body brown above, pale beneath; a white spot at the base of the wings.

Note. This species is one of the two on which Rafinesque has constructed his new genus " Ata-

LAPHA," one of the characters of which is, " no in-
cisors in either jaw !" Vid. prod. de Semiologie.
Amer. Month. Mag.
Inhabit New York.

Species.

2. *Vespertilio pruinosus*, Say. Major Long's
Expedition to the Rocky Mountains, vol. 1. p. 167.

Ears large, short, not so long as the head, hairy
on the exterior side, more than half their length;
tragus, very obtuse at tip, arcuated; canine teeth
large, prominent; incisors one on each side, placed
very near the canine, conical, almost on a line
with it, and furnished with a small tubercle on its
external base; nostrils distant; fur on the back,
black brown at base, then pale brownish-yellow,
then blackish, then white; towards the rump dark
ferruginous; dull yellowish-white on the throat;
wing-membrane, on the anterior lower margin,
hairy; interfemoral membrane, covered with fur;
length nearly four inches and a half.

Inhabits the Western States, and has been observed in Pennsylvania.

3. *Vespertilio arquatus*, Say. Long's Exp. (ut
supra.)

Head large; ears rather shorter than the head,
wide, and at tip rounded, hairy at base; posterior
edge with two slight obtuse emarginations; the
anterior base distant from the eye : tragus arcuat-

ed, obtuse at tip; interfemoral membrane naked, including the tail to one half the penultimate joint.

Total length five inches; tail one inch and a half; expansion thirteen inches.

Inhabits the Western States.

Vespertilio subulatus, Say. Long's Exp. Vol. ii. p. 65. I believe this species to be merely a variety of the V. *caroliniensis*, (Geoff.) from which it differs slightly in colour, and in the form of the auriculum.*

Genus.

Taphozous taphiens, Geoff.
Vespertilio, Schreb. Muller.
Saccopteryx, Illig.

CHARACTERS.

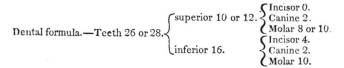

Dental formula.—Teeth 26 or 28.
superior 10 or 12. { Incisor 0. Canine 2. Molar 8 or 10.
inferior 16. { Incisor 4. Canine 2. Molar 10.

Nose not furnished with membranous folds, or operculi; superior lip very thick; ears of moderate size; tail composed of six vertebræ, free above the membrane; interfemoral membrane extensive; posterior border triangular.

---

* It is to be regretted that the dental formula has been neglected in the descriptions of the two last species, which prevents us from arranging them in systematic order with certainty.

Inhabit both continents.

Species.

1. *Taphozous rufus.* Figured in Wilson's Ornithology, vol. vi. *Red Bat of Pennsylvania.* Philadelphia Museum.

Vespertilio rufus, Warden. Description of the United States, vol. v. page 608.

Char. Essent. Fur of a reddish cream colour; membranes of a dusky red; auriculi slender, rounded at the extremity, and situated internally.

DIMENSIONS. Total length four inches; tail as long as the body; spread of the wings twelve inches.

DESCRIPTION. General colour, bright iron gray; fur of a reddish cream colour at base, then strongly tinged with lake, and minutely tipped with white; ears scarcely half an inch long, with auriculi; nostrils somewhat tabular; eyes small; wings furnished with a single hook; interfemoral membrane triangular.

HABIT. Similar to the other VESPERTILIO. The female has been known to manifest the strongest maternal affection; a young lad having taken two young bats of this species, was in the act of carrying them to the Museum at mid-day; being watched by the mother, she followed him through the streets, fluttering round the thoughtless urchin in whose grasp was centred all her hopes, and eventually settled on his bosom, preferring captivity to freedom, with loss of progeny.

Family INSECTIVORA.

Char. Essent. Feet short, armed with robust nails; hind feet always five-toed, resting on the anterior part of the sole; fore feet most generally five-toed; crowns of the molar teeth elevated into sharp tubercles; canine teeth sometimes very long, sometimes very short.

Number of incisors variable. Body covered with hair, or spines; feeding on insects, roots, and fruits.

Inhabit the temperate climates of both continents.

1st Division. Two long incisors before, followed by others, and by small canines shorter than the molars.

Genus.

Sorex, Linn. Erxleb. Schreb. Cuv. Lacep. Illig. *Musaraneus,* Brisson.

CHARACTERS.

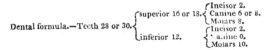

Dental formula.—Teeth 28 or 30. superior 16 or 18. { Incisor 2. Canine 6 or 8. Molars 8. inferior 12. { Incisor 2. Canine 0. Molars 10.

Superior intermediate incisors in form of a double hook, having a short spur situate at their base; inferior incisors elongated, proceeding straight from the alveoles, and are recurved only at their extremity. False canine, particularly the superior, much smaller than the intermediate incisors. Molars with broad crowns, having sharp tubercles, the superior are largest and have the cutting surface oblique; head very long; nose elongated and moveable; ears short and rounded; eyes small but visible.

Tail more or less long, sometimes quadrangular, sometimes partly compressed, at others teretile. Body covered with fine short hair; feet terminated by feeble toes, separate, furnished with hooked nails, not proper for digging the earth; mammæ, both pectoral and ventral, to the number of six or eight; a sebaceous gland on each flank, surrounded by stiff and compact hairs, secreting an oily liquor.

Habit. In summer, living in holes; in winter, penetrating hay-mows; feeding on worms and insects; of slow progression; during the rutting season they diffuse a strong odour; hence their vulgar name, " pole-cat shrew."

Inhabit temperate climates of both continents.

Species.

1. *Sorex constrictus*, Herman, obs. Zool. p. 47. Bodd. Elench. Anim. p. 123. Sp. 4. Geoff. Ann. Mus. d'hist. Nat. t. 17, p. 178. Sp. 6. pl. 3. fig. 1

Sorex cunicularis, Brechstein, Zool. *Musaraigne plaron*, Vic. d'Azyr, Syst. Anat. des anim. tab. method. (Encycl. pl. supple. 4. fig. 6.)

Char. Essent. Ears very small, hairy, entirely concealed by the skin; colour cinereous-black; tail flattened at its base, and at its point, round in the middle.

DIMENSIONS. Total length, two inches seven lines; length of the tail one inch six lines.

DESCRIPTION. Snout more robust than that of the *Sorex araneus*; head broader; fascial line more arched; cartilage at the end of the nose, shorter and thicker, which is owing to the coarse hairs which garnish the nostrils; ears entirely concealed by the hairs; two small canines more than in the other species in the upper jaw; tail flat, slender, and as if strangulated at its origin, whilst the remainder, particularly the middle, is thick, as if swollen, and round, except at the extremity, where it is flattened, and where the hairs unite into a point like those of a pencil; fur thick, long, and very soft to the touch, blackish for the greater portion of its length, and red at the extremity; belly grayish-brown; throat cinereous; feet hairy.

HABIT. Frequents meadows near the water.

Inhabit Europe and the United States. The specimen in the Philadelphia Museum, No. 895, was taken near Philadelphia.

Species.

2. *Sorex araneus,* Linn. Gmel. Daubent. Mem. de l'Acad. des Sciences, 1756, p. 212, pl. 5. *la Musaraigne,* Buffon, hist. Nat. t. 8. pl. 10, fig. 1. Vicq. d'Azyr, Syst. Anat. des Anim. t. 3. pl. 1. p. 33. Geoff. Ann. Mus. t. 17. p. 203. pl. 2. fig. 2. Schreb. tab. 160. *Fœtid Shrew,* Penn. Quadr. p. 307. No. 235.

Char. Essent. Ears large and naked, having within two folds or lobes placed one above the other; colour mouse gray, paler beneath, approaching sometimes yellow or brown; tail square, a little longer than the body.

Dimensions. Total length one inch eleven lines; of the head, eleven lines and a half; of the ears, two lines; of the tail, one inch six lines; of the fore arm, five lines; of the fore-feet, including the nails, three lines and a half; of the leg, five lines and a half; of the hind feet, six lines.

Description. Ordinary weight of the animal, three drachms; hair very fine, softer and shorter than that of the mouse, which it resembles in colour, but is a little browner on the head and body, and of a deeper gray on the inferior parts; all the hairs being of a cinereous colour for the greater part of their length, and brown at their extremity, mixed with a light teint of yellow above, and upon the sides of the head and body, and of a gray colour, mixed with a light teint of yellow, beneath the body; ear within large and naked. having two folds or lobes one above the other, the inferior of which corresponds to the entrance of the meatus auditorius; tail rather swollen, slightly quadrangular; lips, feet, and tail, flesh-coloured, the last of these parts having sometimes a brownish complexion.

Inhabit Europe and the United States. A specimen in the Philadelphia Museum, No. 896, taken near Philadelphia.

Species.

3. *Sorex parvus*, Say. Long's Exped. to the Rocky Mountains, vol. i. p. 163.

Char. Essent. Brownish-cinereous above; beneath cinereous; teeth blackish; tail short, of moderate thickness.

DIMENSIONS. From the tip of the nose to the root of the tail, two inches three-eighths; length of the tail three quarters of an inch.

DESCRIPTION. Body above brownish-cinereous; beneath cinereous; head elongated; eyes and ears concealed; whiskers long; the longest nearly attaining the back of the head; nose naked, emarginate; front teeth black; lateral ones piceous; feet whitish, five-toed; nails prominent, acute, white; tail short, subcylindric, of moderate thickness, slightly thicker in the middle, whitish beneath. The specimen is a female.

Inhabits Missouri, near Council Bluffs.

Species.

4. *Sorex brevicaudus*, Say. Long's Exped. vol. I. p. 164.

Char. Essent. Blackish plumbeous above; beneath rather lighter; teeth blackish; tail short, robust.

DIMENSIONS. From the tip of the nose to the root of the tail, three inches five-eighths; length of the tail, one inch.

DESCRIPTION. Above, blackish plumbeous, when viewed from before; silvery plumbeous when viewed from behind; fur dense, rather long; beneath rather paler; head large ; eyes very minute; ears white, entirely concealed beneath the fur; aperture very large, with two distinct semiseptæ, which are sparsely hairy at tip; snout short, with a slightly impressed abbreviated line above; nose livid brown, emarginate; mouth margined with whitish and sparse hairs; teeth piceous, black at tip, thirty in all, (as in the S. *constrictus*:) incisors of the upper jaw compressed laterally and hooked, white and distinct at base, black and approximate at tip, where they are rather pointed; then follow five minute false molars, black at top, crowns with two tubercles, when viewed with the glass, one external the other internal; the most posterior is without black at tip, or tubercles; true molars three in number, proportionally large, furnished each with four sharp tubercles, and as

many cavities; incisors of the lower jaw, two in
number, black at tip on the inferior surface, white
above; at base compressed laterally, approximate;
at the points slightly divergent, both projecting
forwards in the direction of the base of the lower
jaw, except at the tips, which are slightly curved
upwards; posterior to these are two small false
molars; the true molars three in number, similar
to those of the upper jaw; feet white, the second,
third, and fourth toes nearly equal, the first and
fifth shorter, the former rather shortest; anterior
with but very few hairs, nearly naked: nails nearly as long as the toes; tail with rather sparse hairs,
slightly thickest in the middle, depressed and
nearly as long as the posterior feet; the specimen
a male; the skull in the Philadelphia Museum.

Inhabit Missouri. Mr. G. Ord presented me
with a scull of a *Sorex* from the neighbourhood
of Philadelphia, which has served the purpose of
the above details of the teeth.

Genus.

Scalops, Cuvier, Geoff. Illig.
Sorex, Linn. Erxleb. Bodd.
Talpa, Penn. Shaw.

CHARACTERS.

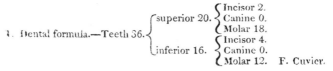

CHARACTERS.

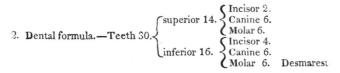

2. Dental formula.—Teeth 30.

superior 14. { Incisor 2. Canine 6. Molar 6.

inferior 16. { Incisor 4. Canine 6. Molar 6. Desmarest

The two intermediate superior incisors very strong and broad, plain and perpendicular to the jaw, and truncated cuneiform; the two external inferior incisors, conical, straight, rather long, and inclosing in their interval two very small, intermediate incisors. A considerable intermediate space in the upper jaw after the two large incisors; a less space in the lower jaw after the lateral incisors.

First and third superior conical teeth, on each side larger than the second; inferior conical teeth increasing from the first to the third.

Crowns of the molars furnished with sharp tubercles, the first being antero-posteriorly compressed, is rather thin, and with two points only, the one external, the other internal.

Snout elongated, terminated with a cartilaginous button.

Eyes very small; external ears wanting; feet very short, pentadactyle; the anterior very broad, having the fingers united to the last phalanx; nails long, flattened, linear, and proper for digging; increasing from the thumb to the third finger, the two remaining decreasing, the external the smallest of all; hind feet very small and very thin: nails small, hooked and arched.

Tail short; body contracted, covered with very short, fine, soft hair, perpendicular to the skin, as in the moles.

Species.

1. *Scalops canadensis.* (Encly. pl. 30, fig. 2. *Musaraigne brune.*)

Sorex aquaticus, Linn. Gmel. Schreb. tab. 158.

Talpa fusca, Penn. Quad. p. 314. n. 245. Shaw, gen. Zool. V. 1. Part. ii. p. 524. *Musaraigne taupe*, Cuv. tab. Element. des Anim.

Char. Essent. Nose elongated, terminated by a cartilaginous button; the feet and tail of a mole; colour grayish-brown.

DIMENSIONS. Total length six inches three lines; of the head one inch three lines; of the tail nine lines.

DESCRIPTION. Nose very much elongated; nostrils but slightly apparent, opening above near the point; a longitudinal groove beneath, commencing at the upper lip; mouth moderately wide; teeth very strong and white; eyes and meatus auditorius concealed by the hair; hands very strong and broad, fingers united to the commencement of the last phalanx; palms naked, bordered with small stiff hairs; above slightly covered with grayish down; nails very strong, long, linear and grooved: posterior feet, small, narrow, naked beneath, covered with down above; nails feeble, hooked, and rather sharp : tail short, covered with hair; colour of the animal grayish-fawn; each hair being mouse-gray at its base, and nearly yellow at its extremity.

HABIT. Analogous to those of the moles, preferring the borders of rivers and creeks.

Inhabit the United States, from Canada to Virginia. A specimen in the Philadelphia Museum, labelled, " American white mole," No. 872.

Species.

2. *Scalops pennsylvanica*, Nob.

I possess the skeleton of a species of this genus, distinct from the *S. canadensis*.

CHARACTERS.

Dental formula.—Teeth 40.
{
  superior 24 { Incisor 2.
                Canine 12.
                Molar 6. false molar 4.
  inferior 16. { Incisor 4.
                 Canine 6.
                 Molar 6.
}

Molar teeth nearly approximate, those of the upper jaw having the crowns slightly indented with a transverse furrow, which is continued along the inner side ; the crowns of the lower molars deeply marked by a transverse groove, which is continued on the outer side of the teeth.

Form of the incisors similar to those of the preceding species.

DIMENSIONS. Length of the body with the head

5

inclusive, four inches six-tenths; length of the tail, one inch three-tenths; length of the head one inch four-tenths; extremities like those of the preceding species.

Note. This species corresponds in the number and arrangement of its teeth, with the genus *Scalops* of F. Cuvier, but the structure of the molars are different from this genus, as described both by Desmarest and Cuvier.

Genus.

Condylura, Illiger, F. Cuvier, Desm.
Sorex, Linn. Gmel. Erxleb. Bodd.
Scalops, Geoff.
Talpa, G. Cuv. Penn. Gmel.

CHARACTERS.

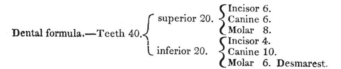

Dental formula.—Teeth 40.
superior 20. { Incisor 6. Canine 6. Molar 8.
inferior 20. { Incisor 4. Canine 10. Molar 6. Desmarest.

Six anomalous superior incisors, implanted in the intermaxillary bone; the two intermediate very broad, contiguous, garnishing the whole border of the jaw, scooped, with their cutting edges rather oblique, having the angle by which they touch more projecting than the external angle; the succeeding incisor on each side, touching the intermediate, resembling a very long pointed canine, somewhat triangular at base, where there exist two very small tubercles, one before, the other behind; the external or lateral incisor the smallest of all, simply conic, slightly compressed, and recurved at the point, placed at some distance from the incisor in form of a canine.

Four inferior incisors flattened, projecting and scooped; the lateral lay in part horizontally on the intermediate, slightly elevated at the extreme border.

Three conical teeth, (false molars, or false canines) in the upper jaw on each side, separated from each other, rather wide, and furnished each with a small pointed lobe at base, and one also posteriorly; five teeth in the lower jaw on each side, similar to these, separated from each other; the first being largest, in which only it resembles a canine, having three lobes, the principal of which is intermediate, the first nearly effaced, and the posterior slightly projecting; the second nearly similar, but shorter and more compressed, with the posterior lobe more apparent than in the preceding; the third has four lobes, a small one anteriorly; a second, the largest of all, and the most apparent, and two small ones posteriorly; the fourth nearly like the third, with this difference, that the first posterior lobe is more internal, which makes the tooth thicker; the fifth differs from the first only in being broader, nearly equal to the first molar; four superior true molars on each side, composed each of two folds of enamel, forming two sharp tubercles on the internal side, and grooved obliquely into furrows on the external side; a spur on the internal base of these teeth: the most anterior being the smallest, increasing to the last, which is smaller than the third; inferior true molars three on each side, presenting like the superior, two folds of enamel; the disposition of these folds being inverse, the points in place of being internal are external.

Snout very much elongated, sometimes furnished with a membranous crest, disposed in form of a star around the opening of the nostrils.

No external ears; eyes extremely small; anterior feet short, broad, five toes furnished with strong nails proper for digging; posterior feet slender, five-toed.

Tail moderately long; body clumsy, covered with very fine soft and short hair, perpendicular to the skin.

HABIT. Analogous to the mole.

Inhabit North America.

Species.

1. *Condylura cristata*, Desm. Mamma. (Encycl. pl. suppl. 4. fig. 7.) *Taupe du Canada.* Delafaille, Essay sur l'hist. Nat. de la taupe, figd. 1767. Buffon, hist. Nat. t. 6. pl. 37.

Sorex cristatus, Linn. Erxleb. Gmel. Bodd.

Radiated Mole, Penn. Syn. Quad. p. 313, n. 243, tab. 28; fig. 1. Desm. Note sur le genre

Condylure, Journal de Phys. 1819. pl. 2. ("Star nosed mole," Philadelphia Museum, No. 876.)

Char. Essent. Nostrils surrounded by a circular membrane, in form of a star; tail, less than half the length of the body.

DIMENSIONS. Total length, four inches; circumference of the fringed disk of the snout, five lines; total length of the hand, six lines; of the foot, ten lines; of the largest nail of the fore feet, two lines and a half; length of the tail, one inch eight lines: distance between the eyes, three lines.

DESCRIPTION. Snout very much elongated, wrinkled, provided with a small bone, and furnished at the point with a naked disk, which encloses in its centre the openings of the nostrils, the borders of which are furnished with cartilaginous points, of a rose colour, moveable, and with a granulated surface, twenty in number; the two superior intermediate ones, and the four inferior intermediate, are united at base, and placed on a plane more advanced than the others; neck not distinct; anterior feet very short, with the hands very broad, naked, scaly; lower cutting surface less marked than in the mole; five short toes, united to the second phalanx, and furnished with strong nails, straight, rather broad, linear, of different relative lengths; hind feet proportionally longer than those of the mole properly so called, being one-third longer than the anterior feet. slen-

der, feeble, naked and scaly; all the phalanges
being free; nails less long than those of the hand,
less broad, but more curved; tail rather slender,
with its vertebræ slightly projecting; the skin
which covers it divided into transverse folds,
scaly; between which project hairs more rare
and stiff than on other parts of the body.

Fur short, very soft, rather coarser and more
sparse than that of the common mole of Europe.
but of the same blackish-gray velvet.

Whiskers composed of stiff hairs, rather long,
elevated, nearly parallel and directed forwards;
the external borders of the hands furnished with
a series of stiff hairs, slightly recurved towards
the palm, which is absolutely naked. Palate
wrinkled transversely; lower jaw very thin and
slender; sixteen vertebræ to the tail.

HABIT. Not sufficiently observed; possesses
the faculty of moving the membrane on the end
of the nose.

Inhabit Canada and the United States; very
common in Pennsylvania and New Jersey.

Species.

2. *Condylura longicaudata*, Desm. Mam. *long-
tailed mole*, Penn. Syn. Quad. p. 314. No. 244.
tab. 16, fig. 2. *Talpa longicaudata*, Erxleb. Syst.
Anim. t. 1. p. 118. Gmel. Syst. Nat. Bodd. p. 126,
sp. 2. (Encycl. pl. 28, fig. 5.)

Char. Essent. No nasal crest; tail as long as one half the body.

Dimensions. Length of the head and body from four to six inches.

Description. Anterior feet broad, and constructed like those of the European mole; hind feet scaly and beset with sparse short hairs; toes long and thin; hair of the body soft, ferruginous brown; tail covered with short hair.

Inhabits North America.

Species.

3. *Condylura macroura*, Nob.

Char. Essent. Nose surrounded with a circular fringed membrane, asteriform; tail nearly the length of the body, round and appearing strangulated at base, becoming suddenly enlarged, slightly compressed and tapering.

Dimensions. Total length, five inches four lines; length of the hands, seven lines; length of the hind feet, one inch; longest nail of the hand, two-eighths. (Extremity of the tail lost.)

CHARACTERS.

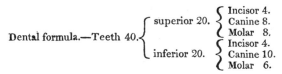

Dental formula.—Teeth 40.

superior 20.	Incisor 4. Canine 8. Molar 8.	
inferior 20.	Incisor 4. Canine 10. Molar 6.	

Note. There is no rule by which to determine in this genus, the distinction of the various kinds of teeth. Thus Desmarest gives them incis. $\frac{6}{4}$, and allows six false molars above, and eight molars proper; whilst F. Cuvier gives as characteristic of his genus *Condylura*, two incis. two canine, ten false molars, and six true molars, to the upper jaw, but the total number of teeth is similar in all; the differences exist only in the names by which the teeth have been designated.*

DESCRIPTION. Snout very much elongated, a longitudinal wrinkle on the upper surface, and on each side; cartilaginous points on the nose twenty in number; hands short and broad, naked, except at the upper border, which is lined with hair; nails strong, short, and flat, with cutting borders, not curved or arched at the extremity, nor pointed as in the *C. cristata;* tail more than one half the length of the body, thick, compressed, and tapering, furnished with coarse scales, clothed throughout with sparse, short, thick hairs; colour of the back, blackish-gray; the snout, fawn colour, darker on the sides. A specimen in the Philadelphia Museum, No. 866.

---

* According to the observations of Dr. Dekay, the total number of teeth in this genus is 44; but 2 of the upper incisors are mere rudiments. His dental formula stands thus:

$$
44. \begin{cases} \text{Above 4 incisor.} \\ \quad\ \ 2 \text{ canine.} \\ \quad 16 \text{ molar.} \\ \text{Below 6 incisor.} \\ \quad\ \ 6 \text{ canine.} \\ \quad 14 \text{ molar.} \end{cases} \begin{matrix} \left.\begin{matrix} \\ \\ \end{matrix}\right\} 8. \\ \ \ 8. \\ \left.\begin{matrix} \\ \\ \end{matrix}\right\} 8. \\ \ \ 6. \end{matrix}
$$

Inhabit the United States, abound in New Jersey.

Genus.

Talpa, Linn. Briss. Erxleb. Bodd. Cuv. Lacep. Geoff. Illig.

CHARACTERS.

Dental formula.—Teeth 44.
superior 22.
{ Incisor 6.
Canine 2.
Molar 14.
inferior 22.
{ Incisor 8.
Canine 0.
Molar 14.

Superior incisors small, vertical, nearly equal in height, the intermediate being broader than the lateral; inferior incisors small, disposed in an arch, slightly projecting.

Canines surpassing the incisors, triangular, compressed, the superior being larger than the inferior, and having two roots.

The three anterior molars of the upper jaw very small, placed in the most narrow portion of the mouth, having nearly the same form as the canines, only smaller; the fourth triquetrous at its base; crown consisting of but one point; the crown of the fifth has a cutting border with two points, the posterior of which is largest, and furnished with a small spur anteriorly, presenting a small point; the sixth is largest of all, in other respects similar to the fifth: the seventh triangular, with the summit exterior and directed transversely.

The two first inferior molars like canine, but smaller; the third cutting, pointed, triangular, with a small spur posteriorly; the three last larger, particularly the penultimate; all composed of an external cutting border, divided into three sharp tubercles, and a double spur, for the two first: one for the posterior.

Head elongated: eyes very small; no external ears.

Extremities short, five-toed, anterior stronger than the posterior, terminated by very broad hands, having the hand always turned outward and backward; the internal border cutting, and the fingers united to the base of the nails, which are slightly arched, long, strong, and cutting; hind feet more slender; toes more feeble, more distinct or separate, and furnished with moderate sized nails.

Tail short, sparsely hairy.

Six abdominal mammæ.

Body covered with short, fine, very soft hair. perpendicular to the body.

(For the anatomy, see the Dict. d'hist. Nat. art. *Taupe.*)

HABIT. Animals eminently organized for burrowing; feeding on insects, larvæ, earth worms, tender roots, &c. having the organs of hearing and of touch very perfect.

Species.

Talpa Europea, Linn. Erxleb. Bodd.

Talpa vulgaris, Briss. regn. Anim. p. 280, n. 1.

la taupe, Buff. hist. Nat. tom. 8. p. 81. pl. 12.

Mole, Pennant, Brit. Zool. p. 52.

Talpa americana, black mole, Bartram's manuscript notes.*

Char. Essent. Fur soft, black, and shining; tail short.

DIMENSIONS. Total length from the base of the tail to the extremity of the snout, five inches; length of the head, one inch six lines; of the tail, one inch two lines; of the fore-arm, eight lines; of the hand, nine lines and a half; of the leg, nine lines; of the longest nail of the fore foot, three lines and a half; of the longest nail of the hind foot, one line and a half.

DESCRIPTION. Body thick, oblong, nearly cylindrical, training on the earth; head pointed, terminated in a snout; eyes exceedingly small, black. situated in the middle of a space of two lines in diameter, destitute of hairs; ears without a concha, only observable externally by the meatus auditorius, the borders of which are slightly projecting

---

* That venerable naturalist, the late Mr. WILLIAM BARTRAM, was accustomed to keep a diary, or " A calendar of natural history," in which he carefully noted his daily observations, almost up to the hour of his death; these were never intended for publication, but since this work went to press, his relative, Maj. Robert Carr, (the present proprietor of the Gardens.) has politely favoured me with a perusal of them.

beneath the skin in the inferior portion of the circle which they form; anterior feet very robust,
thick; fingers short, armed with nails equally long;
wrists concealed in the hair; tail scaly like that
of the rat, but furnished with longer hair; anus
projecting and very distant from the origin of the
tail; fur soft, shining, and of a cinereous colour,
taking different teints, as it is viewed in various
directions; a light teint of fawn on the lower jaw
and middle of the belly.

The following are varieties; *spotted, white,*
yellow, and *cinereous.*

HABIT. Subterraneous, affecting light and cul-
tivated soils; changing locality according to at-
mospherical variations; seeking elevated regions
during the rainy seasons; excavating long galle-
ries which all communicate with each other, parallel to the surface of the soil, and at moderate
depths; elevating the earth into what are denominated *mole-hills*; excavating with their hands, and
raising the earth with their head; feeding on
worms, insects, roots, bulbs of colchicum, &c.; entering in rut early in the spring, and bringing forth
twice annually, four or five at a birth, between
the months of March and August; raising their
young with the greatest tenderness; forming their
nests of leaves, in a spacious chamber, the vault
of which is supported by pillars, and which is
situated in a manner to be sheltered from inunda-
tions.

Family CARNIVORA.

Char. Six incisors in each jaw; molars most generally cutting, sometimes tuberculous; the crowns never furnished with sharp tubercles; canines very strong.

1st *Tribe, Plantigrada.*

Char. Entire soles of the hind feet resting on the soil; five toes to each foot.

Genus.

Ursus, Linn. Schreb. Lacep. Cuv. Geoff. Illig. *Prochilus*, Illig.

CHARACTERS.

Dental formula.—Teeth 42.
superior 20.
{ Incisor 6.
{ Canine 2.
{ Molar 12.
inferior 22.
{ Incisor 6.
{ Canine 2.
{ Molar 14.

Incisors regular; the two exterior stronger and more pointed than the four intermediate; these two teeth in the lower jaw being broad, pointed, having a very distinct lateral lobe at their external base; canines strong and conical; number of molars varying according to age; three very broad, with square crowns, entirely tuberculous; the false molars small, obtuse, and separate; body clumsy, covered with thick fur.

Head thick, with the snout more or less elongated and moveable; tongue smooth; feet pentadactyle, all armed with very strong nails, more or less curved; tail short; six mammæ, two pectoral, and four ventral; no cæcum.

HABIT. Preferring cold or elevated countries for the most part; of slow progression; feeding on wild fruits, roots, herbs, honey, as well as on animal matter; others eating only corrupted flesh; hibernating in winter, during which they bring forth their young from one to five at a birth.

According to the testimony of hunters, they come forth in spring nearly as fat as when they retired, and soon become thin by exercise; which fact was remarked by *Aristotle*.

Inhabit Europe, Asia, and America.

Species.

1. *Ursus arctos*, Linn. Erxleb. Bodd. *Ours*. Buff. t. 8. pl. 31. Perrault, Anim. p. 258. No. 1. G. Cuv. Mènag. des Mus. fig. E. Cuv. Mamm. lithogr. *Brown bear*.

Char. Essent. Fascial line convex above the eyes; snout abruptly diminishing; sole of the feet of moderate length; colour brown.

DIMENSIONS. Total length, three feet four inches, six lines; length of the head, eleven inches three lines; height before, two feet one inch; length of the fore feet, nails inclusive, seven inches two

lines; of the hind feet, eight inches four lines.
(They vary in size from three to five feet.)

DESCRIPTION. (Alpine brown bear, adult.) Body
entirely covered with very thick hair, long and
rather soft, generally of a chesnut brown, deep on
the shoulders, the back, thighs, and legs, and
glazed with yellow on the sides of the head to
the ears, and on the flanks; hair of the feet short
and nearly black, as well as that on the snout,
which is nevertheless in some degree browner;
soles of the hind feet proportionally shorter than
those of the white bear, and longer than those of
the black bear, entirely naked, and marked by
four folds which correspond to the divisions of
the fingers, which are separated from the sole,
properly speaking, by hairs, each finger being
furnished with an elliptical tubercle; anterior half
only of the fore feet naked, and provided posteriorly with a naked tubercle, surrounded with
hair; naked part of the hand marked by three
folds, two of which correspond to two internal
fingers, and the third circumscribes the part
which relates to the two external; fingers furnished with elliptical tubercles like those of the toes.
the middle one being in all cases the longest, and
the others diminishing gradually; nails strong and
cutting; eye small; iris brown; nostrils opening
before a glandular muzzle. and passing to the
sides, curved upwards in form of a slit: ears with
an external concha. very simple and rounded:

tongue smooth, narrow and long; lips very extensible. (F. Cuv.)

HABIT. Frequent the most solitary places, the deepest forests, the highest and most inaccessible mountains; resorting to caverns or hollow trees; hibernating. They copulate in October; the female brings forth in spring, after a hundred and two days of gestation, from one to five young at a birth, according to her age. The brown bear is less ferocious than the polar bear; feeds principally on vegetable substances, and attacks animals only when hard pressed by hunger, when they unite in troops more or less numerous. In order to combat, they raise themselves on their hind legs, and endeavour to suffocate their adversary with their fore paws.

Inhabits the mountains of Europe, Asia, Africa, and western parts of North America. (The identity of the American and European species, not certainly ascertained.)

Species.

2. *Ursus cinereus,* Desm.

Ursus ferox, Lewis and Clark's voyage to the Missouri.

Gray or grizzly bear, Warden. Descrip. des Etats unis, v. 5, p. 609.

Ursus horribilis, Ord. Guthrie's Geog. v. 2, p. 299.

Char. Essent. Hair long, abundant, particularly about the head and neck; colour grayish, sometimes bordering on brown or white; anterior claws elongated; facial line rectilinear, or slightly arched.

DIMENSIONS. Total length, eight feet seven inches six lines; greatest circumference, five feet ten inches; circumference of the neck, three feet eleven inches; of the middle of the leg, one foot eleven inches; length of the claws, four inches five lines.

DESCRIPTION. This animal is best described by Mr. Say, (Long's Exp. to the Rocky Mountains, p. 52,) under the name of *U. horribilis,* but having been taken chiefly from the prepared specimens of a male and female in the Philadelphia Museum, must necessarily be imperfect in some respects, inasmuch as these individuals were captured very young, and brought up in a confined cage, and when killed had not attained a state of maturity and full growth. These circumstances would materially change the quality and colour of the hair, nails, and other superficial characters. Nevertheless, to Mr. Say is due the credit of having first noticed those specific characters which establish this as a distinct species from any previously described. Desmarest in his Mammalogie, so late as 1820, remarks, " the only characters which induce us to place this species here, are taken from its enormous size; for all the information we possess besides, concerning this individual.

is not sufficiently detailed to enable us to distinguish it from the preceding."

From the work first quoted we shall notice those characters which are most permanent : "ears short, rounded; front arcuated; the line of the profile continued upon the snout, without any indentation between the eyes; eyes very small; end of the nose black; sinus very distinct and profound; tail very short, concealed by the hair; anterior feet, claws elongated, slender; fingers with five suboval naked tubercles, separated from the palm, from each other, and from the base of the claws, by dense hair; palm, anterior half, naked, transversely oval; base of the palm with a rounded naked tubercle, surrounded by the hair; posterior feet with the sole naked; the nails moderate, more arcuated and shorter than the anterior ones; the nails do not in the least diminish in width at the tip, but become smaller towards that part only by diminishing from beneath; lower surface of the claws split so as to form a longitudinal groove.

" Length of the prepared specimen, five feet two inches; of the tail, exclusive of the hair, one inch and three quarters."

For interesting particulars concerning the habits of this animal, I must refer to Lewis and Clark's Voyage up the Missouri.

Species.

3. *Ursus americanus*, Pallas, Cuv.
Black bear, (Philad. Museum.)
Ursus gulaire, Geoff.

Char. Essent. Nose nearly on the same line with the forehead, but more arched than in the *Cinereus*; palms of the hands and soles of the feet very short; hair shining black, not curled.

DIMENSIONS. Total length five feet eight inches; length of the tail, one inch six lines.

DESCRIPTION. Facial line less arched than in the brown bear; ears larger and more separated; feet shorter; sides of the nose marked more or less with yellow.

In the state of New York they distinguish two varieties of this species, viz. the long legged and short legged bear.

Inhabits Canada and the United States, from the district of Maine to the Pacific ocean, and as far south as Carolina. Lewis and Clark met them on the Rocky Mountains, and on the borders of Columbia river.

Species.

4. *Ursus maritimus, Polar bear*, Linn. Sabine, append. *Ursus albus*, Briss. regn. anim.
Ours blanc, Buff. suppl. v. 3, pl. 34.
Polar bear, Penn.

Char. Essent. Head elongated; cranium flattened; neck long; sole of the foot very large; hair long, soft and white.

DIMENSIONS. Total length, five feet seven inches one line; of the head, one foot five inches six lines; of the palm of the hand, ten inches two lines; of the sole of the foot, eleven inches nine lines; of the tail, two inches nine lines; height before, three feet four inches.

DESCRIPTION. Body and neck much longer in proportion, head more narrow and more flat than in the brown bear; forehead nearly in a straight line with the nose; snout thicker than in the European species; ears shorter, more round; hind feet about one-sixth of the total length, resting on the entire sole and heel; hair soft, fine, and woolly, very long on the belly and legs, rather short on the head and superior parts of the body; white on all parts; end of the nose, nails, and borders of the eyelids, of a deep black; lips bordering on the violet; interior of the mouth of a pale violet; a small supernumerary conical tooth, situated behind the canine of both jaws, and separated from the first molar by a vacant space.

HABIT. Very voracious and savage, carnivorous, swimming with the greatest facility, and reposing on floating ice. Female brings forth in the month of March, after six or seven months gestation; reposing the young in deep pits made in the snow, where they pass the winter. isolated. and in a lethargic state.

Inhabits the rivers of the frozen ocean, Spitzburg and the most northern coasts of America; Mellvil island, west coast of Davis's strait, according to Sabine.

Genus.

Procyon, Storr, Cuv.
Ursus, Linn. Erxleb. Bodd. Gmel.
Coati, Klein.
Lotor, Tiedmaun.

CHARACTERS.

1. Dental formula.—Teeth 40.
   superior 20. { Incisor 6. Canine 2. Molar 12.
   inferior 20. { Incisor 6. Canine 2. Molar 12.

Inferior incisors regularly arranged.

Canine large and compressed; the three first molars simple, triangular, pointed, distant from each other; the three last tuberculous; the fourth presenting three points on its external border; the fifth almost entirely tuberculous, and the strongest of all; the sixth entirely tuberculous.

Body low set.

Snout pointed.

External ears small, oval.

Tongue soft.

Tail long and pointed, not prehensile.

Feet pentadactyle, armed with rather sharp

nails; during progression the heel does not rest entirely upon the soil.

Six ventral mammæ.

HABIT. Feeding like the bear on animal and vegetable substances; more active than these animals; climbing trees with facility.

Inhabit both North and South America.

Species.

1. *Ursus lotor*, Linn. Erxleb. Bodd.

Le Raton, Buffon, hist. nat. tom. 8. pl. 43.

Procyon lotor, Cuvier, Regne anim. p. 143.

Vulpes americana, Charleton. *Coati Brasiliensium*, Klein. *Agouarapopé*, d'Azara, Essai sur l'hist. nat. des quadr. du Paraguay. *Mapach*, of the Mexicans.

Raccoon of the Americans.

Char. Essent. Colour grayish-brown; snout white, with a brown line passing through the eyes; tail ringed with brown and white.

DIMENSIONS. Length of the body, one foot nine inches three lines; of the head, five inches nine lines; of the tail, eight inches six lines; greatest height one foot.

DESCRIPTION. (Male,) pupil of the eye round; nose prolonged beyond the jaws, but less than the nose of the *Coati*, terminating in a glandular muzzle, at the end of which open the nostrils, which are prolonged on the sides and curve upwards; lips extensible: ears elliptical, very simple; skin of the soles of the feet very delicate; penis almost entirely bony, directed forwards in a sheath; glans rounded, divided by a groove, curving downwards; testicles in part concealed beneath the skin; fore feet five-toed, furnished beneath with thick tubercles, the thumb being shortest, next the little finger, then the finger next the thumb, the two remaining longest and equal; nails proper for digging, long and strong; five elastic tubercles on the palm; one near the wrist, another at the base of the little finger, a third at the origin of the thumb, a fourth opposite the second finger. and a fifth at the base of the two large fingers.

The hind feet similarly constructed.

General colour of the body blackish-gray; paler beneath the belly and on the legs; hairs ringed with black and dirty white; tail tufted, having five or six black rings upon a yellowish-white base; ears whitish; snout whitish before, with a black spot embracing the eye, and descending obliquely to the inferior jaw; the hairs of those parts comprised between this spot and the ear; those of the cheeks and eyebrows, nearly white, and rather long, directed downwards; snout in general covered with short hairs, black above; whiskers long and strong on the upper lip; feet covered with short hairs; the woolly hair of the body being deep gray and very thick. (F. Cuvier.)

Female rather smaller than the male.

Variety, A. *Fawn-coloured raccoon.*
　　　　B. *Brown-throat raccoon.*
　　　　C. *White raccoon.*

HABIT. More active than the bear, but still having the awkward gait of the plantigrade animals; supporting themselves with ease on their hind feet, and holding their food with the fore feet; constantly plunging the food in water, and rolling it between the hands before eating; nocturnal; feeding on roots, fruits, insects, birds, &c.

Inhabit North America, Mexico, West Indies.

In the United States they are found as far north as Lake Ontario.

Genus.

Taxus, Linn. Geoff.
Meles, Briss. Storr. Bodd. Cuv. Illig.
Ursus, Linn. Erxleb.

CHARACTERS.

Dental formula.—Teeth 36.	superior 16.	Incisor 6.
		Canine 2.
		Molar 8.
	inferior 20.	Incisor 6.
		Canine 2.
		Molar 12.

Second incisor on each side of the lower jaw, placed a little farther back than the others; canines strong; superior molars form an uninterrupted series: the first linear and small, the second and third flattened laterally, and having a single sharp point; the penultimate triangular; the last very large and broad.

Of the six inferior molars, the first is rudimental, linear, scarcely apparent; the three following flattened laterally; the fifth being largest and having three sharp points.

Body thick set, low upon the legs; snout somewhat elongated; ears short and round; eyes very small; tongue smooth ; feet five-toed, armed with strong nails ; tail very short; a pouch between the anus and tail, having a transverse orifice, discharging a fetid matter; hair coarse and long.

Habit. Analogous to bears. Inhabit Europe. Asia, and North America.

Species.

1. *Meles labradoria, American badger,* Sabine's appendix to Capt. Parry's Voyage to the Polar sea, p. 649, who proved it a distinct species from the " *Meles vulgaris,*" of Desmarest, with which it had been confounded by all previous authors.

Desmarest remarks, (vide Mammalogie, p. 173) " Le carcajou figurè par Buffon dans ses supplèments. (Encycl. pl. 38, fig. 2.) *Ursus labradoricus,* Gmel. est un vrai blaireau du pays des Eskimaux. il en est venu en France qui avoient ètè pris en Canada."

Char. Essent. Colour of the animal above. ferruginous brown; a broad whitish longitudinal line divides the head above into two equal parts, and is continued along the back; lower surface of the fore feet, black.

8

DIMENSIONS.   Total length of the male, two feet
two inches, not including the tail; female considerably smaller.

DESCRIPTION.   The following details are taken
from well prepared specimens, a male and female
in the Philadelphia Museum, No. 786 and 787.

The back of the animal of a ferruginous brown
colour; hairs at base whitish, then brown, then
tipt with gray; sides of the snout of a dark brown;
those hairs are blackest which cover the upper
surface of the anterior feet; snout contracted,
broad at base, pointed at the extremity; nostrils
open downwards, curving upwards posteriorly, to
form a lateral and vertical slit; end of the nose
continued beyond the upper lip; external ear
small; the borders of the pinnæ, ovoid; a broad
row of reversed hairs anterior to the concha;
nails on the fore claws, strong, equally as long as
the palm, slightly curved and very sharp; nails of
the posterior feet slender, short, and sharp; tail
about the length of the hind leg, covered with
long hairs; hair of the body long, rather coarse.

HABIT.   Frequents the most solitary places;
lives in holes; nocturnal; omnivorous.   When attacked, it defends itself with courage; biting with
tenacity, for which it is well calculated by the
manner of the articulation of the lower jaw; the
coronoid processes being completely locked within the zygomatic arch.

Inhabit North America.

Genus.

Gulo, Retzius, Storr, Cuv. Illig.
Mustela, Linn.
Ursus, Linn. Gmel.
Meles, Bodd. Desm.
Mellivora, Storr.

CHARACTERS.

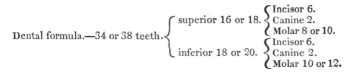

Dental formula.—34 or 38 teeth.

superior 16 or 18.
  Incisor 6.
  Canine 2.
  Molar 8 or 10.

inferior 18 or 20.
  Incisor 6.
  Canine 2.
  Molar 10 or 12.

Second incisors of the lower jaw receding; canines strong; the first two or three superior molars compressed, cutting, unicuspid; the fourth large and bicuspid; fifth small and tuberculous. The first four molars of the lower jaw unicuspid; fifth bicuspid; the last tuberculous; all approximate.

Body low set; sometimes long; head slightly elongated; ears very short and round; tongue sometimes smooth, at other times rough: five distinct toes on each foot, armed with hooked nails; nearly the entire sole of the hind feet resting on the ground; no pouch near the anus; two slight cuticular folds replace them.

HABIT. Carnivorous; analogous to that of the martins.

Inhabit America, north of Asia, and Africa.

Species.

1. **Gulo arcticus**, Sab. Desm. Mammalogie, p.
174. Encycl. pl. 38, fig. 1. *Northern glutton.*
Ursus gulo, Pall. Linn. Erxleb. Schreb.
Meles gulo, Bodd.
Ursus luscus, Linn. Gmel.
Wolverene, Penn.

Char. Essent. Body squat; general colour of
a fine deep chesnut, with a disk nearly black upon
the back.

DIMENSIONS. Total length two feet two inches :
length of the fore leg, eleven inches; of the hind
leg, twelve inches; length of the tail, comprising
the hair at its extremity, which is four inches,
eight inches.

DESCRIPTION. Snout black as far as the eye-
brows; eyes small; between the eye-brows and
ears, of a brownish-white colour; lower jaw and
interior of the fore feet, spotted with white; a tubercle under each toe; four others on the palm
of the hand.

HABIT. Very cruel and voracious; hunting by
night; not hibernating.

Inhabits countries bordering on the north sea,
both of Europe and of Asia. In America they
inhabit Canada, and the uncultivated parts of the
United States, where its depredations are often
experienced by the Indians.

Genus.

Mustela, Linn. Briss. Erxleb. Schreb. Bodd. Cuv. Geoff. Illig.

CHARACTERS.

Dental formula.—Teeth 34 or 38.
- superior 16 or 18.
  - Incisor 6.
  - Canine 2.
  - Molar 8 or 10.
- inferior 18 or 20.
  - Incisor 6.
  - Canine 2.
  - Molar 10 or 12.

Second inferior incisors of each side in a slight degree receding; canines strong; molars cutting; the anterior false molars conical and compressed; sometimes two above and three below, at other times three above and four below; true molars trilobate; the last molar with a blunt crown; body long and thin; arched when the animal is in a state of repose; head small, oval, flat above; jaws short; ears short and round; tongue smooth; feet five toed, armed with sharp crooked claws; small glands near the anus, which secrete copiously an extremely fetid fluid, when the animal is irritated; hair fine and soft; no cæcum; furnished with ventral mammæ.

HABIT. Carnivorous, voracious; killing small quadrupeds and birds, &c.

Inhabit temperate and northern climates in both countries.

Species.

1. *Mustela vulgaris,* Linn. Erxleb. Bodd. *Belette,* Buff. the *Weasel,* Penn. Brit. Zool. p. 39.

Char. Essent. Universal colour of the animal a ferruginous brown, rather darkest on the posterior half of the tail.

DESCRIPTION. Head proportionably broader, thicker, and shorter than the head of the ermines; opening of the nostrils curved backwards inferiorly, forming a lateral slit; ears short, broad, rounded; hands and feet covered with hair on their upper surface; hair at the extremity of the fingers projecting beyond the nails, which are short, strong and hooked.

HABIT. Like its congeners, carnivorous, voracious, very destructive to eggs and poultry; exceedingly alert and rapid in its motions, producing two or three times a year three or five at a birth.

Inhabits North America, abounds in the Atlantic states—and northern parts of the old continent.

Species.

2. *Mustela erminea,* Linn. Gmel. Bodd. Encyc. pl. 83. fig. 2. (Philad. Mus. *ermine,* No. 750) Sab. append.

Char. Essent. General colour during the summer, pale chesnut brown above, and white beneath; general colour during winter, white; tail always black or reddish-brown at the extremity.

DIMENSIONS. Total length, about twelve inches; length of the tail, nearly five inches.

DESCRIPTION. (From a prepared specimen in a winter dress,) general colour white, slightly tinged with yellow along the sides; outer part of the thighs and arms, extremity of the tail penciled with very long hair, about one inch of which is reddish-brown; head, neck and body, elongated; ears broader, but not so long or distinctly rounded as in the preceding species; anterior margin furnished with long hairs which nearly cover the concha; nails entirely hid, from above, by long thick hair, which covers them on the upper surface.

HABIT. Analogous to the weasel.

Inhabit the northern and middle states.

Species.

3. *Mustela lutreocephala*, Nob. Under this name I wish to make known an animal hitherto confounded with the *M. lutreola*, (Pallas, spicil. Zoolog. 14. pl. 31. *Lutra minor*, Erxleb. mem. de. Stock. 1739, tab. 11.) or with the *M. vison*. Linn. Gmel.

It resembles most nearly the " *lutreola*," yet is characteristically distinguished by its form, colour, size and markings; it was indeed noticed as specifically different from the " *lutreola*" by Warden, (descrip. des Etats unis, vol. v. p. 613) who, speaking of the American *Mink*, says " We do not think this Martin (*Mink*) similar to the *M. lutreola*, (Pall.) which is a Swedish animal; although many naturalists have confounded the two. we have reason to believe them different, though both have a common name, and there exists much resemblance in their natural habits."

The specimen here described, was obtained and prepared by Mr. C. W. Peale many years ago, in Maryland.

Char. Essent.   General colour brownish white, lightest beneath; tail ferruginous brown; length of the animal nearly double that of the "*lutreola.*"

DIMENSIONS.   Total length, one foot eight inches: length of the tail, about nine inches.

DESCRIPTION.   In form, the head and ears resemble those of the otter; the hair, the tail, and general proportion of the body, are more analogous to those of the weasel; body long; feet short; toes united to the middle, of equal length, slightly palmated, and furnished with very small sharp nails, nearly covered with hair.

HABIT.   According to Warden, this animal resides in the ground near to streams, in which it pursues its prey, consisting of fish, aquatic birds, rats, mice, insects, moles, and eggs of tortoises; during the night, entering the farm yards and destroying poultry; when famished it demonstrates astonishing boldness.

Inhabits the United States.

NOTE.—*Mustela lutreola,* Sab. append. to Franklin's, Exped. p. 649, was described by Foster, (Philos. Trans.) as the same with the European. *M. Zibellina, (Sable weasel)* Linn. Erxleb.

Bodd. Inhabit Kamtchatka, and agreeably to some authors, the United States; I have no knowledge of their existence in this country.

Species.

4. *Mustela vison*, Linn. Gmel. Desm. Mamm. p. 183. *Le vison*, Buffon, hist. nat. tom. 13. pl. 43. *Minx* of Americans.

Char. Essent. General colour brown, more or less deep; point of the inferior jaw white; tail of a blackish brown; feet demipalmated.

DIMENSIONS. Total length, about fifteen inches. not including the tail.

DESCRIPTION. Long hairs of the body brown. more or less tinged with yellow; next the skin, a thick ash coloured down, of a pale yellow at tip : tail moderately long, blackish ; feet hairy.

HABIT. Living in holes, on the borders of water; female producing from three to six at a birth; manners similar to the preceding species.

Inhabits Canada, and the northern and middle states.

Species.

5. *Mustela canadensis*, Linn. Erxleb. Schreb. *Pekan weasel*, Penn. Quad. p. 331. Desm. Mamm. p. 186. (Encyc. pl. 80. fig. 4.)

Le pekan, Buffon, hist. nat. v. 13. pl. 42. The *fisher*, Philad. Mus. No. 736, from the western states. *Fisher weasel* or *martin* of others.

9

Char. Essent. Head, neck, shoulders, and top of the back, mixed with gray and brown; nose, rump, tail, and extremities of a blackish brown; often a white spot beneath the throat.

DIMENSIONS. Total length, sixteen inches; length of the tail, ten inches.

DESCRIPTION. Body covered with two sorts of hair, for the most part with a down of an ash colour, the ends of which are gray, with some shades of yellow; hairs strong, presenting the same colour with the down, except at the tips. which are gray and black; some hairs of a chesnut colour tipt with black; the general colour resulting from these mixtures, is a gray and yellow on the head, neck, back, shoulders and upper part of the fore leg; flanks more gray than the back; rump blackish; lower part of the fore legs, whole of the hind legs, the fore feet and tail black, with some shades of brown; in some individuals, white between the fore and hind legs, on the breast, and belly.

HABIT. Similar to the preceding.

Inhabits Canada and the northern states.

Fisher weasel, Penn. Quad. p. 328, No. 202.

Mustela pennanti, Erxleb. Syst. Mamm. p. 470, sp. 10.

Mustela melanorhyncha, Bodd. Elench. anim. p. 88, sp. 13.

This is probably a large variety of the preceding, it is an inhabitant of North America.

Total length, twenty-four inches; length of the tail, seventeen inches; ears broad, round, blackish and bordered with white; nose black; whiskers long and silky; face and sides of the neck of a pale brown, or cinereus mixed with black; back, belly, thighs, and tail black, but the base of the last brownish; the sides of the body brown; the feet are broad and very hairy; a nail is often wanting on the hind foot; the nails are sharp, arched and white; tail covered with long hairs.

Species.

6. *Mustela martes*, Linn. Erxleb. Bodd. Schreb. tab. 130. *La marte*, Buff. hist. nat. t. 7. pl. 22. The *martin*, Penn. Brit. Zool. p. 39.

Mustela vison, var. Warden, hist. of the United States, vol. v. p. 613. *Pine martin*, Sab. append. to Franklin's Exped. (Encycl. pl. 81. fig. 4.)

Char. Essent. Colour brown, with a clear yellow spot beneath the throat.

Dimensions. Total length without the tail, one foot six inches eight lines; of the trunk of the tail nine inches nine lines; of the head, three inches ten lines; height before, eight inches; behind, ten inches.

Description. Fur formed of two sorts of hair; the first large, strong, and long, cinereus next the body, then clear fawn, terminated by brown mixed with shining red; the second consists of a fine down, very abundant, not entirely covered by long hairs of a cinereus colour, slightly tinged with white and fawn; end of the snout, breast, the legs and tail, of a blackish brown, in which there is but very little fawn colour; posterior part of the belly, red; borders and interior of the ear whitish, lightly tinged with yellow.

HABIT. Preferring for their haunts the thickest forests; climbing trees in search of birds and their eggs; they also attack small quadrupeds; bringing forth in spring, two or three young at a birth, in the nest of a squirrel or in holes of trees.

Inhabit all the north of Europe and America; have been observed as far south as New England.

Genus.

Mephitis, Cuv. Illig.
Viverra, Linn. Gmel. Bodd.

CHARACTERS.

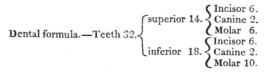

Dental formula.—Teeth 32. superior 14. { Incisor 6. Canine 2. Molar 6. } inferior 18. { Incisor 6. Canine 2. Molar 10. }

Second inferior incisors on each side, out of the range, inclining towards the interior of the mouth.

Canines very strong, conical.

Two false molars above, and three below on each side.

The superior tuberculous teeth very large, and

as broad as they are long; inferior molars furnished with two tubercles on the internal side.

Head short; nose rather projecting; snout obtuse.

Tongue smooth.

Feet pentadactyle, with their palms and soles hairy; toes of the anterior feet, armed with robust nails, arched and proper for digging, nails of the hind feet slightly raised when walking.

Trunk of the tail of moderate length, or very short.

Hair of the body and of the tail often very long, particularly that of the latter.

No cæcum.

Anal glands secreting a liquor excessively fetid. No follicules near the organs of generation.

HABIT. Burrowing in the earth; feeding on small live animals; diffusing, particularly when disturbed, a most nauseous, detestable odour, proceeding from the liquor of the anal glands, which they mix with the urine; with this fluid they wet the tail, and scatter it to a considerable distance.

Inhabits America, and the Isle of Java; those of the latter country have short tails.

A great variety of these animals has been described by M. Cuvier, some of which may hereafter prove distinct species. The following is the species common in North America.

Species.

1. *Mephitis americana.*

Mustela americana, Desm. Mamm. p. 186. (Encycl. pl. 86, fig. 3, *le chinch,* fig. 2. *Le conepate.*)

Var. K. *Moufette* pole cat, Cuv.

Pole cat or *putois* of Kalm, (voy. p. 452.)

Skunk of the Americans.

Char. Essent. General colour of the animal, blackish-brown; a large white spot on the occiput; hairs on the tail long and bushy, white at the extremity; claws of the fore feet strong, and about the length of the palm.

DIMENSIONS. Total length one foot six inches; tail nearly the length of the body.

HABIT. Living near the habitations of man; committing depredations on the poultry, &c. destructive to small animals. In summer they live in rabbit holes, where they collect their provisions. The female brings forth in spring, five or six at a birth. They have been observed to dwell for months near to farm houses, without emitting any odour, provided they be not disturbed.

Inhabits North America, abound in the Atlantic states; there are many varieties, differing in colour and markings. (Several prepared specimens in the Philad. Museum, Nos. 65, 649, &c.)

Genus.

Lutra, otter, Rai. Briss. Scop. Erxleb. Cuv. Shaw. Lacep. Illig. Desm.

Mustela, Linn. Gmel.

Dental formula.—Teeth 36.

superior 18.
- Incisor 6.
- Canine 2.
- Molar 10.

inferior 18.
- Incisor 6.
- Canine 2.
- Molar 10.

The second inferior incisor of each side a little receding in some species; canines of moderate length and hooked; the first superior molar small, blunt, and sometimes deciduous; the second cutting; the third of similar form but thicker; the fourth of moderate thickness, with two external points, and furnished with a strong spur on the inner side; the fifth has three small points externally, with a broad spur internally; inferior molars vary from five to six, the first being often wanting; in other respects they resemble the superior.

Head broad and flat; tongue slightly papillous; ears short and round; body very long and low upon the legs; toes armed with hooked nails, not retractile, and united by a membrane proper to facilitate natation.

Tail not so large as the body, strong, and depressed at its base; body covered with two sorts of hair, a fine soft down, and long brilliant bristles. Two small glands secreting a fetid liquor, situated near the anus.

HABIT. Carnivorous like the martins. but liv-

ing almost exclusively on fish; residing in holes
on the banks of rivers or beaches.

Species.

Lutra brasiliensis, Rai. Geoff. Desm. (Encycl.
pl. suppl. 5, fig. 3.) *Mustela lutris brasiliensis*,
Linn. Gmel. *Saricovienne de la Guyane*, Buffon,
suppl. tom. 6. p. 287. *Lutra canadensis*, Sabine.

Loutre d'Amerique, Cuv. regn. anim. tom. 1. p.
151, et tom. 4, fig. 3. *American otter*, Philadelphia Museum, No. 701, from Delaware state.

Char. Essent. General colour reddish-brown.
with the throat white or yellowish.

DIMENSIONS. Total length, three feet two inches;
length of the head, six inches; of the tail, one foot
five inches; medium height of the body, ten inches.

DESCRIPTION. Head globular; neck very long;
hair rather short, of a reddish-brown, lying flat to
the body; more sparse upon the tail; tail brownish, darkest towards the end; body beneath of the
same colour with the back; lower jaw and throat
of a dirty brown, slightly tinged with yellow.

HABIT. They form groupes more or less numerous, and frequent rivers and fresh water
marshes; feeding on fish.

Inhabit la Guyane, and some parts of North
America. Specimen in the Philadelphia Museum.

Species.

2. *Lutra marina, sea otter.* Erxleb. Desm.

Mustela lutris, Linn. Gmel.
Loutre du Kamtchatka, Geoff. Encycl. pl. 79.
fig. 3.

Char. Essent. Body very much elongated;
tail equal to one-third the length of the body;
hind feet very short; the animal of a lively blackish colour.

DIMENSIONS. Total length two feet ten inches;
length of the tail nine or ten inches; weighing
from seventy to eighty pounds.

DESCRIPTION. Head small and globular; ears
straight, conical, and covered with hair; eyes rather large; iris varying from brown to black; a
nictitating membrane at the internal angle of the
eye, extending over nearly one half the globe;
nostrils black and wrinkled; lips thick; opening
of the mouth, wide; superior jaw armed with fourteen teeth, four of which are sharp incisors; one
canine on each side, and four or five large thick
molars, the first cutting, and the last furnished
with blunt tubercles; one molar additional in the
lower jaw; tongue rather long, slightly notched at
the extremity, covered with corneous papillæ;
legs and thighs short, and placed nearer to the
anus than in other quadrupeds, except in the seals;
toes united by a hairy membrane, and terminated
by a hooked claw; tail thick and depressed: fur
rich, generally black or brownish.

Varietv.   *L. marina*, with a white head, Dict. des Science, Nat. fascic 7, p. 19.

Habit.   During the winter residing sometimes upon the ice, at others, on the borders of the sea; occasionally following the courses of rivers even up to fresh water lakes ; living in pairs ; the female brings forth but one at a time, after a gestation of eight or nine months ; feeding on crustacea, shells, sea worms, fish, fruits cast on shore during the summer, fuci, &c.

Inhabit the coasts of North America, particularly the north-west of this continent ; they exist also on the eastern coast of Kamtchatka, and neighbouring islands.   This animal is hunted for its skin, which is very valuable.

The Canada otter, (*Mustela hudsonica*, Lacep.) is probably the same animal.

Genus.

Canis, Linn. Briss. Penn. Erxleb. Bodd. Cuv Geoff. Illig. Desm.

CHARACTERS.

Dental formula.—Teeth 42.
- superior 20.
  - Incisor 6.
  - Canine 2.
  - Molar 12.
- inferior 22.
  - Incisor 6.
  - Canine 2.
  - Molar 14.

Incisors placed in a regular series, trilobate, when they have not been used; canines conical, sharp, and smooth; superior molars to the num-

ber of six on each side, viz. three small sharp
teeth or false molars with cutting edges, single
lobed; a bicuspid molar, and two small teeth with
flat crowns; the penultimate with two sharp tubercles on the exterior side.

Inferior molars seven, viz. four small molars,
one molar with a blunt point on the posterior part
of the crown, and two tuberculous teeth; jaws
elongated; zygomatic processes moderately arched externally.

Snout pointed, a considerable portion of the
extremity naked and rounded; tongue smooth.

Ears nearly straight and pointed, (in a state of
nature.)

Fore feet pentadactyle; hind feet tetradactyle,
provided with elongated nails, rather obtuse, not
retractile; tail of various lengths, generally straight,
(in a state of nature.)

Mammæ placed upon the breast and abdomen.

HABIT. Omnivorous; voracious; very intelligent; for the most part uniting in troops in order
to hunt down the more peaceable animals on
which they prey; pursuing them by means of
their sense of smell, which is very delicate from
the great development of the schneiderian membrane; seeing and hearing at a great distance;
the female, in a savage state, bringing forth from
three to five at a birth, which they nurse with
great affection, and defend with courage; some
species burrow in the earth, occasionally occupy-

ing the retreats of other animals; but the greatest number establish their retreat in the thickest forests, &c. &c.

Inhabit all parts of the habitable globe, with the exception of some groups of islands situated in the Pacific ocean.

Species.

1. *Canis familiaris*, Linn. Erxleb. Bodd. Desm. p. 130. Encycl. pl. 98, fig. 3. pl. 99, 100—1, 2, 3, 4.

Le Chien, Buff. hist. Nat. tom. 5.

The Dog, Penn. Brit. Zool. p. 23.

Char. Essent. Tail recurved; nose more or less elongated or contracted; nature and colour of the hair various, with the exception that whenever the tail offers the mixture of any colour with white this white is always terminal. This fact has been lately verified in a number of instances by Desmarest, who has lately observed it in several of the more savage species, as the antarctic dog, which has induced him to believe this last named variety to be nearest to the original.

We have very little doubt that the various species of domestic dogs are mere varieties of prolific hybrids, produced by the union of the wolf, (*C. lupus*) with the fox, (*C. vulpes*) or jackall, (*C. aureus;*) which opinion was originally advanced by Pallas. A prolific hybrid of this kind once produced, the progeny would more readily unite with the congeners of either parent, and with each other, and in this manner give rise to the innumerable varieties which at the present day are found scattered over the face of the earth: thus the domestic dog of the North American Indians, bears a strong resemblance to the wolf, not only in its erect and pointed ears, general colour of its body, &c. but this resemblance is further traced in the construction of the cranium and teeth, which partake in some degree both of the dog and wolf; in the former the jaws are less elongated, and display a greater breadth posteriorly; the molar teeth on each side of both jaws being more widely separated; the zygomatic fossæ are less capacious; the surface for the attachment of the temporal muscle less extensive, and the forehead considerably more elevated in the Indian dog; the facial angle of the prairy wolf is twenty six degrees, that of the Indian dog, thirty-five. These differences are yet more obvious when we compare the cranium of the common domestic dog with that of the wolf.

The same observations will apply with nearly equal force to the domestic dog of the East Indies; with this difference, viz. in the latter there exists a strong resemblance to the *Jackall,* to which also it is further allied in its howl, and other less observable particulars; indeed a successful union of the dog and jackall has repeatedly taken place.

In corroboration of the above, we may add that

prolific hybrids have been produced by the union of animals *generically* distinct, between the martin, (*Mustela martes*) and the domestic cat. An account of which is published in one of the early numbers of the New Edinburgh Philosophical Journal.*

* Mr. Sabine states, that during Parry's expedition to the North Pole, the dogs pertaining to the ship, were observed to copulate with the savage wolf; which circumstance he conceives as a convincing proof of identity of species; but the same argument would apply almost equally to prove the identity of the dog and hog.

We are indebted to the late Dr. B. S. Barton, for some very interesting observations concerning the native North American dogs.

"The Indian dog is frequently called by the traders and others, 'the half wolf breed.' His general aspect is much more that of the wolf than of the common domesticated dogs. His body, in general, is more slender than that of our dogs. He is remarkably small behind. His ears do not hang like those of our dogs, but stand erect, and are large and sharp pointed; he has a long, small snout, and very sharp nose; his barking is more like the howling of the wolf. When attacked, and when fighting, he does not shake his antagonist like our dogs; his teeth are very sharp, and his bite sure; when he snarls, which he is wont to do upon the slightest occasion, he draws the skin from his mouth back, presenting all his teeth to view. Our dogs when once attacked by these Indian dogs, always fear and shun them. It is a very curious circumstance, that the Indian dog will never attack or pursue the wolf, which the common dogs so readily do; this fact seems to point very strongly to the origin of the American animal. For the purpose of hunting, the Indian dogs are very useful; but in other respects, they are by no means so docile as the common dogs; they have less

Desmarest, in his "*Mammalogie*," includes all the varieties of this species under three grand divisions.

" 1. *Les matins*. Head more or less elongated; parietals approximating: condyles of the lower jaw on a line with the superior molars.

" 2. *Les espagneuls*. Head moderately elongated; parietals not approximating from their commencement above the temporals, separating on the contrary, and expanding so as to increase the cerebral cavity and frontal sinuses.

" 3. *Les dogues*. Snout more or less shortened; cranium elevated; frontal sinuses considerable; condyles of the lower jaw placed above the line of the superior molars."

In detailing the characters of the common bull dog, (*Canis molossus*, Linn. Gmel.) he omits one of the most principal traits, viz. in this variety, the inferior incisors and the lower jaw project beyond the superior teeth and jaw.

For a detailed account of the varieties of the domestic dog, see F. Cuvier's papers, published in the anal. du mus. d'hist. nat.

Species.

2. *Canis lupus, common wolf,* Linn. Erxleb

fidelity. In short, every thing shows that the Indian dog is a much more savage or imperfectly reclaimed animal than the common dog."*

* Vide. Barton's Medical and Physical Journal. vol. 1. part 2, page 15.

(Encycl. pl. 104. fig. 3.) Schreb. Bodd. *Le lonp,* Buff. hist. nat. tom. 7. pl. 1.

The *wolf,* Penn. syn. Quad. p. 149. No. 3.

Char. Essent. Tail straight; general colour reddish-gray, with a black ray on the fore legs of adults; eyes oblique.

DIMENSIONS. Total length, three feet seven inches; length of the head, ten inches; of the ear, four inches six lines; of the trunk of the tail, one foot three inches four lines; greatest height of the anterior part of the body, two feet five inches; behind, two feet three inches.

DESCRIPTION. Head thick and oblong, terminated by a slender snout; tail thick, tufted, and straight; coat composed of hairs, the longest of which are white at base, then black, then reddish, then black and white at the extremity; those of the head anterior to the opening of the ears, those of the neck and anterior part of the back, of the buttocks, and of the tail, being longest, measuring even five inches; the others much shorter, principally on the snout and ears; all these hairs being stiff and strong, covering a soft cinereus felt; an oblique black band on the wrist in adults; snout black.

The hair of wolves grows white by age, and wolves of northern latitudes become white in winter.

HABIT. Solitary, dwelling in thick forests; prowling at night; attacking generally the sheep, antelope, deer and hare: they also feed on carrion, which they smell at a great distance; they are cunning, distrustful, and intelligent, but much less so than the fox. During the winter, when pressed by famine, they unite in troops in order to attack the larger animals. The female enters in heat during the winter, in which state she continues twelve or fifteen days; she brings forth in the most secret recesses of the forest, after a gestation of sixty-three days, five or six young at a birth, whose eyes are closed, as is the case with dogs. The wolf attains its maturity about the end of the second year, and lives fifteen or twenty years; its voice is a prolonged howl. The dog is generally its enemy, nevertheless instances are numerous of sexual union between the two species, producing a prolific hybrid, partaking more of the nature of the wolf than dog.

Inhabits Europe, southern Africa, North America: the race is totally extirpated from England and Ireland.

Mr. Warden, in his description of the United States, vol. 5. p. 615, says, there is a great variety of wolves in this country, both as regards their size and colour. In the northern states this animal is red or reddish-brown, with a blackish line along the spine, and yellow rays about the ears and on the arms; in the southern states the wolf is entirely black.

In the Missouri country we observe several

11

new species or varieties; one of large size and brown colour was seen in the mountains near Columbia river, between the Great Falls and Rapids; (perhaps the *Canis nubilus*, Say, to be described hereafter?) Another is found on the borders of the Pacific ocean, which burrows like the fox. (This has not been described.) Two other smaller species inhabit woodlands, and show themselves occasionally in the plains; (perhaps *Canis latrans*, Say?)

Mackenzie mentions a little wolf he met with between the sixty-fifth and seventieth degrees of north latitude, which attacks the beavers.

Species.

3. *Canis lycaon*, Linn. Gmel. Erxleb. Schreb. *Loup noire*, Buff. hist. nat. v. 9. pl. 41, and Encyc. pl. 104. fig. 4.

Char. Essent. Tail straight; body totally black.

Dimensions. Intermediate between those of the common wolf and fox.

Description. Resembling the common wolf in form and proportion, but the eyes are rather smaller, and ears longer; hair entirely black.

The black wolf of Florida, of which Bartram speaks as having a white spot on the breast (in the female,) is mentioned as a variety of the *C. lycaon*, by Warden.

Gmelin and Erxleben, have erroneously applied to the *Canis lycaon*, citations which relate to the gray fox of North America.

Inhabits mountainous countries of Europe and North America.

Species.

4. *Canis latrans*, **Prairie wolf**, Say. Long's exped. to the Rocky Mountains, vol. 1. p. 168.

Char. Essent. Hair cinereus gray, varied with black above and dull fulvous cinnamon, and at tip gray or black; longer on the vertebral line.

DIMENSIONS. Total length, including the tail, with the exception of the hair at its tip, three feet nine and a half inches; trunk of the tail, one foot one and a half inches; length of the ears, four inches; length of the fore leg, one foot.

DESCRIPTION. Hair at base, dusky plumbeous, in the middle of its length, dull cinnamon, at tip, gray or black; ears erect, round at tip, cinnamon colour behind; dark plumbeous at base; inside lined with gray hairs; iris yellow; pupil dark blue; lips white; three series of black setæ; sides paler than the back, obsoletely fasciate with black above the legs; legs cinnamon colour on the outer side; a dilated black abbreviated line near the wrist; tail straight, bushy, fusiform, varied with gray and cinnamon, tip black.

HABIT. They are by far the most numerous of our wolves; roaming over the plains in numbers during the night; hunting the deer; sometimes reduced by hunger to eat the wild plums, and other fruits, to them almost indigestible; their bark resembles the dog at first, but terminates in a lengthened howl; these animals are remarkably intelligent.

Inhabit the plains of Missouri, and other regions west of the Mississippi, and not improbably west of the Rocky Mountains.

This is certainly a distinct species from the " *Canis mexicanus*," (Desm. Mamm. p. 199) to which it is most nearly allied; the essential characters of the latter are " general colour cinereus, varied with reddish spots; many blackish bands extending on each side of the body from the spine to the flanks." " Inhabits New Spain."

Mr. Say thinks the " *latrans*" most probably the origin of the domestic dog, so common in the villages of the Indians of this region, some of which still retain much of the manners and habits of this species. (Beautiful prepared specimens in the Philadelphia Museum, brought by the exploring party.)

Species.

5. *Canis nubilus, dusky wolf,* Say. (Long's Exped. to the Rocky Mountains, v. 5. p. 169.)

Char. Essent. General colour dark dusky: the hair cinereus at base, then brownish, then gray, then black; the proportion of black on the hairs is so considerable as to give to the whole

animal a much darker colour than the darkest of
the *latrans*, but the gray of the hairs combining
with the black tips, in the general effect, produce
a mottled appearance; the gray colour predomi-
nant on the sides.

DIMENSIONS. Length from the tip of the nose
to the origin of the tail, four feet three inches and
three quarters; length of the trunk of the tail, one
foot three inches; of the ear, from the anterior
angle to the tip, three inches and three quarters;
from the anterior angle of the ear to the posterior
canthus of the eye, four inches and three quarters; from the anterior canthus of the eye to the
tip of the nose, five inches and a half; between
the anterior angles of the ears, rather more than
three inches.

DESCRIPTION. Ears short, deep brownish black,
with a patch of gray on the anterior side within;
muzzle blackish above; anterior border of the superior lips gray; tip of the inferior jaw, gray, a
line of the same colour extending backwards nearly to the origin of the neck; beneath dusky ferruginous, grayish, with long hair between the hind
legs; a large white spot on the breast; the ferruginous colour narrowed on the neck, and dilated
on the lower part of the cheeks; legs brownish-
black; tail short, fusiform, slightly tinged with
ferruginous, black above near the base and at tip;
the longer hairs on the back, particularly over the
shoulders, resemble a short sparse mane.

The aspect of this animal is far more fierce and
formidable than either the common red wolf or
the prairie wolf, and is of a more robust form.
The length of the ears and tail distinguish it at
once from the former, and its greatly superior
size, besides the minor characters of colour, &c.
separate it from the prairie wolf.

It diffuses a strong and disagreeable odour.

HABIT. Unknown. Inhabits the same countries as the preceding species.

Fox.

Pupil taking the figure of the section of a lens,
in closing.

Species.

6. *Canis vulpes, common fox* (Encycl. pl. 106,
fig. 2.)

Char. Essent. General colour reddish above,
and white beneath; behind the ears black; tail
tufted and terminated by black hairs.

DIMENSIONS. Total length, two feet three inches
six lines; length of the head, three inches; of the
ears, four inches; of the tail, one foot four inches;
height of the body before, one foot one inch three
lines; height of the body behind, one foot two
inches three lines.

DESCRIPTION. Snout pointed; head rather large;
forehead flattened; ears straight, pointed; eyes
very oblique; tail large, touching the ground, ex-

tremely bushy; feet composed of long and thick
hairs, of a more or less deep red; lips, borders of
the mouth, lower jaw, anterior of the neck, throat,
belly, interior of the thighs, white; snout red; behind the ears of a black-brown; feet deep brown
before; tail terminated with black hairs.

Var. 1. *C. alopex*, (Linn.) Var. 2. *Canis cruci-
gera*, (Gesner.)

HABIT. This dexterous and cunning animal
lives in the woods near the dwellings of man;
during the night committing depredations upon
poultry; first killing all within his reach, then
carrying them to his hole, or burying them beneath the leaves; he also destroys rabbits, and
birds, and robs the snares of the hunter, is fond
of eggs, milk, and fruit, particularly of grapes, will
occasionally attack bee hives, and does not re-
fuse fish, insects, &c. The female enters into
heat during the winter; produces once a year,
five or six at a birth, seldom less than three: the
young attain their full growth in about eighteen
months. The duration of their life is about fourteen years; their voice is a species of barking,
produced by a reiteration of precipitate similar
sounds. The fox emits a disagreeable odour. In
cases of extreme danger and surprise these animals have been known to simulate death.

Inhabit northern and temperate climates of both
continents.

Species.

7. *Canis argentatus*, Geoff. Desm.
Renard argentè ou noir, Geoff. collect. du Mus.
Renard argentè, F. Cuvier. Mamm. lithogr. 5 livr.

Char. Essent. General colour soot-black, spotted, or rather brushed with white; extremity of the tail, white.

DIMENSIONS. Total length, one foot five inches; length of the head, six inches; of the tail, eleven inches; height before, one foot one inch; behind, one foot two inches.

DESCRIPTION. Form of the common fox; colour black, sometimes slightly tinged with white in some parts; extremity of the tail for the most part perfectly white; hair silky, thick and fine; feet and snout covered with short hair; eyes yellowish; sometimes a white spot beneath the neck.

HABIT. In captivity some individuals play like dogs, growling like these animals; they hide their superabundant food and dislike the heat.

Inhabit the north of Asia and America. M. F. Cuvier doubts the identity of the European and American species.

Species.

8. *Canis decussatus*, Geoff. collect. du Mus.

Char. Essent. Colour varied with black and white above, with a black cross upon the shoulders; snout, inferior parts of the body and feet black; tail terminated with white.

DIMENSIONS. Same as the European fox.

Inhabits North America—may possibly prove to be a variety of the *argentatus*.

Species.

9. *Canis virginianus, gray fox* of Catesby, nat. hist. Carolin. v. 2. p. 78. Briss. regn. anim. *Canis virginianus*, Erxleb. Gmel. (Encycl. pl. 106. fig. 4.)

Char. Essent. Body entirely of a silver gray colour.

DIMENSIONS and DESCRIPTION. Differing very little from the European fox in size and form. Some doubt has been expressed concerning the identity of this species and the "*Fulvus*," described below. A comparison of the skulls of the red and gray American fox, presents prominent specific distinctions, as has been demonstrated by frequent examination.

Species.

10. *Canis fulvus*, (*renard de Virginie*, Palisot de Beauvois. Mem. sur le renard et le Lapin d'Amerique, dans le Bull. Soc. Philomat.)

Canis fulvus, Desm. Mamm. p. 203.

Chàr. Essent. Colour consisting of different shades of red; beneath the neck and belly, white; breast gray; anterior of the fore legs and feet black: tip of the tail white.

12

DIMENSIONS. Total length, not including the tail, two feet two inches.

DESCRIPTION. Snout obscure red; forehead and cheeks more clear; borders òf the lips, white; interior of the ears, covered with yellowish-white hair; exterior black; top and sides of the neck, shoulders, and fore feet, a lively red; tail varied with black and red, extremity white.

Species.

11. *Canis cinereo-argenteus, tricoloured fox*, Erxleb. Linn. Gmel. *Renard gris*, Briss. Quad. p. 241.

Char. Essent. Upper part of the body, black gray; head reddish-gray; ears and sides of the neck a lively red; throat and cheeks white; inferior jaw black; belly and tail reddish, glazed with black; tip of the tail deep black.

DIMENSIONS. Total length, two feet two inches; trunk of the tail, one foot one inch.

DESCRIPTION. Between the eyes whitish, divided by a black longitudinal line, which is lost upon the forehead; superior lip white; borders of the lips black; beneath the eye an obscure spot, which extends along the cheek nearly to the neck; tail very bushy, covered with hairs about three inches in length.

Inhabits North America and Paraguay.

Species.

12. *Canis velox*, Say. (Long's Exped. to the Rocky Mountains, v. 1. p. 486.)

Char. Essent. Head above ferruginous-brown, intermixed with gray; fur fulvous; hair whitish at base, then black, gray, and brown in succession.

DIMENSIONS. Total length of the animal not more than one half that of the red fox, (*C. fulvus*, Desm.) length of the cranium, four inches three-tenths; distance between the tips of the superior orbitar processes, one inch; between the temporal crests at the coronal suture, half an inch.

DESCRIPTION. The hair is fine, dense and soft; a brownish dilated line passes from the eye nearly to the nostrils; margin of the upper lip, white; orbits gray; margin of the ears, excepting at tip, white; the inner side broadly marginated with white hairs; the neck above has longer hairs, of which the black and gray portions are more conspicuous; beneath the head, pure white; the body slender, and tail rather long, cylindrical and black.

HABIT. This little animal runs with extraordinary velocity, so much so, that when at full speed its course has been by the hunters compared to the flight of a bird. Like the *corsac* of Asia, it burrows in the earth, in a country totally destitute of trees and bushes, and is not known to frequent forest districts.

Inhabits Missouri country; is probably the same animal mentioned by Lewis and Clark, under the name of burrowing fox, vol. 2. p. 351.

Species.

13. *Canis lagopus, isatis fox,* Linn. Gmel. Erxleb. Bodd. *Renard bleu.* Buff. *C. lagopus,* Sabine. append. p. 658. (Encycl. pl. 106. fig. 3.)

Char. Essent. Hair very long, thick and soft; fur cinereus, or of a uniform clear brown in summer; white in winter.

DIMENSIONS. Total length from twenty-two inches to two feet; tail reaching to the ground; about one foot high before.

DESCRIPTION. Head short; snout elongated; ears hairy; soles of the feet covered with long hairs; tail long and very bushy; hairs of the body, about two inches in length, of a cinereus or uniform clear brown colour, changing to a beautiful clear white in winter. The young animal is sometimes of a dark gray colour, sometimes yellowish-white; occasionally marked with a brown line upon the back and a transverse line of the same colour upon the shoulders, on which account they have been called the crucial fox, a name already applied to a species of fox properly so called.

HABIT. Living in the coldest countries of the earth, in mountainous districts, but not in forests. They enter in rut during the month of March.

which state continues about fifteen days, and gestation about nine weeks; its voice is between that of the fox and dog, its skin is very precious.

Inhabits the countries bordering on the frozen ocean in Iceland, Greenland, and the continent of America, according to Sabine.

Genus.

Cat, or *Felis*. Linn. Briss. Erxleb. Bodd. Cuv. Geoff. Illig.

CHARACTERS.

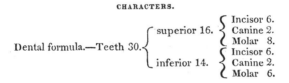

Inferior incisors, forming a regular series. Canine, very strong. Four molars above, viz. two false or conical on each side; one carnivorous, with three lobes and a small tuberculous tooth, wider than long, (the last sometimes wanting,) below, on each side, two false, compressed, simple molars, and one carnivorous bicusped. Head round; facial line short, and slightly arched; zygomatic arches ventricose; jaws short; tongue covered with corneous papillæ, their points directed backwards; nose terminated by a very small muzzle, with the nostrils pierced inferiorly and at the sides; ears short, straight, triangular; pupils contracting sometimes in a vertical line, sometimes in a circle; legs proportionably short; anterior feet pentadactyle, posterior tetradactyle; nails of the fore feet retractile, in a state of repose, elevated and lying obliquely between the fingers; tail more or less long; no pouches or follicles around the organs of generation or anus; glans of the male covered with small corneous papillæ.

HABIT. Very savage; feeding in a state of nature on living animals only, which they seize by surprise and not by chasing, as the dogs are accustomed to do; leaping and climbing with facility; running badly; sense of smell not very acute, but that of sight very perfect.

Inhabit the forests of various climates; none have been discovered in Australasia.

Species.

1. *Felis concolor*, Linn. Gmel. Bodd. Erxleb. (Encycl. pl. 94. fig. 1. and 2.) *Le cougar*, Buff. v. 9. pl. 19. *Gouazoura*, d'Azara, nat. hist. Parg. v. 1. p. 133. *Pouma* of travellers, vulgarly called the *American Lion*.

Char. Essent. Of a deep yellow colour, without a mane or tuft at the end of the tail.

DIMENSIONS. Total length, three feet six inches; length of the tail, two feet three inches; of the head, seven inches nine lines.

DESCRIPTION. Body long and slim; head small; legs strong, short; tail long and training; colour, grayish about the eyes; hairs within the ears white, slightly tinged with yellow, exterior of the ears blackish; those portions of the lips which support the whiskers, black; the remaining portions of the lip, with the throat, white; beneath the neck, pale yellow.

NOTE.—The " *Cougar de Pennsylvanie*," Buff. (hist. nat. suppl. 3. tom. 2. pl. 41.) is most probably a variety. Collinson remarks, that it is lower upon its legs and has a longer tail than this; it is described as being five feet six inches in length; tail, two feet six inches; height before, one foot nine inches; behind, one foot ten inches.

HABIT. Carnivorous, ferocious and cruel without necessity; attacking principally sheep, goats, calves, and colts; living isolated or in pairs, in the depths of forests; leaping with agility and climbing trees with facility.

Inhabit Paraguay, Brazil, United States, as far north as Canada.

Species.

2. *Felis onca, Jaguar,* (Encycl. pl. 92. fig. 2. by the name of *Panther.*) *Yagouarètè,* d'Azara, Fred. Cuvier, Mamm. 17 livr. *Onza* Marcgrave. *Panthère femelle,* Buff. tom. 9. pl. 12.

Char. Essent. Colour yellowish above, white beneath, marked with circular black spots, ranged in five or six lines on each side of the body.

DIMENSIONS. Total length, four feet seven inches; length of the tail, two feet two inches; height of the body, two feet six inches.

DESCRIPTION. Proportions thick and clumsy; hairs short, strong, compact, silky, and rather longer on the inferior parts of the body; base of the fur yellowish, and covered with spots either entirely black, or yellow encircled with black; those of the first sort existing only on the head, tail, extremities and under part of the body; interior of the ear, white; exterior black, with a white spot; commissure of the lips, black, as is also the end of the tail; four mammæ.

HABIT. Living in swampy forests; retiring into dens during the day; they are very fierce, will attack dogs and destroy large domestic animals; they climb trees like cats; bringing forth two young at a birth.

Inhabit Brazil, Paraguay, Mexico and United States, (south-western territory,) occasionally found east of the Mississippi.

Species.

3. *Felis pardalis*, Linn. Erxleb. Bodd. *Ocelot*, Buff. hist. nat. t. 13. pl. 35. No. 36. Shaw, Gen. Zool. v. 1. part. 1. pl. 88. fig. (Encycl. pl. 93. fig. 2.) *Spotted mountain cat.*

Char. Essent. General colour gray, marked with large fawn coloured spots, bordered with black, forming oblique bands on the flanks; two black lines bordering the forehead laterally.

DIMENSIONS. Nearly two feet in length from the extremity of the snout to the origin of the tail, which is about two feet long.

DESCRIPTION. Snout longer and thicker than that of the cat; hairs sparse, grayish fawn above, white beneath; a black line extending on each side, from the nostril to the anterior angle of the eye, and prolonged on the head as far as the occiput, by the side of the ear; small black spots disposed symmetrically between these bands, upon the forehead and head; other small round black spots where the whiskers commence; two rays along the sides of the lower jaw, one above the other, the superior commencing at the posterior angle of the eye, the inferior having two branches before, the lower one directed towards the throat; four longitudinal bands on the top of the neck, of a fawn colour in the middle, the two external ones curved downwards in form of a hook; a small black line between the two middle ones, a black line along the back extending to the origin of the tail, on each side of which is a parallel row of oval black spots, about one inch in length; two other bands also parallel, composed of oval figures, with black borders, and fawn colour in the middle with small round black spots; beneath the third row is a band of more than an inch in width, extending from the shoulders to before the thighs.

13

bordered with black, like the oval figures, and
fawn colour in the middle, with small round
black spots; and lastly a band beneath the latter rather less broad and interrupted; bordered
spots on the rump and thighs; small oval full
spots on the anterior part of the shoulders and
on the thighs, also on the anterior surface of the
paws; transverse lines beneath the neck, one of
which extends from one side to the other, in form
of a collar; breast and belly with small black
spots; tail marked with spots of the same colour,
much larger towards its extremity; (a specimen
of the adult, and very young animal, in Philadelphia Museum.)

Habit. Similar to that of other species of this
genus; climbs trees with facility.

Inhabit Mexico, and the south-western parts
of the United States, particularly Louisiana; also
observed by Mr. Nuttall in the Arkansa territory; vid. Travels into the Arkansa territory, p. 118
Not known to exist east of the Mississippi.

Species.

4. *Felis canadensis*, Geoff. Desm.   *Le lynx du
Canada*, Buff. hist. nat. suppl. tom. 3, pl. 44. *Lynx*.

Char. Essent.   Tail very short, black on the
posterior half; ears terminated by a small pencil
of hairs; colouring of the body grayish, with yellowish or pale brown points below, some black
lines on the head.

Dimensions. Total length, two feet three inches; of the tail, three inches nine lines; of the ears, two inches.

Description. Differing from the *Lynx* properly so called, in the shortness of the tail; body covered with long grayish hairs, mixed with white, spotted and striped with yellow, more or less deep; head grayish, mixed with white and yellow, slightly striped with black in some places; end of the nose and borders of the lower jaw, black; whiskers white, about three inches long; ears furnished with long white hair within, mouse gray externally, external border black, internal border yellowish; pencils of the ears composed of black hairs about seven or eight lines in length; tail short and thick, well furnished with hair, first half reddish-white, last half black; abdomen, hind legs, interior of the fore legs, and end of the feet, of a dirty white; nails white, about six lines in length.

Inhabit Canada, Labrador, &c.

Species.

5. *Felis rufa*, Guldenstaedt, Gmel. Schreb. Rafinesque, Ame. Mon. Mag. 1817, p. 46, sp. 3. " *Chat-cervier*," of furriers.

Char. Essent. Tail short, white beneath and at the point; ears furnished with a pencil of hairs; colour dark or reddish yellow, spotted with brown.

DIMENSIONS. Rather smaller than the common Lynx.

DESCRIPTION. Head and back, of a deep red, with small spots of blackish-brown; throat whitish; breast and belly of a clear reddish-white; extremities of the same colour with the back, with waves of light brown; superior lip presenting some blackish lines upon a reddish-white ground; a little white about the eye.

Inhabit the forests of New York, Pennsylvania. and Ohio.

Species.

6. *Felis fasciata.**

Lynx fasciatus, Rafinesque, Ame. Mon. Mag. 1817, p. 46. Lewis and Clark's expedition up the Missouri.

Char. Essent. Tail very short, white, with the point black; ears furnished with pencils of hair, and black externally; fur very thick, of a brownish-red colour, with blackish stripes and points above.

DIMENSIONS. Large.

Inhabit North America. This species was noticed by Lewis and Clark on the north-west coast; (where there exist several other species of *Lynx*, remarkable for their size and beauty of fur.) It is probably the same as that mentioned by Nuttall. Vid. Travels in Arkansa territory, p. 118.

Species.

7. *Felis montana*, (Encycl. pl. 98, fig. 2.)
Lynx montana, Rafin. ibid. p. 46.
Mountain cat, of the Americans.
Lynx du Mississippi, Buff. t. 8, pl. 53.

Char. Essent. Tail very short, grayish; ears destitute of pencils of hair; exteriorly blackish, whitish or yellow spots within; whitish, with brown spots beneath.

DIMENSIONS. Total length, three or four English feet.

Inhabit New York, Alleghany mountains, and as far south as Florida.

Species.

8. *Felis aurea,** Desm.
Lynx aureus, Raf. ibid. p. 46.
Wild cat, Leray, voy. au Missouri, p. 190.

Char. Essent. Tail very short; ears without pencils; colour, a clear brilliant yellow, spotted with black and white.

DIMENSIONS. One half larger than the domestic cat, tail two inches long.

DESCRIPTION. This species simply indicated by Leray; has been observed on the borders of Yellow Stone river, near the forty-fourth degree of north latitude, and thirty-second west longitude, from the meridian of Washington.

Felis catus, Linn. and others.

Domestic species not indigenous; a variety of the " *Chat sauvoge,*" *Wild cat,* Buff. hist. nat. tom. 6, the essential characters of which are, base of the fur of a more or less obscure gray; marked with blackish longitudinal bands on the back, and transverse ones on the flanks; lips and soles of the feet black; tail surrounded with rings, the end black.

Inhabits all the great forests of Asia, but are rare.

Tribe.

CARNIVOROUS AMPHIBIOUS ANIMALS.

(*Carnivora pinnipedia.*)

Feet short, enveloped in the skin in form of fins; the posterior in the direction of the body; number of incisors variable, often six, and sometimes four above; most commonly four, sometimes two below.

Genus.

Phoca, Linn. Erxleb. Bodd. Cuv. Geoff. Illig. *Otaria,* Peron.

1. Those in which the teeth are furnished with several roots.

CHARACTERS.

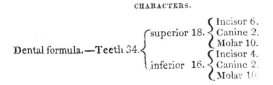

Dental formula.—Teeth 34.

superior 18.
{ Incisor 6.
  Canine 2.
  Molar 10.

inferior 16.
{ Incisor 4.
  Canine 2.
  Molar 10.

A.

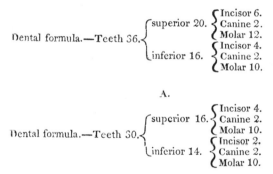

Dental formula.—Teeth 32.
- superior 16.
  - Incisor 4.
  - Canine 2.
  - Molar 10.
- inferior 16.
  - Incisor 4.
  - Canine 2.
  - Molar 10.

B.

Dental formula.—Teeth 30.
- superior 16.
  - Incisor 4.
  - Canine 2.
  - Molar 10.
- inferior 14.
  - Incisor 2.
  - Canine 2.
  - Molar 10.

2. Those in which the teeth have simple roots.

CHARACTERS.

Dental formula.—Teeth 36.
- superior 20.
  - Incisor 6.
  - Canine 2.
  - Molar 12.
- inferior 16.
  - Incisor 4.
  - Canine 2.
  - Molar 10.

A.

Dental formula.—Teeth 30.
- superior 16.
  - Incisor 4.
  - Canine 2.
  - Molar 10.
- inferior 14.
  - Incisor 2.
  - Canine 2.
  - Molar 10.

Incisors varying in their forms, sometimes triangular, sometimes conical, sometimes grooved transversely on their cutting edges, as if bilobate, and more or less distinct from each other.

Canines more or less strong, conical, slightly arched, and most generally proportional to the size of the head, like those animals of the feline race.

Molars resembling the false molars of carnivorous animals, cutting, triangular, but more conical and obtuse; sometimes, though rarely, with little tubercles at their neck.

Head round; snout and lips swollen; nose sometimes prolonged into a species of soft erectile trunk; nostrils susceptible of being completely closed.

Eyes very large, the cornea flat, and the chrystalline lens protuberant; eyelids slightly developed, excepting the nictitating membrane.

Ears wanting altogether, or rudimentary, narrow and pointed.

Tongue conical, papillous, but soft, with the extremity slightly notched; mouth moderately large. bordered by lips susceptible of extension.

Feet five-toed; the anterior displaying externally the hand only; the posterior feet naked; toes slightly distinct, enveloped by the skin which extends beyond them more or less; those of the hand decreasing in length, ordinarily from the internal to the external; the two external of the hind feet the longest.

Tail short and thick, situate between the two hind feet.

Mammæ to the number of four, abdominal; hair in general short, stiff and recumbent; whiskers very strong and abundant; stomach simple, membranous; intestines of equal diameter throughout their length.

Cæcum small.

Habit. Aquatic, visiting the land only for the purpose of copulation, or to bring forth and suckle their young; swimming and plunging with great facility; feeding upon fish, molusca, and sea grass; having the organs of vision constructed for a residence in deep waters; sense of hearing not delicate; that of taste perfect; that of touch obtuse, by reason of the thick layer of fat which surrounds the animal; but the sense of smell is exquisite.

They travel and live in numerous troops, the greatest harmony prevailing amongst them, except during the rutting season, when the males engage in furious combats, disputing the possession of females; the latter bring forth once a year, one or two at a birth, which they nourish and bring up with the greatest care.

Inhabit all seas, especially the Polar, the Mediterranean, the Caspian, and it is said the Lake Baikal, the waters of which are fresh.

Sub-Genus.

1. *Phoca*, Peron.

Characters. No external ears; incisors simply cutting; molars cutting, and with many points; toes of the hind feet terminated by pointed nails placed on the borders of the membrane which unites them.

14

Species.

1. *Phoca cristata*, Sea lion.
Phoca leonina, Fab.

Char. Essent. A sort of moveable hood attached to the top of the head, susceptible of erection and of being extended over the eyes and snout; four superior incisors, of which the lateral are largest; four inferior incisors.

DIMENSIONS. Total length, seven or eight feet.

DESCRIPTION. Forehead of the adult male, carrying a sort of large tubercle, susceptible of swelling like a bladder, and carinated in its middle part; (besides the true nostrils, there exists false ones in the same tubercle, and the number of these false nostrils vary according to the age of the individual;) thirty-two teeth in all, viz. four incisors above and below; one canine, and five molars on each side of both jaws; bristles of the whiskers large, nearly round, and whitish, annulated and compressed at base, obtuse at their extremities; iris brown; hairs soft and long, with a very deep woolly base.

Difference occasioned by age.—At one year, colour white, with the middle of the back livid gray; at two years, of a snow-white, with a narrow brown line on the back: the old ones having the head and feet black; the rest of the body equally black, but checkered with gray spots; the back remaining always obscure.

HABIT. This seal, according to Crantzius (hist. gen. des. voy. t. 19, p. 61.) is very abundant in the straits of Davis; making two voyages thence annually, and remaining there from the month of September to the month of March; it then seeks the shore to bring forth, and returns with its young in the month of June, very thin and emaciated. It departs a second time in July, to go further north, where it probably meets with more abundant nourishment, for it returns in the month of September very fat. Fabricius assures us that they copulate standing.

Inhabit Greenland during the months of April, May and June; the Atlantic coast of North America.

An individual of this species was lately captured in Long Island Sound, fourteen miles from New York; for a particular and interesting description of which, including its anatomy, vid. annals of the New York Lyceum, vol. 1, p. 384, by J. E. Dekay, M. D.

Species.

2. *Phoca vitulina*, Linn. (Encycl. pl. 109, fig. 1.) *Phoque commun*, Buff. tom. 13. pl. 45. Sab. *Sea dog, Sea wolf, Sea calf* of travellers and sailors.

F. Cuvier, obs. Zool. sur les faculties, intellect. du *Phoque commun*, Ann. du mus. t. 17, p. 337.

Char. Essent. Six superior incisors; four in-

ferior; nails rather strong; bristles of the whiskers, undulating; colour of the animal, grayish-
yellow, more or less glazed with brown, according to age; hair abundant and thick.

DIMENSIONS. Total length, from the extremity
of the head to the end of the feet, three feet
three inches six lines; of the head, six inches six
lines; trunk of the tail, three inches four lines;
circumference of the body, posterior, to the fore
feet, one foot six inches.

DESCRIPTION. Body elongated, diminishing in
thickness from the chest to the tail; neck very
short; head round, having at its anterior portion
much analogy to that of the otter; snout broad,
flat, and truncated; upper lip very moveable, provided with whiskers; six incisors above, four below; four canine and five cutting lobate molars
on each side of both jaws; ears marked only by a
small tubercle at the anterior borders of their
orifices; meatus auditorius opening anterior to
the tympanum at the side of the eye; posterior
portion of the head very thick, without occipital
or saggital crests; feet short, five-toed; the nails
are largest on the hind feet, thick, long, free, and
of a black colour; hair compact, not incumbent
posteriorly as in other seals; general colour of
the body of a grayish-yellow, more or less undulated with brown.

HABIT. These animals are much more intelligent than could be expected from beings purely

aquatic; they become attached to man, and execute at his command various actions not very accordant with their natural habits. In captivity they feed on fish; remaining a considerable time under water without breathing, as they are enabled to close their nostrils accurately by means of a muscular apparatus, which has been described by M. de Blainville, (Bull. Soc. Philom.) Their voice is a sort of barking, rather weaker than that of a dog, which they utter during the evening or when the weather is about to change.

Inhabit the northern seas; frequent the coasts of Spitsbergen, Greenland, North America, Russia, Norway, Baltic, Holland, England and France.

Species.

3. *Phoca groenlandica*, Mull. prodr. p. 8. *Phoca semilunaris*, Bodd. *Harp seal*, Shaw, gen. Zool. tab. 71.

Char. Essent. Six incisors above, four below; general colour of the adult male, whitish; forehead black; a large conical black spot on each flank; nails strong.

DIMENSIONS. Total length, six feet; circumference, four feet.

DESCRIPTION. This species though confounded with the preceding, is nevertheless very distinct in size, number of molar teeth, and in colour, which resembles that of the *Phoca oceanica*, but it differs also from the last in the number of incisor teeth.

Total number of teeth, thirty-two; viz. six incisors above, four below; two canine and twelve
molars in each jaw on both sides; head long, depressed; snout very prominent; whiskers gray,
slightly compressed and undulating in the middle,
sharp towards the point; eyes, ears, tongue, and
feet, like those of the common seal; hair very
short, incumbent, brilliant.

HABIT. Feeding on fish, particularly the *Salmo
arcticus ;* copulate in the month of July; the females bring forth in the month of March, or beginning of April, generally one, rarely two at a
birth, on the ice at a distance from land.

Inhabit the coasts of Greenland, from whence
they depart in the month of March, and return in
May; depart again in the month of July and return in September; they also visit Spitsbergen.

Species.

4. *Phoca fetida*, Mull. prodr. 8.   *Phoca hispida*
Schreb. tab. 86. Erxleb. Bodd. Gmel.   *Phoque
neitsoak*, Buff. hist. Nat. suppl. tom. 6.

Char. Essent.   Six incisors above, four below;
general colour a pale brown, varied with white
above, dirty white beneath; hairs erect; nails
strong.

DIMENSIONS.   (According to Fabricius,) total
length, upwards of four feet and a half.

DESCRIPTION.   Dental system similar to that of
the common seal; head short, rounded; length of

the snout nearly equal to one third that of the head; whiskers pale, pointed, compressed; eyes small, with the iris brown; the feet, ears, tongue, and tail, are also similar to those of the common seal; body nearly elliptical; back very much arched; belly flat; hair thick, nearly straight, soft to the touch, long and fine; colour nearly brown, varied with whitish; belly white, with some brown spots.

Habit. The old males emit a very stinking and nauseous odour, which taints their flesh and fat; the latter is very fluid; feeding principally on fish and crustacea: copulating in June, bringing forth in February.

Inhabits the least frequented coasts of Greenland.

Species.

5. *Phoca barbata*, Mull.

Phoca barbata, Oth. Fabr. Erxleb. Bodd. Gmel. *P. major*, Parsons, phil. trans. (Encycl. pl. 3. fig. 1.) *Grand phoque*, Buff.

Char. Essent. Six incisors above, four below; thumb of the hand shorter than the fingers; general colour blackish.

Dimensions. Total length about ten feet.

Description. Dental system like that of the common seal; head elongated; snout broad; openings of the ears larger than in other species; fore feet long, having the middle toe longest, the lateral smallest, (which is the case in no other species;) body elongated, robust; general colour livid above, white beneath, then blackish, or entirely black in old individuals.

Inhabits the high seas of Greenland.

Species.

6. *Otaria ursina,* sea bear.
Ursus marinus, Steller.
Phoca ursina, Linn. Gmel. Erxleb. Bodd.
Ours marin, Buff.
Chat marin, Krachenninikow, hist. du Kamtschat. (Encycl. pl. 109, fig. 1.)

Char. Essent. Six incisors above, of which the two lateral resemble canine ; colour brown : posterior toes terminated by a large, narrow, cuticular membrane.

DIMENSIONS. Total length, six feet ten inches six lines; tail, one inch ten lines; ears, one inch six lines.

DESCRIPTION. Body thin posteriorly; head round, mouth small, six incisors above, four below; two canine above and below, very pointed; six sharp molars above, five below; ears pointed, conical; anterior feet entirely free, excepting the carpus, metacarpus, and fingers, where the skin is naked, wrinkled above, and smooth below; thumb longer than the fingers, which decrease successively; posterior extremities five-toed, of which the thumb is as long as the three following; hair thick, erect; colour blackish, spotted with gray on the body, and yellowish or reddish on the feet and flanks ; beneath the hair a species of blackish fur; females differing in size and colour.

Habit. Very similar to that of the *Otaria jubata*, living in troops; the old males live separate, or dispute the females; gestation endures eleven months.

Inhabit the seas of Kamtschatka, the southern part of America, according to Forster, and North America, according to some authors.*

Genus.

Trichechus, Linn. Schreb. Cuv. Lacep.
Odobenus, Briss.
Rosmarus, Scopoli.
Manati, Bodd.
Morse.

CHARACTERS.

Dental formula.—Teeth 24.
superior 14. { Incisor 2. Canine 2. Molar 10.
inferior 10. { Incisor 0. Canine 0. Molar 10.

Two small incisors above in the young animal only and of the form of molars; two superior ca-

---

* *Otaria* is a subgenus of Peron. *Character.* Small external ears; six incisors above, four middle, with double edges, the external simple and smaller ; four inferior, forked ; all the molars simply conical ; nails flat and thin ; hair less rare than in ordinary seals.

nine or enormous tusks, longer than the head,
oval, laterally compressed, arched inferiorly, obtuse at the extremity; the internal ivory granu-
lous, excessively hard, and disposed in curved
lines as in the ivory of elephants; superior molars rather small, nearly cylindrical, with simple
crowns truncated obliquely, the first three situated more internally than the others, the third being the largest and the fifth the smallest; at a
certain period two of these teeth fall; the inferior
molars of similar form and decreasing regularly
from the first to the last; body elongated and conical like that of the seal; head round, snout
swollen; no external ears; tail very short; anterior feet or fins, like those of the seal, with five
toes, armed with very sharp nails; posterior feet
in the same direction with the body, horizontal,
with five toes united by a membrane, the two external the longest.

Species.

Trichechus rosmarus, Linn. Gmel. Erxleb.
Odobenus, Briss.
Equus marinus, Rai, syn. quad. p. 191.
Manati trichechus, Bodd.
Le morse, Buff. t. 13. pl. 54. Vulgarly *Sea cow,*
Sea horse, the *Morse*, &c.

Char. Essent. Lips very much swollen, with
strong whiskers: two long tusks directed down-

wards; hair very rare upon the body, short and reddish.

DIMENSIONS. Total length, eleven feet; of the tail, four inches; of the fore feet, one foot seven inches; hind feet one foot one inch; of the tusk out of the mouth, eleven inches.

NOTE.—The *Morse* attains to eighteen feet in length, and from ten to twelve in circumference.

DESCRIPTION. Head of moderate size relative to the body, rounded, obtuse; maxillary bone and anterior part of the head very much swollen; tusks in some individuals two feet long, rather converging; eyes small, brilliant; orifices of the ears situated far back; body thickest at the breast, tapering to the tail, which is comparatively longer than in the seal; neck short; skin very thick, mucous blackish, with some scattered, short, stiff, reddish or brownish hairs, more obvious on the legs: posterior feet very broad; four ventral mammæ: penis of the male very long and thin.

HABIT. Very similar to that of the seal, living in troops composed of a hundred individuals; females bringing forth in winter on the ice or land, one at a time, which at birth is as large as a pig a year old.

Inhabit the northern Atlantic, where they abound, and the Polar Regions of the Pacific ocean; at present but one species is known. These animals are hunted for their oil, their skin and tusks, the ivory of which is more homogeneous than that of the elephant, and does not tarnish by time.

Family MARSUPIALIA.

Char. Growth of the young premature; frequently a pouch formed by a fold of the skin in the female, enclosing the mammæ, and destined to receive the young fœtusses at birth; in some instances lateral folds exist as rudiments of this pouch. The *Marsupial bones* are peculiar to both sexes.

Scrotum and testicles, situate anterior to the penis, the glans of which is usually bifurcated; uterus communicating with the vagina by two narrow canals; thumb of the hind foot sometimes wanting, at others very distinct, without nail and opposable to the other toes; dental system very different in the various genera; canines sometimes wanting in one or both jaws; incisors varying from two to six or ten in number, in most instances the number varies in each jaw.

First division.—Long canines and small incisors in both jaws; abdominal pouch in the female sometimes wanting.

Genus.

Didelphis, Linn. Erxl. Bodd. Cuv. Geoff. Illig.

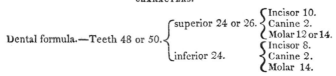

Dental formula.—Teeth 48 or 50.

superior 24 or 26.
{ Incisor 10.
Canine 2.
Molar 12 or 14.

inferior 24.
{ Incisor 8.
Canine 2.
Molar 14.

Superior incisors small; the two intermediate rather longer and separate from the others; the inferior very small, nearly equal, slightly compressed and obtuse; canines strong, compressed and rather disposed outwards; the inferior smallest. Superior molars, the first three false, triangular, compressed, the anterior being much smaller and separated from the others; crowns of the posterior furnished with indentations and sharp points; the first three inferior molars false; the crowns of the remainder furnished with points.

Head long, conical; snout very pointed; mouth wide; eyes placed very high, oblique; ears large, thin, nearly naked, borders rounded; tongue ciliated on its borders and prickled over with small points; whiskers long and abundant; five separate toes to all the feet; thumb of the hind feet, (which are plantigrade,) strong, rather long, opposable and nailless; nails of the other toes crooked.

Tail rather long, round, scaly, and destitute of hair for the greatest part of its extent; hair which covers the body, rather compact, often of two kinds; stomach simple and small; cœcum moderate.

HABIT. Manner of living analogous to that of the martins, but inactive and nocturnal; hiding during the day in bushes, holes or branches of trees; feeding on birds, eggs, reptiles, insects and fruit. Bringing forth a great number of young, which at birth are yet in an embryotic state, with only rudiments of limbs and tail, becoming immediately attached to the teat of the mother by the mouth, which bleeds when forcibly separated; less than one fourth of an inch long (in the opossum,) at the period of birth, when until very lately no traces of placenta or umbilical cord had been discovered. M. E. Geoffroy de St. Hilaire, (Annales des Sciences Nat. 1824,) has just announced the discovery of the vestiges of a placental organization, and of an umbilicus, observed in a very small fetus of the " *Didelphis virginiana*." These observations have served to enlighten a most mysterious subject, and in the generation of the opossum, brings us back to the more usual, if not the more regular course of nature; in common with other mammifera, these animals do in fact pass through the various stages of gestation, changing only their locality at different periods. Thus they exist as ovum in the ovaries, embryon in the uterus, and fetus in the pouch. This interesting subject is as yet by no means divested of obscurity.

Inhabit all America.

Species.

1. *Didelphis virginiana*, Penn. Gmel. *Manicou*, Bonnaterre, *Opossum*, of the Americans, *Sarrigue*, *des Illinois*, Buff. *Virginian opossum*, Shaw, v. 1. part 2. pl. 107, (Encycl. pl. 246. suppl. 7. fig. 1.) *Woapink*, of some of the Indian nations.

Char. Essent. Covering woolly, mixed with black and white, traversed with white bristles; ears black and white; head nearly white.

Dimensions. Total length, one foot two inches nine lines; of the tail, eleven inches; of the head, four inches; of the ears, one inch.

Description. Body rather thick; head very pointed; facial line straight; nostrils separated by a vertical groove; covering composed of a mixture of fur and wool, of a dirty white near the skin, brown at the extremity, and traversed by hairs longer and often white; general teint more deep upon the back; head white; around the eyes and base of the ears brown, the latter being whitish at their extremity; feet brown; belly white; tail hairy one fourth its length, the remainder scaly and whitish; thirteen mammæ, twelve disposed in a circle around a central one.

Habit. Frequenting woods and fields; visiting the farm yards at night, committing depredations on the poultry.

The young at birth weighing only one grain, and remaining in the maternal pouch until they have

attained the size of a mouse, and are covered with
hair; when they venture out, it is only for a short
distance, re-entering at the first signs of danger;
female producing from fourteen to sixteen at a
birth; gestation continues for twenty-six days;
the young remain in the pouch about fifty days
after their birth, about which time their eyes
open.

In captivity they are sluggish and by no means
ferocious; they capture their prey by cunning
and not by chase; their tail is prehensile, which
enables them to suspend themselves on the limbs
of trees, and thus fall upon and seize their prey;
when discovered they seldom attempt to effect
their escape, but on such occasions their cunning
in simulating death in order to avoid destruction
is proverbial; they are omnivorous and fond of
persimmons and apples; the flesh of the female is
eaten, and when roasted, is said to resemble a
young pig in flavour; the male emits a strong
odour; the urine fetid.

Inhabit the eastern coast of the American continent, from Paraguay to the Great Lakes; they
abound in the middle states.

Order GLIRES, *Gnawers.*

Glires, Linn. *Rosores,* Storr.

Char. Two large incisors in each jaw, separated from the molars by a vacant space. No canine teeth; molars sometimes compound, with flat crowns; sometimes with blunt tubercles. Extremities terminated by a variable number of toes furnished with claws. Thumb sometimes rudimentary or wanting, never opposable to the fingers. Mammæ varying in number; orbits not separate from the temporal fossæ; zygomatic processes moderately arched, thin and curved inferiorly.

Inferior jaw articulated by a longitudinal condyle; posterior extremities generally longer than the anterior; stomach simple; intestines long; cœcum voluminous when it exists.

Nourishment, purely vegetable in those species which have compound molars with flat crowns; mixed with animal substances in those which have simple molars with tubercular crowns.

Habit. Generally nocturnal and timid; triturating their food with their molars after having torn it with their long incisors, which have angular summits, and are produced from their roots as they are worn at the points.

Inhabit both the old and new continents; not found in the south-sea islands.

16

SECTION I.

Gnawers with clavicles.

Char. Clavicles complete, often very strong.

Genus.

Castor, Linn. Briss. Schreb. Cuv. Geoff. Illig.

CHARACTERS.

Dental formula.—Teeth 20.
$$\left\{\begin{array}{l}\text{superior 10.}\left\{\begin{array}{l}\text{Incisor 2.}\\ \text{Canine 0.}\\ \text{Molar 8.}\end{array}\right.\\ \text{inferior 10.}\left\{\begin{array}{l}\text{Incisor 2.}\\ \text{Canine 0.}\\ \text{Molar 8.}\end{array}\right.\end{array}\right.$$

Incisors very strong; anterior faces, even and flat; posterior faces angular; molars compound, their crowns nearly plane, presenting circumvolutions of enamel and grooves on their sides, viz. three external and one internal on the molars of the upper jaw; one external and three internal on those of the lower jaw; eyes small; ears short and round; five toes to each foot, the anterior short and not separate; the posterior longer and united by a membrane; tail broad, depressed, oval, naked, and scaly. Two pouches containing an unctious and odoriferous matter, situate on each side of the male organs of generation. The salivary glands very large.

Species.

1. *Castor fiber*, Linn. Erxleb. Schreb. tab. 175.

Le castor, ou *Le bièvre*, Briss. regn. anim. p. 133.
Le castor, Buff. hist. nat. t. 8. pl. 36. F. Cuvier,
Mamm. Lithogr. (Encycl. pl. 79. fig. 1. and 2.)
Sabine, append. p. 659. Long's exped. vol. 1. p.
46. *Common beaver*.

Char. Essent. Fur consisting of two sorts of
hair; one coarse and brownish; the other a very
fine down, more or less gray.

DIMENSIONS. Total length, two feet six lines;
of the head, five inches; of the tail, one foot;
breadth of the tail, four inches; height before,
ten inches four lines; behind, eleven inches;
length of the fore arm, four inches; from the
wrist to the end of the nails, two inches four
lines. Some individuals attain to three feet in
length.

DESCRIPTION. Snout short and thick, furnished
with strong whiskers; facial line rather arched;
summit of the head flattened; eyes rather small,
of a blackish colour; ears short and rounded;
neck short; body rather thick and short, particularly at its posterior part.

Back arched; tail very flat, broad, oval, and
naked, the skin of which is covered with scales,
generally of an hexagonal form, thicker beneath
than above. The fine soft hair is of a silver-gray
colour, offering some differences of shades; the
coarser hair, long, stiff, and elastic; gray for the
first two-thirds of its length, and terminated by a

reddish-brown, from whence results the general
colour, which is more brilliant above than beneath;
whiskers black; hair of the head and hands or
feet, shorter than that on other parts.

The varieties of this species resolve themselves into the white, black, olive, variegated, and
yellow.*

Some doubts have been expressed relative to
the identity of the American and European beaver,
founded chiefly on some difference observed in
their habits. (The European beaver does not
construct huts.) We are inclined to the opinion
of their identity, the more especially as no differences are observable on comparing their skulls.

HABIT. Frequenting the shores of rivers, streams,
or lakes; in the summer remaining solitary in
their holes; in winter uniting in troops, in a species of hut, which they construct with the greatest ingenuity in the banks; intercepting the current to form dams, which they effect by the aid
of dikes, in form of an arch, the convexity of
which is opposed to the current, and which is
composed of stones, mud, and the branches of
trees interlaced.

The huts are established on these dams, and
formed of nearly the same materials as the dikes:

* The late Mr. Bartram has indicated two species of beaver
as inhabiting the United States, viz. " Great beaver of Canada,"
and " Lesser beaver of Florida and Carolina." Manuscript
notes, penes me.

the huts are two stories high, each story eighteen inches in height; logs composing these cells have been observed measuring two feet in length, sixteen inches in circumference, and weighing fourteen pounds; it is evident from the marks on the ends of these logs, that they have been all cut through with the teeth, and notched at the end, so as to interlock with each other in the same manner as logs fashioned by human industry for the purpose of constructing the common log houses. The base of the lower chamber is under water, as is also the hole by which they enter.

They feed on the bark of the willow, poplar, and cotton wood tree; they swim well, in which action they are aided by their posterior palmated feet, and flat tail. The female brings forth at the commencement of spring, two or three at a birth, after a gestation of four months. They arrive at maturity in two years; the duration of their life is about fifteen years. Such are, nearly, the manners of the North American beaver; those which exist in Europe do not build, but dig holes in the earth on the borders of rivers.

The fur of these animals is exceedingly valuable; but from the constant and universal destruction to which they are subjected, we must, before long, be deprived of this luxury.

For further very interesting particulars concerning the habits of this extraordinary animal, vid. Long's Exped. to the Rocky Mountains.

Inhabit North America, from Canada to the thirtieth degree of north latitude; on either side of the Rocky Mountains. Siberia, and northern and temperate Europe.

Genus.

Osteopera, Nobis.

CHARACTERS.

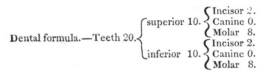

Dental formula.—Teeth 20.
superior 10.
{ Incisor 2.
{ Canine 0.
{ Molar 8.
inferior 10.
{ Incisor 2.
{ Canine 0.
{ Molar 8.

Inferior incisors slender, laterally compressed, nearly pointed, not approximate, convex anteriorly; molars nearly similar to those of the beaver; head very broad and flat; snout rapidly attenuated; eyes widely separated; zygomatic arches exceedingly large, descending beneath the inferior molars, scabrous and convex externally, forming within large osseous pouches communicating with the mouth, anterior to the molars; lower jaw proportionably small and slender; the condyloid extending above the coronoid process.

Species.

1. *Osteopera platycephala.*

Char. Essent. Head flat, ventricose at the sides; snout obtuse; eyes widely separated.

DIMENSIONS of the cranium compared with that

of the full grown Canadian beaver: (the extremity of the snout of the *Osteopera*, together with the upper incisors, have been destroyed.)

	New Genus.		Castor fiber.	
Total length of the skull, -	Inches 6	0	5	0
Length of the frontal bone, - - -	2	5	1	5
Breadth of do. - - -	1	8	1	0
Length of the parietal bone, - - -	3	0	1	7
Breadth of do. - - -	2	3	1	6
Length of the zygomatic arch, - - -	3	6	3	0
Breadth of do. - - -	2	0	1	2
Width across from one zygoma to the other,	4	0	4	0
Breadth of the palate bones between the molars,	0	4	0	8
Length of the zygomatic fossa, - - -	1	7	2	3
Breadth of do. - - -	1	2	1	0
Length of the lower jaw not including the incisors,	4	0	4	0
Breadth of the same including the molars, -	1	3	1	5
From the top of the coronoid process to the base of the jaw, - - -	1	2	2	4

DESCRIPTION. Frontal bone nearly double the length and breadth of that of the common beaver, flat and scabrous, forming on each side a similunar ridge, projecting into the orbits; orbit of the eye small, and nearly circular, which is due, principally, to the extraordinary development of the zygomatic processes of the temporal and jugal bones, which are produced downward and backward, so as to conceal the posterior half of the lower jaw, together with the teeth, anteriorly arched, scabrous, and ventricose; the jugal portions being developed anteriorly and inferiorly so as to form on each side a *bony antrum*, or cavity, capable of containing in all two or three ounces of fluid, and communicating with the mouth by large oblong openings, immediately anterior to the molar teeth; the cavity projecting posteriorly into the orbit, with which it has no communication; anterior to the orbit, above the cavity, is a bony canal, capable of admitting the little finger, somewhat analogous to the infraorbitar foramen observed in the skull of the genus *Cavia.*

The structure of the inferior jaw is equally remarkable, and adapted in every respect to the peculiarities of the upper jaw; the whole of the lower jaw is more slender and narrower than that of the beaver. In order to admit a free passage from the bony cavities into the mouth, the molar teeth and alveolar processes of the lower jaw are elevated, and the latter are separated from each other anteriorly, so as to leave a capacious opening, of an oval form, from the sack into the mouth; the coronoid process very small, and not projecting so high as the condyloid; the latter also small, rounded above and compressed; angles of the lower jaw rounded; the inferior incisors slender in proportion to those of the beaver, arched on the anterior surface, not approximate, slightly divergent at their extremity, somewhat analogous to the incisors of the squirrel; the crowns of the molars are plain, though they do not appear to have been much worn, and are traversed by three, sometimes four folds of enamel, which, in several of the teeth, have no connexion with the enamel

which encircles them; in others they consist of
re-entering folds, as in the teeth of the beaver;
thus displaying, in a remarkable manner, the extent to which this portion of the structure of the
teeth may differ in the same individual : in those
instances where the transverse plates of enamel
are distinct from the encircling enamel, there are
no grooves on the side of the tooth; in other instances, the sides are grooved, as in the teeth of
the beaver, except that portion buried in the
socket, which is smooth in most instances. In all
other details, this skull bears the closest analogy
to that of the beaver. The animal was full grown,
as is evinced by the teeth and other particulars.

HABIT and LOCALITY. Nothing further is known
concerning the history of this animal, than that
its skull was found more than thirty years ago on
the shore of the river Delaware, and presented to
the Philadelphia Museum; when first discovered
it was nearly perfect; by rough usage it has since
lost the upper incisors, and part of their alveoles.
This cranium has been frequently examined by
the curious, and by them regarded as a *lusus na-
turæ ;* the characters which it presents are certainly unique of their kind; the bony cavities
communicating with the mouth, which must have
served as receptacles for provision, &c. distinguish
this skull from that of all other animals, and particularly the beavers, to which, in other respects,
it bears so near a resemblance. That it is not a

17

monstrous production of nature, is fully demonstrated by the well defined characters of the jaws and teeth, as well as by the harmonious adaptation of its various parts. It is further, not in the least degree fossilized, nor does it appear to have been totally buried in the ground, inasmuch as one side of the jaw has been bleached by exposure to the sun.

The first question which presents itself for solution is, from whence came the animal? are we to consider it as the type of a genus which has become extinct and yet not fossil? or does it owe its present locality to accident, having been brought from some distant and unexplored country, and heretofore escaped the eye of the naturalist?

The present existing genera to which it is most nearly allied, being known to inhabit only Europe and America, would militate against the latter opinion, and induce us to believe, that this animal did inhabit the countries near which its remains were first discovered, its residence like that of the beaver, being on the banks of rivers.

The skull being recent, and not in the least decomposed, the animal could not have been long dead when first discovered. It is most probable that in the instance before us, we are presented with the remains of the type of a genus which has become extinct since the settlement of North America, or if it still exists has retreated to the most inaccessible and unexplored forests, which is at least very uncertain. It is more than probable that many species have disappeared and are entirely lost since the present state of the surface of our globe.

Suppose an animal to inhabit the shores of the great rivers of America previous to the discovery of this continent, and not to be endowed with the instinct of emigration, to become surrounded by the habitations of civilized man; hemmed in, and cut off from all resources by the march of civilization, the natural consequences would be destruction.

It may be necessary further to remark, that all the fossil beavers hitherto discovered, resemble the recent species.

Genus.

Fiber, Cuv. Geoff. Illig.
Ondatra, Lacep. Geoff.
Castor, Briss. Linn. Erxleb. Bodd.
Mus, Gmel.

CHARACTERS.

Dental formula.—Teeth 16. superior 8. Incisor 2. Canine 0. Molar 6. inferior 8. Incisor 2. Canine 0. Molar 6.

Superior incisors plane and chissel form; inferior sharp, and rounded anteriorly; molars compound, presenting transverse zigzag plates.

Anterior feet, four-toed; the thumb rudimentary; the posterior, five-toed; all very distinct, with their borders furnished with stiff hairs, which serve in place of the membranous feet of aquatic mammifera.

Tail long, linear, laterally compressed, the skin of which is naked and granular, with a few scattering hairs; glands near the pubis, secreting a whitish odoriferous matter, which is discharged by two ducts, either at the base of the glans of the male, or in the ureter of the female.

Six ventral mammæ.

Species.

1. *Fiber zibethicus*, Desm. Mamm. p. 279. Sab. Append. p. 659.

Rat musquè, Sarrazin, Mem. de l'Acad. Roy. des Scien. de Paris, 1725. *Rat musquè du Canada*, Briss. regn. Anim. *Castor zibithecus*, Linn. Erxleb. Bodd. *Ondatra*, Buff. (Encycl. pl. 67, fig. 7.) *Ondatra* of Canada. *Mus zibethecus*, Gmel. vulgarly, *Musk-rat*.

Char. Essent. General colour brown, tinged with red above; cinereus beneath.

Dimensions. Total length, one foot seven lines; of the tail, nine inches.

Description. In external appearances very analogous to the water-rat, but differing in the compressed form of the tail; snout short and thick; eyes large and lateral; ears short, oblique, rounded, and entirely covered with hair; whiskers very large; fur soft and shining, composed of two sorts of hair, the longest reddish-brown on the superior parts of the body; cinereus-red on the flanks, breast, and belly; down or interior hair of the back very fine and soft, of a cinereus colour near its roots, and reddish-brown at its points; that of the inferior parts of a clear gray, and brilliant; feet covered with short and shining hair; tail three-fourths the length of the body, compressed, covered with small scales of a blackish-brown colour; between these are small black hairs, which are longest on its borders.

Habit. Living in small families on the borders of waters; swimming with facility; feeding on roots, fruits, &c. copulating in spring, at which period in particular, they shed a strong odour of musk; female bringing forth five or six young annually.

Inhabit Canada, and the northern and middle states.

According to Bartram, the "Musk-rat is never seen in Carolina, Georgia, or Florida, within one hundred miles of the sea coast, and very few in the most northern parts of these regions; which must be considered a most favourable circumstance in a country where there is so much banking, and draining of the land, they being the most destructive creatures to banks."—Vid. "Travels in North America."

Genus.

Arvicola, Lacep. Cuv. Desm.
Lemmus, Geoff.
Hypudœus, Illig.
Mus, Briss. Linn. Erxleb. Bodd.

CHARACTERS.

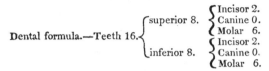

Dental formula.—Teeth 16.
superior 8. { Incisor 2. Canine 0. Molar 6.
inferior 8. { Incisor 2. Canine 0. Molar 6.

Incisors of the upper jaw large, cuneiform; the inferior sharp.

Molars compound; crowns marked with zigzag lines of enamel; the largest situated anteriorly, the smallest posteriorly.

Fore feet having the rudiment of a thumb, and four toes furnished with weak nails; the posterior with five toes, armed with claws, not palmated or furnished with hairs on their borders.

Tail hairy, cylindrical, nearly as long as the body. From eight to twelve pectoral and ventral mammæ.

HABIT. Burrowing in the earth, feeding principally on grain and bulbous roots; some are omnivorous.

Inhabit both the old and new continent.

Species.

1. *Arvicola amphibius.*

Mus amphibius, Linn. Erxleb. Bodd. Schreb.
Mus aquaticus, Briss. *Rat d'eau,* Buff. (Encycl.
pl. 68. fig. 9.) Water-Rat.

Char. Essent. Colour blackish-gray, slightly
mixed with yellow, more clear beneath; tail longer
than one-half the body, black; ears short, hairy.

DIMENSIONS. Total length seven inches; of the
head, one inch seven lines; of the ears, five lines
and a half; of the trunk of the tail, four inches six
lines.

DESCRIPTION. Head short; snout swollen; ears
slightly apparent, hairy; tail rather more than one-
half the length of the body, furnished with short
and sparse hairs; colour of the fur blackish-gray
above, more clear beneath, composed of hairs, the
points of which are yellowish, but the greater part
of the base clear cinereus-yellow; some larger hairs
of a blackish-brown colour, longer than the rest, and
placed on the top of the neck; down or fine hair
covering the skin, generally of a grayish colour.

VARIETIES. *Mus amphibius niger,* Linn.
Mus amphibius maculatus, Linn.
Mus amphibius paludosus, Linn.

HABIT. Living in holes on the sides of banks of
rivers, dams, &c.; they swim well, but are obliged
to come to the surface of the water to breathe
every half minute: feeding on water-plants and
herbs; also insects, spawn, and frogs, &c. The

female brings forth in the month of April, five or six at a birth.

Inhabit all Europe, Asia, and North America. From Canada to Carolina according to Penn. Arct. Zool. Carolina, according to Lawson.

Species.

2. *Arvicola xanthognatha.* *Meadow Mouse.* Leach, Miscellanea, vol. i. pl. 26. p. 60.

Arvicola xanthognatus, Sabine, append. p. 660.

Char. Essent. Fawn coloured, varied with black above, clear cinereus-gray beneath; cheeks yellowish.

DIMENSIONS. Total length five inches.

DESCRIPTION. Tail black above, and white beneath; feet brownish, white beneath. This species has some resemblance to the *Arvicola vulgaris,* (*Mus terrestris*, Linn.)

Inhabits the borders of Hudson's Bay, state of Ohio, Pennsylvania, &c.

The exploring party under Major Long observed this animal on the Ohio. Vid. Exp. to the Rocky Mountains, vol. i. p. 369.

Species.

3. *Arvicola palustris*, (nobis.)
Marsh campagnol.
Arvicola riparius, Ord, Journal of the Phil. Acad. of Nat. Sciences, vol. iv.

Char. Essent. Body above dark grayish-brown; pale plumbeous beneath; snout rather elongated, reddish-brown at its extremity; ears moderately long, sparsely bordered with hair.

Tail short, sparsely hairy.

DIMENSIONS. Total length, from the tip of the nose to the base of the tail, very nearly six inches; length of the tail two inches and three-tenths.

DESCRIPTION. Body elongated, thickest behind, covered above with soft fur, plumbeous at base, and tipped with gray and brown, from whence results the general colour, dark grayish-brown above, lighter on the flanks and sides, becoming reddish-brown on the end of the snout, and beneath the tail, between the hind legs; belly, inside of the legs, and throat, of a pale plumbeous colour, occasioned by the hairs being plumbeous at base, and white at the extremity; head long and narrow; snout rather elongated; facial line straight; ears situate far back, moderately long, internal border lined with sparse hair, posterior surface nearly naked; whiskers fine long hairs, white and black; inferior incisors very long, distinct, gently recurved at top, laterally compressed, very sharp and pointed, yellow on the anterior surface, and convex; upper incisors much shorter and cuneiform.

Molar teeth unusually long at the crowns, and so deeply grooved laterally, that when viewed in this direction, these animals appear to possess six

18

or eight, in place of three molars on each side, the usual number; eyes large, situate six-tenths of an inch from the extremity of the snout.

Legs small, terminated ⊢ five clawed toes behind, four before. The fore feet brown above: middle toe the longest, then the next on each side, the outer one small, all furnished with hooked nails; the thumb tubercle very small, and furnished with a scarcely visible nail.

The three middle toes on the hind feet nearly equal; the two remaining toes very small, particularly the interior; all furnished with nails similar to those on the fore toes.

Tail small and short, sparsely covered with brownish hair.

Habit. Living in marshes on the shores of rivers; they dive well, and swim with facility; their habits in many respects resemble those of the *Arvicola amphibius;* they bring forth six or eight young at a birth; feeding principally on the wild rice, (*Zizania aquatica.*)

Inhabit the swamps along the shores of the Delaware. (Specimens in the Philadelphia Museum.)

Species.

4. *Arvicola hortensis,* (nobis.)

Char. Essent. Body ferruginous-brown above; plumbeous, intermixed with yellow beneath; hairs coarse, standing more or less obliquely from the body, giving the animal a shaggy appearance; ears broad, oval; head globular; snout contracted, conical; tail more than one-half the total length.

DIMENSIONS. Total length, from the tip of the nose to the origin of the tail, five inches and five-tenths; length of the tail two-inches and seven-tenths.

DESCRIPTION. Body covered with rather long, coarse hair, of a dark plumbeous colour for the greater portion of its length next the skin, but reddish or dusky brown, sometimes grayish at the extremity, standing more or less obliquely from the body, which occasions the plumbeous colour of the inferior portion to show through in some places, giving the animal a motley, shaggy appearance; beneath the throat of a dirty yellow-ish-white; belly ochreous-yellow, intermixed with plumbeous; tail rather thickly invested with black-ish-brown hair, lighter beneath; head rather broad; snout contracted, conical; facial line arched; ears six-tenths of an inch broad, the same in height, hairy within, sparsely hairy without; coarse, stiff hairs lining the anterior borders; whiskers, nume-rous, fine, long hairs, both black and white.

Molar teeth rather oblong, deeply grooved at their crowns, and marked by several transverse curved lines of enamel; the grooves extending nearly one-half the length of the sides of the bodies; the lower incisors rather shorter, the upper rather longer than in the preceding species.

Feet small, brown above; the number of toes and nails, their form and situation, do not materially differ from the same parts in the preceding species.

HABIT. Mr. Ord discovered these animals in Florida in the year 1817 or 1818, and presented specimens to the Philadelphia Museum, where they have remained ever since, undescribed. He states that they frequent the ruined gardens of deserted plantations; feed on seeds, grain, &c.; they are very abundant also on the borders of marshes, and constitute the principal food of the Marsh-Hawk, as we are informed by Mr. T. Peale.

NOTE.—The molar teeth of this species present some differences from those of the common *Arvicola,* and resemble somewhat those of the genus *Lemmus ;* but the following, among other characters of this latter genus, " *ears very short,*" and " *tail very short,*" &c. will not apply to the present species; in all other respects it resembles the *Arvicola* much more closely than any other genus; it must consequently be referred to the former, or establish a new genus; the latter alternative would be as unwarrantable as to make distinct genera of the two existing species of Elephants.*

* *Some weeks after the above description had been drawn up, and read before the Philadelphia Academy of Natural Sciences,* Messrs. Say and Ord thought it necessary to describe the same animal, and to construct from it a new genus, which they name " *Sigmodon.*" For this distinction they have no other founda-

Species.

5. *Arvicola floridanus.*
Mus floridanus, Ord, Nouv. bull. de la Soc. Phi-

tion than a slight and unimportant variation in the form and
direction of the plates of enamel, which traverse the crowns of
the molars, and the partial division of the root into rudimentary
radicles. On similar distinctions, F. Cuvier has founded his *divi-*
sions of the genus *Arvicola,* which " differ from each other in the
number of parts of which the teeth are composed."

It could be shown, if necessary, in a number of instances, that
greater differences are observable in the different teeth of the
same individual, than have served those gentlemen, in the present instance, to construct a new genus; who, in their description of the animal, have entirely neglected to point out any
generic distinctions in the *external characters,* (which, in reality,
correspond with the genus *Arvicola.*) This neglect is the more
extraordinary, as in their former descriptions they have dwelt
upon the *external* characters of animals, and, in some cases, to
the exclusion of any observations on the structure of the teeth,
as was instanced in the " *Mus floridanus.*" The slight variations
in the teeth noticed above, provided they be accompanied with
well marked differences in the external characters of the animal, may form good grounds for *specific* distinctions, but surely
cannot be received as sufficient reason for the construction of a
new genus, according to the established laws which regulate
naturalists in similar instances; particularly as nature acknowledges no such distinction, inasmuch as the food, the manners,
the habits, and we may add, the external characters of this animal, correspond with those of other species of the genus *Arvicola.*

We have dwelt the longer on the principles involved in this
dispute, believing that, if the precedent be established, it might
prove fatal to the best interests of science.

Note.—The description of the present species is drawn from
one of the three individuals presented to the Museum by Mr. Ord.

lomat. Decem. 1818. *Mus floridanus*, Say, Long's
Exped. to the Rocky Mountains, vol. 1. p. 54.

Char. Essent. Body robust, black plumbeous;
sides, rump, and origin of the tail, ferruginous-
yellow; fur plumbeous near its base; all beneath
white.

DIMENSIONS. Total length including the tail,
nearly sixteen inches; tail, seven inches; ear, nine-
tenths; greatest breadth, one inch.

DESCRIPTION. Head gradually attenuated to the
nose, plumbeous, intermixed with gray; ears
large, prominent, patulous, obtusely rounded,
naked or furnished with sparse hairs behind, and
on the margin within; eyes moderate, prominent;
whiskers, some white, some black bristles, the
longest surpassing the tip of the ears, arranged
in six longitudinal series; tail hairy, as long as
the body, above brown; legs subequal, robust;
feet white; toes annulate beneath; thumb minute;
palm with five tuberculous prominences; nails
concealed by the hairs; sole with six tubercles;
the three posterior ones distant from each other.
(Say.)

HABIT. Feeding on vegetables, such as the
green bark of trees, and the young shoots of
plants; their nests are large, and composed of a
great quantity of brush. This species is well
known in some districts under the name of large
hairy tailed rat, and is by no means rare in Flori-

da; it is as large as the ordinary stature of the Norway rat, and equally troublesome; infesting houses, but gives place to the Norway rat.

Inhabit Florida and the borders of Mississippi river. Two prepared specimens in Philadelphia Museum; one from Florida, presented by Mr. Ord, the other from Mississippi, presented by Maj. Long's exploring party.

A beautiful figure accompanies Mr. Ord's description of this animal, in vol. 4 of the Journal of the Philadelphia Academy of Natural Sciences.*

* Since this work went to press, we have received No. 1} of the Journal of the Academy of Natural Sciences, in time to follow up the eventful history of this animal. In vol. 4, p. 345, of the work above quoted, there is an essay entitled " A New Genus of *Mammalia*, &c. proposed by T. Say, and G. Ord; read March 8, 1825." The name of the proposed genus is "*Neotoma*." There appears to have been some mistake relative to the date, wherein it is stated that the new genus "*Neotoma*" was proposed; at any rate, it is very certain that on the evening of the 8th of March, the identical animal on which this new genus is founded, was described by those gentlemen as an "*Arvicola*," and this after an attentive examination of the teeth. It was not until this description of the "*Arvicola floridanus*" had passed through the press, that it was recalled by the authors, and the new name substituted. In order to avoid confusion, it will be necessary for naturalists to remember that the animal under notice, is at present described as pertaining to three or four distinct genera. The first notice of this animal, is an imperfect description by Mr. Ord, in the Bull. de la Soc. Philom. 1818, who named it "*Mus floridanus*," (its identity with the genus *Mus*, was doubted from the first, by the French natural-

Species.

6. *Arvicola Pennsylvanica.**

ists.) A more complete description occurs in Maj. Long's exped. to the Rocky Mountains, vol. 1, p. 54. 1819—20, where Mr. Say has adopted in an unqualified manner the name given by Mr. Ord. Thus it remained until the attention of these gentlemen was particularly directed to the dentition of this animal, by the observations of M. Desmarest, in his " *Mammalogie.*" They now described the animal as an *Arvicola*, (to which, in reality, it belongs.) Finally, observing that the molar teeth of the animal were furnished with " *roots*," they have constructed the new genus " *Neotoma.*" (The *division* is sufficiently *novel*, it must be confessed, and if adopted, would destroy the whole fabric of classification.)

F. Cuvier has not mentioned the *roots* of the molar teeth of those species from which he has drawn the characters of the genus *Arvicola* ; a circumstance so apt to vary even in the teeth of the same animal, this able naturalist considered as beneath his notice in a work which has for its object *a description of the teeth considered as zoological characters.* (" Dents des mammifères considerèes comme charactèrès zoologiques.") Notwithstanding this, Messrs. Say and Ord, consider the " roots" of the teeth as of sufficient importance to establish generic distinctions. In the present instance, at least, they admit, that in the softness of the fur, and in the tail being clothed with hair, the " *Neotoma*" resembles the *Arvicola ;* to which I would add, that in all other external characters, this species resembles the *Arvicola*, as closely as the different species of that genus resemble each other.

The description which Messrs. Say and Ord have given of the *teeth* of the " *Neotoma*," (always excepting the roots,) so exactly corresponds with M. Cuvier's description of the teeth of the genus Arvicola, that we are tempted to believe the former to be a literal translation. (Vid. Dents des mammifères. &c. F. Cuvier; first division, page 155.)

The Campagnol or *Meadow Mouse* of Pennsylvania. Warden's Descrip. of the United States, vol. v. p. 625.

Described in Wilson's Ornithology, vol. vi. pl. 50. fig. 3. *Arvicola Pennsylvanica*, Ord. Guthrie's Geography.

DESCRIPTION. Colour above a brownish-fawn; beneath grayish-white; eyes very small; ears short and round.

DIMENSIONS. Total length, from the origin of the tail to the extremity of the nose, four inches; tail three-fourths of an inch.

HABIT. Feeding on bulbous roots; injurious to river plantations, making holes in the banks. According to Mr. Ord, the female brings forth only two young at a birth; the teats of the female are situated very near the organs of generation; she carries her young between the hind legs.

Probably a variety of the *Arvicola xanthognathus*, described p. 136.

Genus.

Lemmus, Link, Cuv. Geoff.
Hypudæus, Illig.
Georychus, idem.
Mus, Linn. Pallas. Gmel. Bodd.
Glis, Erxleb.
Lemming.

CHARACTERS.

Dental formula.—Teeth 16. superior 8. { Incisor 2. Molar 6. inferior 8. { Incisor 2. Molar 6.

The anterior face of the superior incisors convex and smooth; the inferior sharp; molars compound, with plane crowns, presenting angular plates of enamel; ears very short and rounded; eyes very small; anterior feet sometimes five-toed. sometimes four-toed, with claws proper for digging; posterior feet five-toed; tail very short and hairy; (this genus differs from the preceding chiefly in the disproportion of the fore legs, and shortness of the tail.)

HABIT. Social animals, great travellers, feeding chiefly on vegetable food.

Species.

1. *Lemmus hudsonius,* Sab. append. p. 669.
Mus hudsonius, Pallas. Schreb. Gmel. (Encycl. pl. 69. fig. 6.) *Lemming of Hudson's Bay.*

Char. Essent. Of a clear cinereus colour; four fingers, and a rudiment of a thumb on the fore feet; the two internal nails (in the male) appear very large and double; no apparent external ears.

DIMENSIONS. Total length about five inches.

DESCRIPTION. Body short and swollen; head large; eyes very small; feet short; fur soft, generally of a cinereus-gray colour, which is owing to the points of the hairs, the bases of which are brownish.

Inhabit Labrador and northern parts of North America.

NOTE.—The following species are noticed by

Rafinesque, which we mention as mere indications of varieties, or perhaps some new species. 1. *Lemmus vittatus;* inhabits Kentucky. 2. *L. talpoides,* also of Kentucky. 3. *L. noveboracensis,* together with the *Mynomes pratensis,* figured by Wilson, Amer. Ornithol. vol. vi. tab. 50. fig. 3. which is an *Arvicola.*

Genus.

Mus, Linn. Erxleb. Briss. Cuv. Geoff. Illig. &c. *Rattus,* Penn. the *Rat.*

CHARACTERS.

Dental formula.—Teeth 16.
- superior 8.
  - Incisor 2.
  - Canine 0.
  - Molar 6.
- inferior 8.
  - Incisor 2.
  - Canine 0.
  - Molar 6.

Superior incisors cuneiform; the inferior compressed and sharp.

Molars simple, crowns furnished with blunt tubercles, the anterior being the largest both above and below; snout rather elongated; ears oblong or rounded, nearly naked; no pouches.

Anterior feet with four clawed toes, and a wart covered with an obtuse nail in place of a thumb; the posterior feet moderately elongated, with five clawed toes; tail long, tapering, naked and scaly. Some of the hairs on the body are longer, and more stiff than others; for which are sometimes substituted flattened spines, similar to those on the body of the echimys.

Habit.   Omnivorous, lascivious, and nocturnal.
Inhabit all climates and countries of the earth :
some species have become cosmopolites.

Species.

1. *Mus rattus*, Linn.
Mus domesticus major, Rai.   *Le rat*, Buff.
Rattus niger, Penn. Syn. Quad. p. 299.   The
Black rat.

Char. Essent.   Black above, deep cinereus beneath; tail a little longer than the body.
Dimensions.   Total length seven inches; of the
head one inch nine lines; of the tail seven inches
six lines.
Description.   Head elongated; snout pointed;
inferior jaw very short, and much less projecting
than the superior; eyes large and projecting;
ears naked, large, broad, and nearly oval; whiskers long; five flat toes on the hind feet, and four
on the anterior, with a nail representing a thumb;
lateral nails, both before and behind, very short;
tail nearly naked, and furnished with scales disposed in rings, the number of which amount in
some instances to two hundred and fifty; ordinary colour of the animal, cinereus black, lighter
beneath; whiskers black; small white hairs covering the top of the feet; mammæ to the number of twelve.
Habit.   Bold, courageous, and great depreda-

tors, their manners resemble those of the common rat.

Inhabit France, Germany, England, &c.

We are inclined to believe this species indigenous to the United States, where they were very numerous about fifty years ago, though they have become very rare on the Atlantic coast since the arrival of the *Norway rat*, (*Mus decumanus*, Pall.) and are found at the present time, (though rarely) in the western states, having like the aboriginal Indians, receded before their European invaders. We are credibly informed by an eye witness of the fact, that the *Norwegian rat* did not make its appearance in the United States any length of time previous to the year 1775.

The *Norway rat*, it appears, was originally a native of Persia, or of India, and was unknown in England previous to 1730, or in France before 1750. According to Pallas, it made its first appearance in Siberia and Russia about the year 1766.

The *Mus musculus*, (Linn.) *Common mouse*, is most probably not indigenous, though like the preceding species, it inhabits all climates.

Species.

2. *Mus sylvaticus*, Linn. Erxleb. Bodd. Schreb. tab. 180. *Mus agrestis major*, Gesn. *Mus domesticus medius*, Rai. *Mus campestris major*, Briss. Regn. Anim. p. 171. No. 4. *Mulot*, Buff. hist. nat. t. 7. pl. 41. *Field mouse.*

Char. Essent. Reddish-gray above; whitish beneath; tail a little shorter than the body.

DIMENSIONS. Total length, four inches two lines; of the head, one inch two lines; of the trunk of the tail, three inches six lines.

DESCRIPTION. Larger than the *Mouse*, or the *Campagnol*; less than the *Black rat*; head larger and longer than that of the mouse; eyes larger and more projecting; ears longer and broader; legs longer. The upper surface and sides of the head and neck, superior parts of the body, and external surface of the fore feet, covered with fine short hair, of a fawn colour, tinged with black, each hair cinereus the greater part of its length, then fawn colour, then black at the extremity; side of the snout and inferior surface of the head and body, as well as the interior of the feet whitish, tinged with blackish or cinereus, where the hair is longest; on the breast, a yellowish spot, with a blackish tinge; tail brownish above, whitish beneath.

HABIT. Living in woods and neighbouring fields; burrows in the ground and amasses provisions, which consist chiefly of grain; female producing more than once annually, and several at a birth.

Inhabit all Europe and United States; several varieties found in the vicinity of Philadelphia.

Two other species of *Mus* are noticed by Rafinesque as inhabiting the United States.

1. *Mus leucopus.*

Char. Essent. Colour brownish-fawn above, white beneath; head yellow; ears large; tail as long as the body, pale brown above, gray beneath: feet white.

DIMENSIONS. Total length five inches.

2. *Mus nigricans,* (black rat, or wood-rat.)

Char. Essent. Colour blackish above, gray beneath; tail black, longer than the body.

DIMENSIONS. Total length, six inches. (Monthly Magazine, 1818.)

The last mentioned species is nothing more than the *Mus rattus,* Linn.

Genus.

Pseudostoma, Say, Long's Exped. to the Rocky Mountains, vol. i. p. 406.

Geomys, Rafinesque, Month. Mag.

CHARACTERS.

$$\text{Dental formula.—Teeth 20.}\begin{cases} \text{superior 10.} \begin{cases} \text{Incisor 2.} \\ \text{Canine 0.} \\ \text{Molar 8.} \end{cases} \\ \text{inferior 10.} \begin{cases} \text{Incisor 2.} \\ \text{Canine 0.} \\ \text{Molar 8.} \end{cases} \end{cases}$$

The incisors are not covered by the lips, but always remain exposed to view; they are strong, and truncated in their entire width at tip; the superior ones are each marked by a deep longitudinal groove near the middle, and by a smaller one at the inner margin.

The molars, to the number of eight in each jaw, penetrate to the base of their respective alveoles without any division into roots; their crowns are simply discoidal, transversely oblong-oval, margined by enamel, but which is not elevated into crests or dividing ridges; the anterior tooth is double, in consequence of a profound duplicature in its side, so that its crown presents two oval disks, of which the anterior one is smallest. The molars of the upper jaw incline obliquely backwards; those of the lower jaw obliquely forwards.

Head and body large, so as to produce a clumsy aspect; cheek pouches voluminous, exterior to the mouth, from which they are separated by the common integuments; they are profoundly concave, opening downwards and towards the mouth.

Legs short; fore feet large; hind feet small; (Say.)

This animal is, with great propriety, separated from the genus *Cricetus*, (hamster,) Lacep. Cuv. Geoff. Illig. from which it differs in the following particulars.

1. In having four molar teeth on both sides of each jaw. 2. In having five toes to the anterior feet. 3. In the form of the crowns of the molar teeth, which are tuberculous in the *Cricetus*, and plane in the *Pseudostoma*. 4. In the length of the elongated nails on the fore feet. 5. In its enormous cheek pouches, and in other particulars to be observed in the description.

Species.

1. *Pseudostoma bursarius*, Shaw, Trans. Lin. Soc. Lond. and General Zool. vol. ii. part 1. p. 100. pl. 138. under the name of *Canada Rat*.

Mus bursarius, Lin. Trans. vol. v. p. 227. pl. 8.

Mus saccatus, Mitchill, Med. Repos. 1821.

Geomys cinereus, Rafinesque, Monthly Mag. 1817, p. 45. Vulgarly *Sand-rat*, *Goffer*, *Pouched-rat*, *Salamander*, &c.

Char. Essent. Body covered with reddish-brown hair, plumbeous at base; feet white; anterior nails elongated; posterior ones short, and concave beneath.

DIMENSIONS. Total length from nine to eleven inches.

DESCRIPTION. Body elongated, subcylindrical; hair reddish-brown, plumbeous at base; rather paler beneath; cheek pouches capacious, covered with hair both within and without; eyes black; ears hardly prominent; feet five-toed, white; anterior hair robust, with large, elongated, somewhat compressed claws; middle nail much the longest, then the fourth, then the second, then the fifth, the first being very short; posterior feet slender; nails concave beneath, rounded at tip, the external one very small; tail short, hairy at base, nearly naked towards the tip.

HABIT. Walking awkwardly, but burrowing with great rapidity. so that the difficulty of obtaining specimens, may be in a great measure attributed to the facility with which the animal passes through the soil, in removing from the vicinity of danger; they cast up mounds of loose earth, which, like those of the blind rat, (*Spalax typhlus*) have no exterior opening; these elevations have been aptly compared by Lewis and Clark to the heaps of earth emptied from a flower-pot. The mounds are of various dimensions, from the diameter of a few inches to that of several yards. So entirely subterranean is the habit of this animal, that it is rarely seen; and many persons have lived for years surrounded by their little edifices without knowing the singular being by whose labours they are produced. (Say.)

Inhabit United States, from Lake Superior to Florida, and as far west as the Missouri.

The late Professor Barton, (Medical and Physical Journal,) was of opinion that the *Mus bursarius* of Shaw, was similar to the *Toucan* of Hernandez, and the *Tuza* or *Tozan* of Clavigero, and says that the cheek pouches in the figures given by Shaw, are represented in an inverted position.

We have seen the specimen described by Professor Mitchell, and observed that it had lost its tail.

Genus.

Gerbillus, Desm. F. Cuvier.
Meriones, Illiger.
Mus, Pallas, Pennant.
Dipus, Gmel. Bodd. Schreb. Oliv. Geoff.
Sciurus, Erxleb.
Jerboa.

CHARACTERS.

Dental formula.—Teeth 16.
superior 8. { Incisor 2. Canine 0. Molar 6.
inferior 8. { Incisor 2. Canine 0. Molar 6.

Molars similar in both jaws; the first being the largest, having three tubercles, which divide the crown equally lengthwise; the second having two, and the third, one; head elongated; cheeks rather projecting; ears moderately long, rounded at the extremity; anterior feet short, with four clawed-toes, and a rudiment of a thumb; the posterior long, or very long, terminated by clawed-toes, having each its proper metatarsal bone; tail long, more or less hairy.

HABIT. Living in holes, which they dig in the earth; leaping forcibly with their hind legs; one species hibernates.

Inhabit the temperate climates of both continents.

Species.

1. *Gerbillus canadensis*, Desm. Mamm. p. 321.

Mus canadensis, Penn. *Dipus canadensis,* Davies, Trans. Lin. Soc. v. iv. p. 155. *Canadian jerboa,* Shaw, Gen. Zool. vol. ii. p. 192. pl. 161. (Encycl. pl. suppl. 11. fig. 3.)

This species has not been hitherto correctly described. The following description is taken from a well prepared specimen in the Philadelphia Museum.

Char. Essent. Yellowish above; white beneath; ears rather short; tail nearly naked, longer than the body, without a tuft of long hair at the extremity.

DIMENSIONS. About the size of a mouse.

DESCRIPTION. Head small, narrow, pointed; facial line slightly arched; fore legs very short, four-toed, with a rudiment of a thumb; hind legs very long, five-toed; thigh and leg nearly of equal length; nails small, shaped like those of the mouse; ears of moderate length, with elevated and rounded borders, hairy within and without; colour yellowish-fawn above, whitish beneath; whiskers very long, fine and black; tail longer than the body, tapering, marked by several nodes, nearly naked, a few fine whitish hairs surround its extremity.

Inhabit the middle states; noticed by Maj. Long's exploring party at the base of the Rocky Mountains. Exped. to the Rocky Mountains. v. ii. p. 17.

Species.

2. *Gerbillus labradorius.*

Mus labradorius, Sab. p. 661. append. to Franklin. Penn. Arct. Zool.

DESCRIPTION. Body nearly four inches long; forehead arched, and projecting so as to turn the nose towards the earth; mouth placed far below, small; upper lip slit; ears large, round, and placed far back; whiskers long, black, and projecting, forming two tufts; back, brown above; under parts white, without a dividing line; hind legs long, (one inch and a half,) covered with short hair, having five toes, four long, a shorter one placed on the inside; fore feet short, with four toes; tail two inches and a half long, covered with black hair above, white below, showing the joints of the bones.

Inhabit Labrador. (As usual, Mr. Rafinesque has indicated numerous species.)

Genus.

Arctomys, Gmel. Schreb. Geoff, Cuv. Lacep. Illig.

Mus, Linn. Pall. Bodd.

Glis, Briss. Erxleb.

Marmot.

CHARACTERS.

Dental formula.—Teeth 22.
- superior 12.
  - Incisor 2.
  - Canine 0.
  - Molar 10.
- inferior 10.
  - Incisor 2.
  - Canine 0.
  - Molar 8.

Incisors very strong, anterior face rounded; the inferior slightly compressed; molars simple, their crowns presenting ridges and blunt tubercles; the anterior and internal one is most projecting; body thick and clumsy; head large, flat above, without pouches for the most part; eyes large; ears short and rounded; feet robust, those before terminated by four distinct toes and a rudiment of a thumb; the posterior five-toed; nails of all the feet strong, compressed, and slightly hooked.

Tail hairy, moderate, or short.

HABIT. Burrowing; living in societies more or less numerous, becoming lethargic during the cold season; feeding on vegetables during the summer; becoming excessively fat; when tamed, they are sufficiently docile; and one species at least, (*Monax*) was never observed to eat animal food.

Inhabit both continents, some preferring northern and elevated countries.

Species.

1. *Arctomys monax*, Gmel. Schreb. tab. 208. *Monax*, Edwards, av. vol. ii. p. 104. *Maryland Marmot*, Penn. Quad. p. 270. N. 178. *Glis monax*, Erxleb. *Le Monax*, ou *Marmotte du Canada;* Buff. *Cuniculus bahamensis*, Catesby, Carolin. p. 79. tab. 79. *Wood-chuck*, in Maryland. *Ground-hog*, in Pennsylvania.

Char. Essent. Brown above; paler on the sides

and under the belly; snout bluish-gray and blackish; tail about half the length of the body, covered
with blackish hairs.

DIMENSIONS. Total length from fifteen to
eighteen inches.

DESCRIPTION. Body clumsy, low set; snout rather
longer than in the Marmot properly so called; ears
rounded; nails long and sharp; colour ferruginous-
brown, less deep on the flanks and inferior parts
of the back, bluish-gray about the snout; tail
covered with blackish hairs.

HABIT. The ground-hog digs deep holes in
clover fields, or on the sides of hills, or under
rocks in the woods in the neighbourhood of fields:
these holes are deep and slanting, generally consisting of several compartments, with one or more
entrances; they pass the winter in a state of
lethargy; feed on herbs and fruits, but delight in
clover, of which they destroy immense quantities:
the female produces five or six at a birth: when
tamed, they become sufficiently docile, and never
eat animal food; when intercepted from their
holes, they prefer giving battle to a dog rather
than attempt to effect their escape by retreating;
they are more than a match for a dog a size larger
than themselves.

Inhabit North America; abound in the middle
states. The above remarks are made from an individual that lived perfectly tame for several months.

Species.

3. *Arctomys empetra*, Gmel. Schreb. tab. 210.
Quebec Marmot, Penn. Quad. p. 270. n. 199. tab.
24. fig. 2.

Glis canadensis, Erxleb. *Mus empetra*, Pall.
(Encycl. pl. 67. fig. 4. under the name of *Marmotte du Canada*.)

Char. Essent. Colour blackish-brown, spotted
with white above; ferruginous-red beneath; tail
short, blackish at the end.

DIMENSIONS. Total length eleven inches; of the
tail two inches.

DESCRIPTION. Colour blackish-brown, spotted
with white above, which is owing to the hairs of
this part being blackish at their base, then annulated with white, and terminated with black; top
of the head of a uniform brown, passing into reddish-brown on the occiput, and to black on the
end of the snout; cheeks and chin of a dirty grayish-white; breast and fore paws red; feet black;
tail rather short, with abundant black hairs; a
variety has only the reddish teint less lively.

HABIT. Unknown.

Inhabit Canada and the environs of Hudson's
Bay.

Species.

3. *Arctomys ludoviciani*, Ord, Guthrie's Geog.
v. ii. p. 302, 1815. Say. Exped. to the Rocky

Mountains, v. i. p. 451. *Arctomys missouriensis*, Warden's descrip. of the United States, vol. v. p. 627, 1820. *Prairie dog*, Lewis and Clark's Exped. up the Missouri. (A well prepared specimen in the Philadelphia Museum, presented by Lewis and Clark.)

Char. Essent. Colour a light dirty reddish-brown above, intermixed with some gray, also a few black hairs, this hair is of a dark lead colour next the skin, then bluish-white, then light reddish, then gray at tip; the lower parts of the body are of a dirty white colour.

DIMENSIONS. Total length sixteen inches; of the tail two and three quarter inches; hair at its tip three quarters of an inch.

DESCRIPTION. Head wide and depressed above; eyes large; iris dark brown; ears short and truncated; whiskers of moderate length, and black; a few bristles projecting from the anterior portion of the superior orbit of the eye, and also from a wart on the cheek; nose rather sharp and compressed; all the feet five-toed, covered with very short hair, and armed with rather long black nails, of which the anterior one of the fore foot nearly attains the base of the next, and the middle one is half an inch in length; the thumb is armed with a conical nail, three-tenths of an inch in length; the tail is rather short, banded with brown near the tip, the hair excepting near the body is not plumbeous at base.

HABIT. This interesting little animal is very sprightly, and has received the inappropriate name of *Prairie dog*, from a fancied resemblance of its warning cry to the hurried barking of a small dog; this sound may be imitated with the human voice, by the pronunciation of the syllable, cheh-cheh-cheh, in a sibilated manner, and in rapid succession, by propelling the breath between the tip of the tongue and the roof of the mouth.

As particular districts, of limited extent, are in general occupied by the burrows of these animals, such assemblages of dwellings are denominated *Prairie dog villages*, by hunters and others. These villages differ widely in the extent of surface which they occupy; some are confined to an area of a few acres; others are bounded by a circumference of many miles. The entrance to the burrow is at the summit of the little mound of earth cast up by the animal during the progress of excavation. These mounds are sometimes inconspicuous, but generally somewhat elevated above the common surface, though rarely to the height of eighteen inches. Their form is of a truncated cone, on a base of two or three feet, perforated by a comparatively large hole at the summit, or in the side. The whole surface, but more particularly the summit, is trodden down and compacted; the hole descends vertically one or two feet, whence it continues in an oblique direction downwards. A single burrow may have many occupants, as many as seven or eight individuals have been observed sitting upon one mound. They delight to sport about the entrance of their burrows in pleasant weather; at the approach of danger they retreat to their dens; or when its proximity is not too immediate, they remain barking, and flourishing their tails on the edges of their holes, or sitting erect to reconnoitre; when fired upon in this situation they never fail to escape; if killed, they instantly fall into their burrows, beyond the reach of the hunter. They pass the winter in a lethargic state, and defend themselves from its rigours by accurately closing up the entrance of the burrow: they construct for themselves a very neat globular cell with fine dry grass, with an aperture at top large enough to admit the finger, and so compactly formed, that it might almost be rolled over the floor without receiving injury. The burrows are not always equidistant, though they occur usually at intervals of about twenty feet. (Say.)

These animals would appear to be very innocent, as we are informed by Gen. Pike, (in his Expedition,) that he has observed " the *Marmot*, the *Rattle-snake*, the *Horned frog*, (*Agama cornuta, nob.*) of which the prairies are full, and the *Land turtle*, seek refuge in the same hole." He further states that the Indians name this animal

" *Wish-ton-wish*," which they pronounce with a sharp voice, in order to mimic the voice of the animal.

Inhabit North America, abounding in the Missouri country.

Species.

4. *Arctomys tridecemlineata.*

Sciurus tridecemlineatus, Mitchill, Medical Repository, No. 2. vol. vi. January, 1821.

· *Arctomys hoodii*, Sabine, Trans. Lin. Soc. vol. xiii. p. 590.   1822.

Striped and spotted Ground-squirrel, Say, Long's Exped. to the Rocky Mountains, vol. ii. p. 174.

This beautiful little animal has been improperly placed under the genus *Sciurus*, from which it is essentially different, and corresponds with the genus *Arctomys* in the following particulars.   1. In the form and appearance of the whole body in general; 2. in the form of the head and ears; 3. in the length, direction, and form of the tail; 4. in the form and proportion of the legs; 5. in the form and length of the nails; and, 6. in some of its manners and habits.   In justice to Mr. Desmarest, we must remark that he has expressed some doubts of the propriety of arranging it under the division in which he had placed it, but not having seen the animal, he was unable to say which genus it most resembles.

Char. Essent. Colour a deep chesnut above, striped with six white lines, alternating with an equal number of longitudinal rows of white spots; white beneath.

DIMENSIONS. Total length six inches five-tenths; of the tail, less than two inches.

DESCRIPTION. Head small, rather flattened above; snout conical; body elongated, low set, thickest behind; extremities short, nearly of equal length; feet covered with hair even to the base of the nails; colour of the animal above of a deep chesnut, and marked with six longitudinal lines, commencing at the occiput, and running the whole length of the body, alternating with a series of white oblong spots, commencing at the shoulders, and continuing along the body; the middle dorsal line is composed of these spots, about eighteen in number, which commence at the nucha and are continued to the base of the tail; throat, breast and belly nearly white; tail short, surrounded with hairs longer than on the body, rather bushy. and of a whitish colour, mixed with black; feet whitish, covered with fine hairs, and terminated by five clawed toes before and behind. Nails on the three middle toes of the fore feet long, subulate, blackish; the middle toe nail is the longest; the external and internal toes and nails very short; hind feet broad and flat; the three middle claws nearly equal; the external and internal nails like those of the fore foot very short. The whole ani-

mal resembles the *Arctomys missouriensis*, except
in colour, size and markings.

TEETH. Molars five above and four below,
crowns rather concave, borders slightly tuberculous, roots long and distinct from each other;
superior incisors rather small, cuneiform, plane
on the anterior surface, and of a yellow colour;
inferior incisors proportionably long, nearly cylindrical at base, chisel shaped at top, separate and
divergent. Furnished with large cheek pouches
lined with hair both internally and externally.

HABIT. According to Mr. Say, (who observed
this animal when descending the Arkansa,) they
burrow in the earth, and do not *voluntarily climb
trees*. They inhabit an extensive portion of North
America, extending at least from the more northern lakes to the Arkansa river, and most probably
in that direction into Mexico, and westward to the
Rocky Mountains. They were not uncommon in
the vicinity of Engineer Cantonment. According
to Sabine, they inhabit also the northern parts of
Canada.

Mr. Nuttall long since obtained specimens of
this species near the Mandan village on the Missouri, and in the year 1814 he presented skins of
it to several of his scientific friends in London.
He states that he has seen tippets worn by the
Indians of the Upper Missouri, which were made
of the skins of this elegant species, sewn together.

(A specimen in the Philadelphia Museum. brought by Major Long's exploring party.)

Species.

5. *Arctomys franklinii*, Sabine, Trans. Lin. Soc. vol. xiii. tab. 27. p. 587.

Gray American Marmot.

Char. Essent. Head furnished with small ears: snout very obtuse; tail elongated; body variegated fuscus.

DIMENSIONS. Total length, not including the tail, eleven inches; of the tail to the end of the hair five inches.

DESCRIPTION. Face broad, nearly covered with rigid hairs (black and white;) nose bare and very blunt; ears broad, covered with short hairs; short black whiskers on the cheeks, and similar hairs grow thinly distributed above and below the eyes; throat dusky white; upper incisors short, and of a reddish colour; inferior incisors twice the length of the upper, and paler; upper part of the body with short hairs, dark at the base, in the middle dingy-white, then first black, next yellowish-white, and tipped with black; the whole a variegated dark yellowish-gray; the hair on the sides is longer, has less black, and is without the yellow tinge; that on the belly is dark at base, and dingy-white above; tail with long hairs banded with black and white, tipped with white, the whole appearing indistinctly striped with black and

white; feet broadish; toes thin and gray, covered
with hairs; on the fore feet the second from the
inside is longest; the outer shortest, and placed
far back; the three middle hind toes nearly equal;
the extremes shorter and far back; claws horn
colour, those on the fore feet long and sharp, those
on the hind toes shorter.

Species.

6. *Arctomys richardsonii,* Sabine, Trans. Lin.
Soc. vol. xiii. tab. 28. p. 589.

Tawny American Marmot.

Char. Essent. Ears short; snout acute; tail
moderate; body fuscus.

Dimensions. Nearly the size of the preceding
species, but more slender.

Description. Top of the head covered with
short hairs, dark at the base and light at the tips;
face narrow; nose tapering and sharp, bare at the
end, above covered with short light brown hairs
joining and mixing with those on the top of the
head; ears oval and short; cheeks swollen, covered with light brown hairs; whiskers short, growing from the cheeks, and a few long and rigid
hairs above the eyes; throat dirty white; upper
part of the body covered with soft short hairs,
dark at the base, above fulvous; in the middle of
the back, the hairs are like those on the top of
the head, but lighter; sides with longer hairs,
showing dark at base when raised. the ends a

smoky white, the under parts similar, but a little dashed with ferruginous; tail three inches and a half long to the end of the hairs, slender, and thinly covered with long hairs, which are at the base of the same colour as the body, but above of three distinct colours, first black, then dark, and lastly light at the upper extremity; legs rather long and slender; feet narrow; claws horn colour, arched and sharp; on the inner side of the fore feet, a small toe placed far back, with an obtuse claw, in which it differs from the other species of this genus; outer toe and claw of the fore feet much shorter than the remaining three, of which the middle one with its claw is longest; of the hind toes, the two extremes shorter and placed back, the others nearly of equal length.

Species.

7. *Arctomys pruinosa,** Gmel. Syst. Nat. i. 144. Turt. Linn. **Hoary Marmot**, Penn. Hist. Quad. ii. 389. Penn. Arct. Zool. i. 112. Schreb. Quad. 745, Shaw's Zool. iii. 121.

Size of a rabbit; tip of the nose black; ears short and oval; cheeks whitish; crown dusky and tawny; hairs usually rude and long, those on the back, sides, and belly, cinereus at the root, black in the middle, whitish at the tip, so that the animal has a hoary appearance; tail black, mixed with rust colour; legs black; claws dusky.

22

This specimen was supposed to have come from the northern parts of North America.

Species.

8. *Arctomys parryii,* Dr. Richardson's Appendix to Franklin's Expedition.

Gray Arctic Marmot.

Ground-squirrel, Hearne's Journey, p. 141.

Quebec Marmot, Foster, Philos. Trans. lxxii. p. 378.

Arctomys alpina, Parry's Narrative, 2nd voyage, p. 61.

Char. Essent. "A. palmis pentadactylis; rostro obtusissimo; buccis sacculiferis; auriculis brevissimis; cauda elongata, apice nigra; corpore supra maculis albis nigrisque confluentibus marmorata, subtus ferrugineo."

DIMENSIONS. A size larger than the *A. franklinii,* and less than the *empetra.* Total length, to the base of the tail, twelve to fourteen inches; trunk of the tail four inches, with the hair five inches and a half.

DESCRIPTION. Body broad and flattish, with thick legs; head depressed; nose blunt and covered with a dense coat of short brown hairs; margin of the mouth hoary; eyes large and dark coloured; orifice of the auditory passage large; ear very short, consisting merely of a flat, semi-oval flap, projecting about two lines; pouches ample, opening into the mouth anterior to the grinders; teeth, primores white, with chisel shaped cutting edges, wearing away, and frequently channelled inside, those in the upper jaw short and somewhat truncated; lower one-third longer, rather narrower, and terminated by nearly a semicircular outline; molars five above and four below, posterior largest; some adults with only four above, their crowns are bounded by an irregular bending plate of enamel, intersected by two transverse ridges of unequal height, and presenting a few obtuse points; back covered with soft fur, consisting of a soft down of a dark smoke-gray at the roots, pale fresh-gray in the middle, and yellow-gray at tips; this arrangement produces a crowded assemblage of ill defined irregular and confluent whitish spots, margined and separated by black and yellowish-gray; these spots assume a transverse arrangement on the posterior part of the back; throat and all underneath brownish-red and brownish-yellow, or rather a colour intermediate; colours of the back and belly run into each other. Tail flattish and subdistichous, the hairs of which the animal is capable of expanding like a feather, in which state the tail is brown along the middle, tipped and margined for two-thirds of its length with black; feet with short depressed claws, large, blackish, slightly arched, and grooved underneath; on the inside of the fore feet, and high up, there is a small toe or thumb armed with a small nail; palms naked and with callous protuberances, three at the base of the toes, the thumb inserted into the largest.

Habit and geographical range like the preceding species.

Genus.

Sciurus, Briss. Linn. Erxleb. Bodd. Cuv. Geoff. Illig. *squirrel.*

CHARACTERS.

Dental formula.—Teeth 22. $\begin{cases} \text{superior 12.} \begin{cases} \text{Incisor 2.} \\ \text{Canine 0.} \\ \text{Molar 10.} \end{cases} \\ \text{inferior 10.} \begin{cases} \text{Incisor 2.} \\ \text{Canine 0.} \\ \text{Molar 8.} \end{cases} \end{cases}$

(NOTE.—The fifth molar exists only in the young individual.)

Superior incisors flat before, and cuneiform at the extremity; the inferior pointed, and laterally compressed.

Molars with tuberculous crowns.

Body elongated; head small; ears straight, moderate and rounded; eyes large. Anterior feet with four long toes, distinct, armed with compressed and horned nails, with a tubercle covered with an obtuse nail, in place of a thumb; posterior feet very large; tarsi very long; five elongated distinct toes, with hooked nails.

Tail long, often furnished with hairs disposed in two rows like the feathers of a quill: *distichous.*

Eight mammæ, of which two are pectoral; six ventral.

Habit. These animals, evidently constructed for climbing, pass their life on the summits of trees; their posterior extremities, much longer than their anterior, are disposed for embracing the branches; they are full of life and agility, and feed principally on dried fruits, which they carry to the mouth with their hands, making use of their stumpy thumbs as points of support. They construct near the tops of high trees, a round nest, formed of small branches of leaves and of moss. They bring forth four or five young at a birth.

Inhabit the whole earth, with the exception of New Holland, and the greatest part of South America.

1. Sub-genus, *squirrels properly so called.*

Species.

1. *Sciurus cinereus*, Schreb. Tab. 213. *Sciurus caroliniensis* and *cinereus*, Gmel. *Ecureuil gris de Caroline*, Cuv. Reg. Anim. *Petit-gris*, Buff. (Encycl. pl. 74. fig. 3. *Le pitit gris.*) *Gray Squirrel.*

Char. Essent. General colour, of a grayish-fawn, spotted with black above; white beneath; borders of the flanks, a fawn colour, more or less pure; ears without pencils of hair.

Dimensions. Total length ten inches six lines;

of the head two inches six lines; of the ears eleven lines; of the trunk of the tail seven inches six lines.

DESCRIPTION. Superior parts of the head and neck, as well as the back, covered with hairs, gray at their base, and afterwards divided into two or three zones, alternately of a clear fawn, and black, which produces a general complexion of gray, approaching to yellow; sides of the neck, and particularly the haunches, spotted with white; flanks slightly spotted with black, which leaves the fawn colour nearly pure; abdomen white; legs covered with gray hair at their base, and reddish-fawn at their extremities; sides of the head and snout reddish; ears rounded, covered with very short hair; whiskers black; tail composed of hair marked with zones alternately fawn and black, and terminated with white; from whence it results when the tail is flattened, that it is surrounded from right to left with a white line, then with a black line, and its middle fawn colour, spotted with black.

VARIETY. Blackish-gray, more or less approaching black.

HABIT. Living in large troops and feeding on nuts and grain; very destructive to the produce of the latter. In winter they retire to holes in old trees where they have amassed their provisions, and where they bring forth their young.

Inhabit Pennsylvania and most parts of the

United States; they appear to retire before the intrusion of a smaller species, (the *S. hudsonius.*) In 1749, a premium of three pence a head was offered for their destruction, which amounted in one year to 8000*l.* sterling, which is equal to about 1,280,000 individuals killed.

Species.

2. *Sciurus capistratus,* Bosc. Ann. Mus. t. 1. p. 281. *Sciurus vulpinus,* Gmel.? Schreb. 213. B. Brown, Nouv. Illust. de Zool. pl. 47. Charlevoix, t. 1. p. 237. *Ecureuil à Masque,* Cuv. Regn. Anim. t. 1. p. 205. (Encycl. pl. suppl. ii. fig. 2.) *Fox Squirrel.*

Char. Essent. Colour iron-gray or black above; head black, with the end of the snout always white, as are also the ears.

Dimensions. Total length about two feet from the end of the snout to the extremity of the tail, and three inches in diameter.

Description. Head oval, rather elongated, black at its summit; cheeks black, mixed with brown; top of the nose and lips white; ears round, white, hair on the exterior longer than on the interior; body covered with two sorts of hair, the one black, with the superior half white, the other white with the superior half black; chin, breast and belly white; feet grayish-brown; tail as long as the body, covered with long hairs, black at their base, white at their extremity, and the intermediate parts of which are twice annulated with white, and twice with black; from whence it results that the tail, when it is flattened, appears to have a double border, white and black.

Var. 1. *S. capistratus niger.* V. 2. *S. capistratus nigriventer.*

HABIT. Dwelling in pine forests; the seeds of the pine constitute their principal nourishment; they enter in heat during the month of January; their young are capable of running by the month of March; they differ little for the rest in their habits from the common gray squirrel.

Inhabit New Jersey and South Carolina, principally in the neighbourhood of Charleston, where they are found in the company of the gray Squirrel.

Species.

3. *Sciurus rufiventer,* Geoff. Collect. du Mus, Desm. Nouv. Dict. d'Hist. Nat. t. 10. p. 103.

Char. Essent. Colour, grayish-brown above; a lively red beneath; feet brown; tail nearly the length of the body; the colour of the back at base blackish at the extremity.

DIMENSIONS. Total length six inches six lines; tail without the hairs nearly the length of the body.

DESCRIPTION. Reddish-brown, bordering on black on the head, neck, back and flanks; feet reddish-brown; these hairs are slate-gray at base; beneath the jaws and throat dirty reddish-white;

belly and inside of the legs nearly pure red;
whiskers black, and as long as the head; ears
reddish, and covered with short hairs; extremities
of the feet of a blackish-brown; tail brownish at
base, blackish beneath and at the extremity, reddish on the middle upper surface.

Inhabit southern states. The above description
is taken from a specimen in the Philadelphia
Museum, brought from near New Orleans, and is
without doubt, distinct from the Gray Squirrel.

Species.

4. *Sciurus niger*, Linn. Erxleb. Screb. tab. 215.
Sciurus mexicanus, Hernandez, Mex. p. 582. fig.
2. *Black Squirrel*, Catesby, Carrol. vol. ii. p. 73.
Bartram, Voy. in North Amer. vol. ii. p. 31. (Encycl. pl. 74. fig. 2.)

Char. Essent. Colour deep black above,
brownish-black beneath; ears black and not pen-
cilled with hair; tail black.

DIMENSIONS. Total length about eight inches,
tail proportionably shorter than that of the gray
squirrel.

DESCRIPTION. Top of the head, back, tail, and
extremities of the feet, covered with hair of a deep
black colour, without any mixture of red or fawn
colour; throat, breast, and belly, of a black approaching to a brown colour; hair of the flanks
black, and having each a brown ring, which di-
minishes about these parts the intensity of the

23

black colour; ears short and black; hair of the tail ringed like the flanks; covering consisting of brown fur, traversed with long hairs, which are alone apparent; each of these are brown at base, then marked with a teint more clear for a small extent, and terminated with black; those of the posterior part of the back being the longest and entirely black, as well as those on the top of the head.

Some individuals have white at the end of the tail, nose and feet, also like those of Catesby's, (copied in the Encyclopædia) around the neck.

Inhabit North America. This species differs from the black variety of the *S. capistratus* in its small size, the softness of its hair, and because its nose and ears are not regularly white. It is separated from the black variety of the Gray Squirrel by the shortness of its tail.

Species.

5. *Sciurus magnicaudatus.*

Sciurus macrourus, Say, Long's Exped. to the Rocky Mountains, vol. i. p. 115.

The specific name by which this species has been designated, has already been applied to designate a squirrel totally different, viz. the *Ceylon Squirrel*, Penn. Quad. p. 408. which is the *S. macrourus*, Gmel. Schreb. tab. 217.

Char. Essent. Body above on each side mixed

gray and black; side of the head and orbits pale ferruginous; cheek, under the eye and ear, dusky.

DIMENSIONS. From the nose to the tip of the trunk of the tail one foot seven inches and one-fourth; trunk of the tail from the base to the tip nine inches one-tenth; length of the ears three-fourths of an inch; tail more voluminous even than that of the *S. cinereus.*

DESCRIPTION. Fur on the body plumbeous, black at base, then pale cinnamon, then black, then cinereus, with a long black tip; ears bright ferruginous behind, the colour the same to the base of the fur, which in the winter dress is prominent beyond the edge; within dull ferruginous, the fur slightly tipped with black; whiskers black in about five series, of which the four inferior ones are more distinct, hairs slightly flattened; mouth margined with black; teeth reddish-yellow; head beneath, neck and feet above, pale ferruginous; belly paler; fur pale plumbeous at base; palms black; anterior toes, four; thumb tubercle not longer than its lobe in the palm, and furnished with a broad, flat nail; posterior toes, five; tail beneath bright ferruginous, the colour extending to the base of the fur, with a submarginal black line; above mixed ferruginous and black; fur within pale cinnamon, with the base and three bands black; tip ferruginous.

The fur of the back in the summer dress is from three-fifths to seven-tenths of an inch long; but in the winter dress the longest hairs on the middle of the back are one inch and three-fourths in length, but the colours do not vary, and it is only during the winter that the ears are fringed. (Say.)

Inhabit the United States. The most common species on the banks of the Missouri river.

Species.

6. *Sciurus quadrivittatus*, Say, Long's Exped to the Rocky Mountains, vol. ii. p. 45.

Char. Essent. Head brownish, intermixed with fulvous, marked with four white lines; sides fulvous; beneath whitish.

DIMENSIONS. Total length four inches and one-fourth (without the tail;) of the tail three inches: of the hair at the tip of the tail nearly one inch.

DESCRIPTION. Head brownish, marked by four white lines, of which the superior one on each side passes from the tip of the nose immediately over the eye to the superior base of the ear, and the inferior one passes immediately beneath the eye to the inferior base of the ear; ears moderate, semi-oval; incisors reddish-yellow; back with four white broad lines, and alternate mixed black and ferruginous ones; sides fulvous; beneath whitish; tail moderate, hair black at base, then fulvous, black in the middle, and pale-fulvous at tip; beneath fulvous with a sub-marginal black line; thumb of the anterior feet, a prominent tubercle.

HABIT. Nestling in holes, and on the edges of rocks, and do not ascend trees by choice. The nest is composed of a most extraordinary assemblage of the burs of the *Xanthium*, branches, and other portions of the large upright *Cactus*, small branches of pine trees, and other vegetable productions, sufficient in some instances to fill the body of an ordinary cart; what the object of so great, and apparently so superfluous, an assemblage of rubbish may be, we are at a loss to conjecture; we do not know what peculiarly dangerous enemy it may be intended to exclude by so much labour; their principal food, at least at this season, (July) is the seeds of the pine, which they readily extract from the cones.

Inhabit the Rocky Mountains, about the sources of the Arkansa and Platte. (Say.) A specimen in the Philadelphia Museum.

Species.

7. *Sciurus lateralis*, Say, Long's Exped. to the Rocky Mountains, vol. ii. p. 46.

Char. Essent. Above brownish cinereus; each side of the back marked with a dull yellowish-white dilated line, broader before.

DIMENSIONS. Rather larger than the *S. striatus*.

DESCRIPTION. Above brownish-cinereus, intermixed with blackish; on each side of the back is a dull yellowish-white dilated line, broader before; margined above and beneath with black, originating upon the neck anterior to the shoulder. and not attaining the origin of the tail; no appearance of a vertebral line; thigh, neck, anterior to the commencement of the white line, and top of the head, tinged with ferruginous; orbit whitish; tail short, thin, with a submarginal black line beneath; nails of the anterior feet elongated; thumb tubercle furnished with a broad nail; sides dull yellowish-white; beneath pale, intermixed with blackish. (Say.)

Inhabit about the base of the Rocky Mountains, where they were first observed by Lewis and Clark, on their expedition to the Pacific Ocean. A specimen in the Philadelphia Museum, brought by the exploring party under Maj. Long.

Species.

8. *Sciurus grammurus, lined tail squirrel,* Say. Long's Exped. to the Rocky Mountains, v. ii. p. 72.

Char. Essent. Body cinereus; fur very coarse; three black lines on each side of the tail.

DIMENSIONS. Length to the origin of the tail eleven inches; of the tail nine inches.

DESCRIPTION. Body cinereus, more or less tinged with ferruginous; fur very coarse, much flattened, canaliculate above, plumbeous or blackish at base, then whitish or ferruginous, tip brownish; above the neck and shoulders the whitish is prevalent; from the middle of the back, the sides, and the exterior surface of the legs, the ferruginous colour

prevails, the terminal brown of the feet being ob-
solete; superior and inferior margins of the eyes
white; tail moderate, whitish; fur trianulate with
black; the base and tip of each hair being whitish; beneath whitish, tinged with ferruginous;
thumb tubercle armed; iris burnt amber colour,
pupil black.

HABIT. Nestling in holes and crevices of rocks,
and do not appear to ascend trees voluntarily; in
the stomachs of those killed, were found the buds
and leaves of a few small plants, common among
the rocks.

Inhabit near the Rocky Mountains on the head
of the Arkansa; frequent about the naked parts
of the sand stone clifts, or where are only a few
cedar bushes. (Say.)

Species.

9. *Sciurus striatus*, Klein. Pallas, Glir. p. 378.
Gmel. Schreb. Tab. 221. *Sciurus lysteri*, Rai.
Syn. Quad. p. 216. *Sciurus caroliniensis*, Briss.
Regn. Anim. p. 155. *Le suisse*, Buff. t. x. pl. 28.
Vulgarly the *Ground squirrel*. (Encycl. pl. 76.
fig. 4.) Desm. Mamm. p. 339.

Char. Essent. Body a brown fawn colour
above, with five longitudinal brown rays and two
white; rump red; inferior parts white; tail blackish above, red and bordered with black beneath.

DIMENSIONS. Total length five inches: of the

tail two inches six lines; of the head one inch six lines.

DESCRIPTION. Top of the head, reddish-gray-brown colour; eye-lids whitish; a black line parting from the external of the eye is directed towards the ear; a reddish-brown line on each cheek; ears short, rounded, covered with very fine hair, of a reddish-brown within, and of a grayish-brown without on the anterior border, and of a whitish-gray on the posterior; top of the neck, shoulders, and base of the dorsal fur of a grayish-brown, spotted with white; five longitudinal black bands slightly touched with red on the body, the intermediate commencing at the occiput, and the lateral at the shoulders, all terminating towards the rump, which is of nearly a lively red; inferior parts of the flanks and sides of the neck of a more pale red; two white bands, one on each side, separating the two lateral black bands; exterior surface of the fore feet, gray-fawn colour; exterior of the thighs and hind feet above red; superior lip, chin, throat, belly and face, with the interior of the extremities, of a dirty brown; tail reddish at its base, blackish above and red beneath, with a black border. All the hairs of the superior parts of the body, are gray at base; those of the tail red or reddish at base, then black, and terminated with dirty white.

HABIT. Digging holes in the earth having two openings and as many lateral branches, in which holes they accumulate provisions for winter, which they transport in their cheek pouches; such articles as seeds, roots, nuts, &c. Copulate in March.

Inhabit Northern Asia, from the Kama and the Dwina to the extremity of Siberia; North America, from Canada to Carolina, and west of the Mississippi. (Variety, perfectly *white, albino.*)

Species.

10. *Sciurus hudsonius*, Gmel. Schreb. Tab. 214. Foster, Act. Angl. v. lvii. p. 378. Penn. Syn. Quad p. 280. Tab. 26. fig. 1. Pall. Glir. p. 376. *S. vulgaris*, Var. F. Erxleb. (Encycl. pl. 75. fig. 1.) vulgarly *the Chick-a-ree.*

Char. Essent. Colour reddish-brown above, whitish cinereus beneath; a single black line on each flank.

Dimensions. Total length seven inches seven lines; of the head one inch ten lines; of the tail five inches.

Description. Superior parts of a reddish-brown, more or less deep, and more or less spotted with black; top of the head and anterior part of the members of the same colour, but of a complexion rather more clear; lower jaw, beneath the throat, breast, belly, and anterior surface of the thighs, of a dirty white, lightly tinged with yellow; a well defined black line on each flank, separating completely the colour of the back from that of the

24

belly; tail of a similar colour to the body, bordered with black; whiskers very long and black.

Inhabit North America, from Hudson's Bay to
the middle states.

NOTE.—*S. rubralineatus*, (Warden, Desc. des
etats unis,) is probably a variety of the *S. hudsonius.*

Species.

11. *Sciurus ludovicianus*,* Custis, Barton's Med.
and Phys. Jour. vol. ii. part 2. p. 47.

Char. Essent.   Body and upper part of the tail
dark gray; the belly, inside of the legs and thighs,
and under part of the tail, reddish-brown; ears not
bearded; tail longer than the body, very broad.

DIMENSIONS.   About the size of the *Sciurus vulpinus.*

Inhabits the shores of Red River.

Genus.

Pteromys, Cuv. Geoff. Illig.

Sciurus, Rai, Briss. Klein. Linn. Gmel. Erxleb.
Bodd.

CHARACTERS.

		Incisor	2.
Dental formula.—Teeth 22.	superior 12.	Canine	0.
		Molar	10.
	inferior 10.	Incisor	2.
		Canine	0.
		Molar	8.

NOTE.—In very old individuals the two anterior
molars of the upper jaw are wanting.

The terminations of the superior incisors cunei-form, with their anterior surfaces smooth; the two inferior laterally compressed and sharp.

The crowns of the molars are furnished with blunt tubercles.

Head slightly rounded; snout prolonged; ears rounded; eyes large.

Anterior feet with four elongated toes, armed with elongated and compressed claws; a rudimentary thumb furnished with an obtuse nail; the posterior feet disposed for climbing, with five clawed toes, very much separated; skin of the flanks very extensive, clothed with hair above and below, joining the anterior with the posterior members, and forming a species of parachute; an osseous appendage to the feet, destined to sustain this membrane of the flanks.

Tail long, hairy, sometimes distichous; hair generally soft.

HABIT. Nocturnal, feeding on dry fruits and nuts like the squirrels, to which they are nearly related in their habits.

Inhabit North America and Asia, Southern Asia. and the Indian Archipelago.

Species.

1. *Pteromys volucella, American Flying Squirrel. Sciurus volucella,* Pallas, Nov. Quad. e Glir. Ordin. p. 353. Gmel. Syst. Nat. Schreb. tab. 222.

Polatouche, Buff. t. 10. pl. 21. Shaw, Gen. Zool.
vol. ii. part 1. p. 155. tab. 150.

Assapan, F. Cuv. Mamm. Lithogr. 8th livraison,
(Encycl. pl. 77. fig. 4.)

Char. Essent. Colour reddish-gray above, white
beneath; tail nearly as long as the body; lateral
membranes presenting a simple lobe posterior to
the wrists.

DIMENSIONS. Total length four inches ten lines:
of the head one inch six lines; of the trunk of the
tail three inches seven lines.

DESCRIPTION. Superior surface of the head, of
the body, of the tail, and exterior surface of the
limbs, of a gray colour, with a slight brush of red;
the hairs of these parts being cinereus at base, and
reddish-yellow at their extremity; eyes surrounded with a blackish-ash colour, with a white spot
above each; borders of the membrane also passing
into a brown above; beneath the body, from the
end of the snout to the origin of the tail, white,
with a slight teint of yellow on the borders of the
membrane, and on the inner sides of the thighs
and legs; upper surface of the tail of a clear brown
colour, the inferior of a yellowish-white; whiskers
black, and about two inches in length.

HABIT. Living in little troops on trees, feeding
on nuts, seeds, grains, buds of the birch tree, &c.

Inhabit the United States, from Canada to Virginia.

Genus.

Hystrix, Briss. Linn. Schreb. Cuv. Geoff. Lacer
Illig. Klein.
   Cavia, Klein.
   Coendu, Lacep.
   Porcupine.

CHARACTERS.

Dental formula.—Teeth 20.
superior 10.	Incisor 2.	
	Canine 0.	
	Molar 8.	
inferior 10.	Incisor 2.	
	Canine 0.	
	Molar 8.	

Superior incisors very strong, smooth anteriorly,
cuneiform at their extremity; the inferior strong
and slightly compressed laterally.

Molars compound, with flat crowns, surrounded
with a line of enamel, which traverses more or
less deeply the external and internal borders, and
appears to cut the tooth into two parts; a few circular lines of enamel of a larger or smaller size.

Head strong; snout thick and tumid; ears short
and rounded; tongue beset with spiny scales; anterior feet four-toed, posterior five-toed, all armed
with powerful nails; a rudiment of a thumb with
an obtuse nail to the fore foot.

Spines more or less long on the body, sometimes intermixed with hair; tail more or less long,
sometimes prehensile.

HABIT. Herbivorous, living principally on

fruits, grains and roots; digging holes, or else living in the hollows of old trees.

Inhabit North and South America, Southern
Europe, Africa, and India.

1. Subgenus. *Porcupines* properly so called .
tail not prehensile.

Species.

1. *Hystrix dorsata*, Gmel. Erxleb. Bodd. Schreb.
tab. 169. *Hystrix hudsonis*, Briss. Regn. Anim.
p. 128. *Hystrix pilosus americanus*, Catesby, Carol. app. p. 30. *Cavia hudsonis*, Klein. Quad. p.
51. *Urson*, Buff. l. 12. pl. 55. (Encycl. pl. 65
fig. 1.)

Bear Porcupine.

Char. Essent. Spines short, in part concealed
by brown hair; tail elongated; no mane; long
bristles on the head and neck.

DIMENSIONS. Total length two feet one inch
of the tail eight inches; the longest nails one inch
three lines.

DESCRIPTION. Snout thicker and shorter than
that of the common Porcupine; ears very small,
entirely covered by the hair; base of the hairs
very thick, and beset with spines, the largest of
which are two inches and a half long, and are
situated about the rump; these spines being partly
white and partly brown or blackish, tipped with
black; those of the rest of the body are covered
with long, strong hairs, of a blackish-brown colour.

terminated with yellowish-white; a cinereus coloured down next the skin; simple stiff bay-colour-
ed hair on the tail; belly, legs and feet equally
covered with hair, but of a blackish-brown, as well
as the snout.

HABIT. They make their nests or dwelling
place beneath the roots of hollow trees; they fly
the water and fear to soil themselves; they sleep
much, and feed principally on the bark and leaves
of the hemlock, (pinus canadensis) and basswood,
(tilia glabra;) they have been known to strip trees
of their foliage, in the same manner as the sloths;
they are, however, fond of sweet apples, corn, &c.
which they eat holding in their fore claws in a
sitting posture. The Indians say they are excellent food. When they are discovered on the
ground, which seldom happens, they do not strive
to get out of the way, but on being approached,
immediately spread the spines situated near the
tail over the whole of the back.

The female brings forth annually, three or four
at a birth, after a gestation of about forty days.

Inhabit the northern parts of the United States.
According to the account of Mr. F. Cozzens,
(Vid. Annals of the Lyceum of Nat. Hist. of New
York, vol. i. p. 190, 1824,) to whom we have
been chiefly indebted for the above details concerning the habits of this singular animal: of late
years they have multiplied greatly, and have become numerous near the Oneida lake, and in the

north-western part of New York.   Their quills
are dyed of different colours by the Indians, and
used as ornaments in giving a border to mocca-
sins, wampum, leggings, &c.

Genus.

Lepus, Briss. Linn. Schreb. Cuv. Geoff. Lacep.
Illig.   *The Hare.*

CHARACTERS.

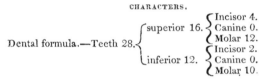

Superior anterior incisors, large and cuneiform,
having a longitudinal groove in front; the posterior small and accurately applied in the direction
of their length to the superior; inferior incisors
with cutting square edges; the six superior molars on each side (of which the anterior is smallest,) have flat crowns, with transverse, projecting
plates of enamel; inferior molars nearly similar
to the superior.   Head rather large; snout thick;
ears very long; eyes very large, projecting laterally; interior of the mouth furnished with hairs.

Anterior feet rather short and thin, five-toed;
the posterior feet very long, four-toed; all the toes
laying close to each other, and armed with moderate sized nails, slightly arched; palms and soles
hairy.

Tail short, hairy and elevated; a fold of skin forming a sort of pouch in each groin.

Mammæ to the number of six or ten. An enormous cæcum, with a spiral lamina which runs its whole length.

The infra-orbitar cavity is cribriform in the skeleton.

Habit. Nocturnal, timid, exclusively phytivorous.

Inhabit both continents under all latitudes.

Species.

1. *Lepus americanus*, Erxleb. Gmel. Schoepf. Naturf. 20. p. 20.

Lepus hudsonius, Pall. Glir. part 1. p. 30. Bodd. *American Rabbit*.

Char. Essent. Colour, a grayish-fawn, varied with brown; nucha fawn; beneath the neck and belly white; ears shorter than the head, without black at the extremity; tail grayish above, and white beneath.

Dimensions. Total length one foot two inches; of the head three inches six lines; of the ears two inches three lines; of the tail two inches.

Description. Ears shorter in proportion than those of the Hare or European Rabbit; thumb of the fore feet very short and elevated; colour very similar to that of the European Rabbit, varied with blackish-brown and reddish, more red about the shoulders than elsewhere, whitish-gray about the breast, white under the belly, a whitish spot before the eyes, and another behind the cheeks; ears of a uniform grayish-brown; feet reddish before, with the point of the foot fawn colour; upper surface of the tail of a similar colour with the back, beneath white; fur becoming whiter during the winter, but the ears and tail remaining always of the same gray.

HABIT. Burrowing in the earth, preferring dry places; female bringing forth three or four times annually, from five to ten at a time; period of gestation endures about six weeks; the female will receive the embraces of the male immediately after delivery. In the domestic state the latter is apt to destroy the young.

Inhabit the whole extent of the United States.

Species.

2. *Lepus glacialis*, Sabine, Suppl. to captain Parry's voyage, 1819—20.

Char. Essent. Colour white; ears black at the tips, longer than the head; nails robust, broad and depressed.

DIMENSIONS. Larger than the *L. variabilis*, (which is two feet four inches two lines from the end of the snout to the anus,) the average weight being about eight pounds.

DESCRIPTION. The ears are longer in proportion to the head than those of the common hare, (*L. timidus*,) and much longer than those of the *L.*

variabilis; the ears of the common hare are usually considered one-tenth longer than the head,
those of the present species are from one-fifth to
one-seventh; the fore teeth are curves of a much
longer circle, and the orbits of the eye project
much more than those of either of the other species; the claws are broad, depressed and strong;
those of the *L. timidus* and *variabilis* being on the
contrary, compressed and weak; the hind leg is
shorter, in proportion to the size of the animal,
than in the *variabilis;* the fur is exceedingly thick
and woolly, of the purest white in the spring and
autumn, excepting a tuft of long black hair at the
tip of the ears, which is reddish-brown at base;
the whiskers are also black at the base for half
their length. In some of the full grown specimens
killed in the height of summer, the hair of the
back and sides was a grayish-brown towards the
points, but the mass of fur beneath still remained
white; the face and the front of the ears were a
deeper gray; the fur is interspersed with long
solitary hairs, which in many individuals were
banded with brown and white in the middle of
summer. The hares which Mr. Hearne describes
in his northern voyage, as inhabiting the continent
of America as high as the seventy-second degree
of latitude, are stated to weigh fourteen or fifteen
pounds when full grown and in good condition.
The largest hare killed at Melville Island did not
weigh nine pounds; were it not for this difference

in size, they might be supposed, from other parts of their description, to be the same species. (Sab.)

Inhabit the Arctic Circle, Greenland, the southern coast of Barrow's straits, and the north Georgian islands, where they are very abundant. They feed in ravines, near the bottom of steep clifts by the sea-side, which they ascend with great agility on being alarmed, and secure themselves amongst the loose stones near the top of the clifts. None were seen during the winter, but it does not seem probable that they had deserted the island.

Note.—Perhaps may be referred to this species also, the Greenland hare, or Rekalek, which remains entirely white, even in summer, with black at the end of the ears; the young being whitish-gray; the female bringing forth eight young at a time. The food of this animal consists principally of the tender herbs, which grow along the brooks on the slopes of the Greenland Mountains.

Species.

3. *Lepus virginianus*, (Nobis) *Varying hare*, Warden's Descrip. of the United States, vol. v. p. 632, in a note.

Char. Essent. Grayish-brown in summer, white in winter; the orbits of the eyes surrounded by a reddish-fawn colour at all times; ears and head of nearly equal length; tail very short.

DIMENSIONS. Total length from the tip of the nose, along the back to the root of the tail, sixteen inches; length of the ears four inches.

Warden states that the largest hares are eighteen inches total length, and weigh from seven to eight pounds.

DESCRIPTION. (Winter dress, at the commencement of spring.) General colour a snow-white, at the end of the snout intermixed with fawn; ears within naked, bordered with brown hairs intermixed with white; externally their anterior surface is reddish-brown; posterior surface white, slightly marked with dark plumbeous at tip; fur fine, soft, and long, most abundant on the breast, plumbeous at base, then reddish, then pure white; tail very short; legs longer and more slender, ears longer in proportion to those of the common American rabbit, (*L. americanus,*) nails long, slightly arched, subulate, and compressed at base, entirely covered by the hair which projects from the top of the foot; incisors above and below of nearly equal length; the inferior straight and cuneiform; the superior slightly arched, and marked by a longitudinal groove near the inner margin; whiskers, some entirely white, some black, others white with black at their base.

HABIT. These animals never burrow, but frequent meadows, &c. near the base of mountains, and when pursued retreat into hollow trees; they

bring forth several times a year, three or four at
a time, after a gestation of about thirty days.

The above description is taken principally
from a prepared specimen in the possession of
Mr. C. Bonaparte, and was killed on the Blue
Mountains, in the state of Pennsylvania.

Inhabit the southern and middle states, and
most probably as far north as New England.

Note.—It is most probably this species alluded
to by Mr. Lewis, in his *Notice of Animals discovered in the Missouri country.* " A species of
hare, apparently the *Lepus variabilis,* or varying
hare, which is common in Hudson's Bay, New
York, Pennsylania, Virginia, &c." (Vid. Barton's
Med. and Phys. Journal, vol. ii. part 2. page 159.)

ORDER, EDENTATA.

Character. No incisors in either jaw. Sometimes canine and molar teeth, at other times molars only, often none whatever. Four extremities terminated by a variable number of toes, armed with large nails, never constructed like hands. The orbitar and temporal fossæ united.

Nourishment phytivorous, insectivorous, or carnivorous, according to the species.

HABIT. Generally very slow in their movements; some destined to climb trees, some to burrow in the earth, others to swim, &c.

Inhabit South America, Africa, the Indian Archipelago, and New Holland. In North America, they are found only in a fossil state.

1st *Tribe, Tardigrada.*

Char. Face short.

Canines and molars, or molars only; claws very long and hooked.

Inhabit South America. Fossil locality, North and South America.

Genus.

Megatherium, Cuvier. (Foss.)

CHARACTERS.

Dental formula.—Teeth 10. $\begin{cases} \text{superior 6.} & \begin{cases} \text{Incisor 2.} \\ \text{Molar 4.} \end{cases} \\ \text{inferior 4.} & \begin{cases} \text{Incisor 0.} \\ \text{Molar 4.} \end{cases} \end{cases}$

Molars with broad crowns, marked with transverse angular eminences.

Zygomatic arches entire, furnished at their anterior base with a very large descending apophysis as in the sloths.

Lower jaw having its posterior or angular rising portion very broad; and its anterior or projecting portion grooved.

Nasal bones very short; upper maxillary bones very much elongated forwards; seven cervical vertebræ, sixteen dorsal, and three lumbar. Tail very short, if there existed any?

Clavicles perfect.

Posterior extremities much more developed than the anterior. Five toes to each foot, three only of which are furnished with very powerful hooked claws, the others rudimentary.

Species.

1. *Megatherium cuvieri.*

Megathère, Cuvier, Magas. Encycl. an 4. Descrip. d'un squelette conservè dans le Mus. de Madrid. Traduct. de Garriga. Cuv. Ann. du Mus. tom. v. page 376. pl. 24 et. 25. Ejusd. Recherch. sur les Ossemens Fossiles, 1 edit. tom. 4. *Animal du Paraguay.* *Megatherium*, S. L. Mitchill, Ann. of the Lyceum of Nat. Hist. New York, vol. i. p. 58. W. Cooper, ejusd. vol. i. p. 114.

Char. Essent. Crowns of the molar teeth marked with transverse angular eminences.

Dimensions. Total length of the body twelve foot; height at the withers five feet three inches.

Description. The characteristic traits are those peculiar to the genus.

Habit (presumed.) The immense thickness of the branches of the lower jaw, which even surpasses that of the elephant, would appear to indicate that this animal was not restricted to eating leaves, but like the elephant and rhinoceros, comminuted the branches of trees also. Its compact teeth, transversely grooved, are instruments very proper for this purpose.

Locality. The skeleton, nearly entire, of the Paraguay animal, has been found one hundred feet beneath the sandy diluvial, in the neighbourhood of the river Luxan, three leagues south-west of Buenos Ayres; two other skeletons less complete have been sent to Spain, one from Paraguay, the other from Lima. In North America the remains of this animal have been recently discovered in the marshes of Skidaway island. on the sea-coast of Georgia.

Genus.

Megalonix, Jefferson.

Char. Molars cylindrical, simple, hollow in the centre of their crowns, with the margins of the enamel projecting.

Species.

1. *Megalonix jeffersonii. Megatherium jeffersonii.* Desm. Mammalogie, p. 336.

Megalonix, Jefferson, Trans. of the Amer. Philos. Soc. No. 30. p. 246.　Cuvier, Recherche sur les Ossem. Foss. 1 edit. tom. 4.　Ejusd. Ann. du Mus. tom. v. p. 358. pl. 23.

Characters of the species are those peculiar to the genus.

DIMENSIONS.　One-third smaller than the preceding; about the size of an ox.

DESCRIPTION.　The remains of this animal present the unguicular phalanges very voluminous, and very much resembling those of the large toes of the *Megatherium* of Cuvier, and consequently like those of the Sloths and Ant-eaters; the radius and ulna are very similar to the corresponding bones of the same animal, differing only slightly in the form and dimensions of the various articular surfaces and apophyses; the fore feet have five toes, of which the thumb and little finger are rudimentary, and the others armed with robust claws; the teeth of this species more nearly resemble those of the Sloth than any other known animal.*

HABIT, (presumed.)　Possessing teeth similar to the Sloths; like them the *Megalonyx* was most probably herbivorous, their feet being so nearly alike, it is presumed that their motions were also similar to these animals.

---

* With the exception of the teeth of the *Chlamyphorus truncatus.*　Vid. Ann. of the Lyceum of Nat. Hist. New York, No viii. p. 235. pl. xxi. 1825.

Locality. The bones of the *Megalonyx* were found for the first time in 1796, at the depth of two or three feet, in Green-briar county, western part of the state of Virginia.

Order PACHYDERMATA.

Char. Sometimes three sorts of teeth, sometimes two only.

Four extremities solely destined for progression, the toes of which are furnished with nails or hoofs, varying in number.

No clavicles. Organs of digestion not constructed for rumination; stomach simple, membranous, or more or less divided by membranous septæ; animals of this class are generally herbivorous, some of them, nevertheless, can occasionally subsist on animal food.

Habit. Varying with the organization.

Inhabit all warm and temperate countries of the earth.

---

1. *Family* PROBOSCIDEA.

Char. Superior incisors in form of tusks; molars compound, few in number.

Five toes to each foot; nose prolonged into a great trunk, cylindrical, and moveable in every direction, and terminated by an organ of touch and prehension; form massive; skin very thick; nourishment purely vegetable.

Inhabit the warm countries of the old world. (Living species.)

Genus.

Elephas, Linn. Briss. Erxleb. Bodd. Cuv. Geoff. Illig.

CHARACTERS.

Dental formula.—Teeth 10.	superior 6.	Incisor 2.
		Canine 0.
		Molar 4.
	inferior 4.	Incisor 0.
		Canine 0.
		Molar 4.

Superior incisors in form of tusks, often very large, cylindrical, curved downwards, and elevated at their points, formed of a close osseous texture, and offering lines more hard and compact, convergent, and intersecting so as to form very regular, curvilinear lozengers; these tusks are besides surrounded by a very light layer of enamel, properly so called.

Molars composed of vertical and transverse laminæ; these laminæ are each formed of an osseous substance, enveloped in enamel, and all united together by a solid inorganic substance or cement; the molars proceed obliquely forwards from the bottom of the jaw; body very large, rather short, and situated high upon the legs; head very large; neck very short; proboscis very much elongated, moveable in all directions, enclosing the two nasal tubes, and terminated by a moveable appendage which performs the function of a finger; eyes very small, lateral; external ears flat and very large, lateral; tongue fleshy, smooth, and very thick; legs very long, thick, and terminated by five toes, which are only apparent through the hoof placed at the base of the foot, and of which one or two are wanting in the hind foot; tail moderate, terminated by a tuft of coarse hairs; two pectoral mammæ; skin very thick, rugous, rather loose, naked in the living, hairy in the fossil species.

Frontal and maxillary sinuses very large, and extending over the greatest portion of the cranium; openings of the anterior nares very high; proper bones of the nose small, triangular, and thick; inferior jaw pointed before, with its symphysis grooved; articular condyles of the large bones of the extremities, disposed in a vertical line; head of the femur in the axis of the bone; acetabulum situate rather beneath the pelvis; stomach simple; intestines voluminous; cæcum enormous.

Liver composed of two lobes; no gall bladder.

Habit. Powerful, robust, endowed with much intelligence, using their trunk with great address,

which is at the same time the seat of smell and
touch. They live in troops, at the head of which
is an old male or female; they feed on leaves,
roots, and fruits; all food and drink passes from
the trunk to the mouth, except during infancy;
the young sucking the mother, like other animals,
with the mouth; the female is capable of receiving
the male at the age of fifteen years; gestation lasts
twenty-two or twenty-three months.

The young, which is mostly single, sucks for
two years; loosing the milk tusk in about thirteen
months, those which succeed grow during the
remainder of life; they begin to cut their milk
molars at the end of six weeks, and these are
complete in three months: the second molars
have appeared at the end of two years; the third
force these out at the sixth year; the fourth push
forwards the third at the ninth year; the number
of laminæ in the tooth increases in the order in
which they appear: the number in each tooth varies from four to twenty-three.

It is probable that the life of these animals endures for two hundred years, they having been
kept in a domestic state for one hundred and
twenty or one hundred and thirty years. They
are fond of music.

Their voice, which is commonly a weak whistle,
becomes terrible when they are irritated.

When domesticated, these animals consume

about two hundred pounds of food daily; they sleep during the night in a recumbent posture.

Species. None living on the continent of America.

Fossil Elephants.

Species.

1. *Elephas primogenius*, Blumenbach. *Mammoth of the Russians*, Cuv. Mèm. de l'Inst. Part. Phys. tom. 2. Ejusd. Ossem. Foss. 2. edit. t. 1. p. 75. pl. 2. *Le squelette.*

Char. Essent. Head elongated; forehead concave; alveoles for the tusks, very large, marked by ribbands of enamel parallel to each other and very close; inferior jaw obtuse before.

DIMENSIONS. Very little larger than the Indian elephant; form rather more contracted.

DESCRIPTION. M. Cuvier, by a minute examination of all the bones which have been collected of this species, which are very numerous, is convinced that they present remarkable differences from those of the two living species; the fossil elephant resembles the Indian more than the African species, in the form of the cranium, but it differs particularly. 1st, In the form of its molar teeth, which are much larger, and possess parallel borders; as well as in the crowns which have a much greater number of parallel plates of enamel. 2d, In the more contracted form of the inferior jaw, the symphysis of which is rounded, in place of being pointed; finally by the extreme length of the alveoles for the tusks, which must have modified in a singular manner the form and structure of the trunk. The tusks are very long, more or less spirally arched and directed outwards.

In the Petersburg Museum, there is an individual preserved, with portions of its skin and flesh, discovered a few years past by Mr. Adam, enveloped in ice, in Siberia.

When first noticed, it was nearly in a perfect state of preservation, and was covered with two sorts of hair, viz. a reddish wool, thick and bushy, and a thick and black main on the neck and along the back.

LOCALITY. In Europe, these remains abound in northern countries, also in France, Italy and Germany. In America they are also scattered over a great range of country, but are more frequently met with in the States of Kentucky, North and South Carolina, Pennsylvania, &c. From observations lately published in the Phil. Jour. Acad. Nat. Sciences, (vid. vol. iii. p. 65.) there would appear to have existed two distinct species in the United States.

These remains are most generally discovered in the diluvial deposites which fill vallies, or on the borders of rivers; in our own country they are mixed with the remains of the Ox, Deer, and Mastodon; in Europe, also with the Rhinoceros.

Mr. Cuvier is of opinion that these animals must have lived and died in those countries and situations in which their bones are discovered at the present day, and that all the individuals then existing perished, simultaneously and suddenly, from some great catastrophe, concerning the nature of which we are unacquainted. The entire body with its flesh, discovered in Siberia, proves that the animal was seized by the ice immediately after its death, and the thick coat of wool and hair with which it was covered would well adapt it for a residence in cold climates. The isolated bones, which are met with every where, are often observed to have marine animals attached to them, which establishes, in an incontestible manner, that since their dispersion they have been covered by the ocean, under which they have been buried a considerable time.

Genus.

Mastodon, Cuvier, (fossil.)

CHARACTERS.

Dental formula.—Teeth 10.
- superior 6.
  - Incisor 2.
  - Canine 0.
  - Molar 4.
- inferior 4.
  - Incisor 0.
  - Canine 0.
  - Molar 4.

Incisors in form of tusks, a transverse section of which presents in the interior a homogeneous,

27

dense structure, composed of concentric laminæ, which vary from two to four-tenths of an inch in thickness, and do not display those curvilinear lozenges so conspicuous in the tusk of the Elephant.

Note. This difference of structure noticed in the tusks of the Mastodon and Elephant, first observed by Cuvier, is overlooked by Desmarest, who attributes to each a similarity of structure; the fact, as above stated, we have repeatedly verified by observation.

Molars rectangular, formed simply of an osseous substance, surrounded with enamel, without cement or cortical matter, having their crowns elevated into large points, disposed in pairs, varying in number, according to the age and position of the tooth, from six to ten; these molars advance in the jaws in proportion as they become developed; their crowns displaying, when half worn, as many lozenges of enamel as there were originally points to the tooth; very old animals have only one molar on either side of each jaw.

The *Os incisivum* is prolonged and pierced with large alveoles for the tusks.

Inferior jaw terminated before by a point, in which is a canal.

Neck very short; extremities very long, and terminated by five toes; tail moderately long; seventeen pairs of ribs, of which six are true.

Species.

1. *Mastodon giganteum*, Cuvier, Recherches sur les Ossemens Fossiles, nouv. edit. tom. 1. p. 206. pl. 1 and 7. Peale's account of the skeleton of the Mammoth, 4to. *Mammoth* of the Americans. *Father of Buffaloes* of the North American Indians. *Animal of Ohio* of the French.

Char. Essent. Molars rather broad in proportion to their length, their crowns displaying, when half worn, lozenges of enamel.

DIMENSIONS. Height at the withers from ten to eleven feet; length from the end of the snout to the posterior part of the pelvis, from fifteen to sixteen feet and a half.

This difference arises from the inaccurate manner in which the skeleton in the Philadelphia Museum is articulated; though this is the most perfect specimen hitherto discovered, the upper part of the head is destroyed, and the tusks are placed in an inverted position; the tusks are nine feet in length; each molar weighs twelve pounds.

DESCRIPTION. In the general structure of the skeleton, there is considerable analogy to the fossil Elephant; it is proportionably longer than the Elephant, and from which it differs in the structure of the tusks and molar teeth, as noticed above.

HABIT. Phytivorous, feeding most probably chiefly on leaves, limbs and tops of young trees, &c.

LOCALITY. The remains of this animal, hitherto

discovered only in North America, are in some instances better preserved than most other fossils, though this depends, in a great measure, on the nature of the soil from whence they are disinterred. They are most frequently met with beneath the surface of dried marshes, situated in the valleys of the largest rivers, as the Mississippi, Missouri, Hudson, Ohio, &c. They not unfrequently occur in the State of New York and New Jersey in diluvial deposites. The most perfect and largest specimen of a molar tooth we have yet seen, was fished up from the ocean at Long Branch, on the shore of New Jersey; now in the cabinet of Dr. Morton.

The remains of this extinct species have not been found south of lat. 31, or north of 43, near to lake Erie. The colour of the enamel is found to vary with the soil in which they occur.

Besides the present, five other species of this genus have been described by M. Cuvier, from South America and Europe.

Among a collection of fossils, such as the Elk, Buffaloe, &c. lately presented by Maj. Long, from Big-bone-lick, in the state of Kentucky, is the molar tooth of a species of *Mastodon* somewhat different from the many others we have examined, and which approaches in some respects, the *Mastodon tapiroides*, of Cuvier; though the specimen is not sufficiently perfect to enable us to decide with certainty.

Species.

2. *Mastodon angustidens, the narrow tooth Mastodon,* Cuvier, Ann. Mus. tom. 8. p. 405. Recherches, sur les Ossem. Foss. 2 edit. tom. 1. p. 250. pl. 1. fig. 1, 2, 3, 7. pl. 2. fig. 6, 7, 8, 9, 10, 13. pl. 3. fig. 1, 2, 3, 4, 5, 8. pl. 4. fig. 1, 2, 3, 6, 7. *Animal de Simore,* Réaum. Mem. de l'Acad. des Sc. Annèe. 1715, p. 174.

Char. Essent. Molars narrow and elongated, their crowns presenting from detrition, disks of enamel, in form of trefoils.

DIMENSIONS. One third less than the *Mastodon giganteum,* and less elevated on the legs.

DESCRIPTION. The cones of the crowns of the molars, marked by grooves more or less deep, sometimes terminating in several points, sometimes accompanied by other smaller cones on their sides or intervals, from whence it results that mastication produces upon this crown, at first, small circles of isolated enamel, and afterwards trefoils or figures of three lobes, but never lozenges; the first molar, small, with four tubercles, and appearing to project perpendicularly; the second with six tubercles, projecting from behind forwards. as likewise the third, which has ten tubercles; all these teeth do not appear to have existed at the same time in the mouth, the first becoming developed and used, then the second, then the third, which appears alone to occupy the alveolar border, and which is sometimes truncated to such a degree, as to represent only a cuneiform substance of ivory, surrounded by festooned enamel.

LOCALITY. The teeth of this animal have been found, first at Simore (Gers) in a sandy rock or in sand; they are coloured with iron, and become blue when burned. They are known by the name of *Western turquoises.* They are still met with at Sorde, near to Dax, (Landes) in diluvial stratæ. At Trèvoux, (Cote-d'or) in sand; at Santa Fe dé Bogota, at a place called the *" Field of Giants,"* at an elevation of one thousand three hundred toises above the level of the sea. On Mount Follonico, near to Mount Pulciano, in the Val d'Arno, in Piemont; and lastly, the specimen before us, was found in Club-foot canal, connecting Newbern to Beaufort, in the state of North Carolina.

This tooth is in the cabinet of Mr. Wagner, of Philadelphia.

An immense number of fossil bones were disinterred many years ago at Big-bone-lick, by Dr. *Goforth,* for an account of which, Vid. " Cramer's Navigator," eighth edition, 1814, append. p. 260.

Among these bones the author notices the " paw of an unknown animal of a size sufficient to fill a flour barrel; it had four claws, and when the bones were regularly placed together, measured from the os calcis to the end of either middle claw, five feet two inches.

" The bones of this paw were similar to those of a bear's foot. Where I found these bones, I found large quantities of bear's bones at the same time, and had an opportunity of comparing and arranging the bones together, and the similarity was striking in every particular except the size.

" The vertebræ of the back and neck when arrayed in order with the os sacrum and os coccygis, measured nearly fifty feet, allowing for cartilages; though I am not confident the bones all belonged to one animal. I had some thigh bones of the *incognita* of a monstrous size when compared with my other bones, which I much regret I neither weighed nor measured.

" These bones were all obtained at *Big-bone-lick*, in the state of Kentucky, three miles from the Ohio river. This *Lick* was formerly a salt-marsh; we generally dug through several layers of small bones in a stiff blue clay, such as deer, elk, buffaloe, and bear's bones, in great numbers, many of them much broken; below which was a stratum of gravel and salt water, in which we found the larger bones, some nearly eleven feet deep in the ground, though others were found on the surface. These bones were never regularly connected together, but lay scattered in various directions."

It will be readily perceived that in the above account of the bones of the *incognita*, the Doctor has confounded the vertebræ and claws of several individuals; his descriptions of the same are too loose and inaccurate to enable us to form any positive conclusions on the subject, but from other circumstances connected with their history, we have reason to believe that they belonged to the *Megatherium* or *Megalonix*; be this as it may, the subject is replete with interest, and highly deserving of further investigation; any information concerning them, must be sought for from some European naturalist, as all these bones were taken to England, by Mr. Thomas Ash, (author of " *Travels in America*," published in London in 1819,) he having basely stolen the same from Dr. Goforth.*

* The villany and theft of this Thomas Ash, cannot be too publicly and generally known, and we subjoin an extract from the work above quoted, detailing the particulars of this transaction.

" Dr. Goforth, had for several years been engaged in collecting the Mammoth and other enormous bones, at the Big-bone-lick, at a great expense and labour. In the year 1804 or 1805, he conveyed about five tons of these bones to Pittsburg, with a view of transporting them to Philadelphia. The bones, however, remained in Pittsburg for some time. Mr. Ash had passed through Pittsburg, and descended to Cincinnati. There learning that Dr. Goforth had a very valuable collection of big bones, he soon ingratiated himself into the Doctor's good graces, and entered into written articles to become his agent for the sale of the bones; New Orleans being fixed upon as the market. Accordingly, Mr. Ash returned to Pittsburgh in 1806 or 1807, with an order for the bones, which were in the possession of Dr. Richardson, who delivered them to Mr. Ash, (or

2nd *Family.* PACHYDERMATA, properly so called.

Char. Three sorts of teeth, in the greatest number, at least two in the remainder; feet terminated by four toes at most, and two at least, excepting in the Pecari, in which one lateral toe is not developed.

Genus.

Sus, Linn. Briss. Erxleb. Cuv. Geoff. Illig.

CHARACTERS.

Dental formula.—teeth 42 or 44.
- superior 20 or 22.
  - Incisor 4 or 6.
  - Canine 2.
  - Molar 14.
- inferior 22.
  - Incisor 6.
  - Canine 2.
  - Molar 14.

Inferior incisors directed obliquely forwards, with cutting edges; superior incisors conical.

Canines strong, projecting from the mouth, and curving upwards, sometimes very long, destitute of proper roots, and growing during life.

Molars simple, the anterior small and narrow, the last four furnished with blunt tubercles, dis-

---

Arvil, the name he then went by.) The bones were boated by Mr. Ash to New Orleans, where he made a feint to sell them, and was offered seven thousand dollars for them. He observed that the sum was not one tenth their value, and from New Orleans he shipped them to London," (Vid. append. p. 259.)

28

posed in pairs; nose elongated, cartilaginous, truncated at the extremity, and furnished with a small bone.

Eyes small; pupil round.

Ears considerably developed and pointed.

All the feet having four toes, two large intermediate only resting on the soil, and two more small, elevated and placed a little backwards, each furnished with small triangular hoofs.

Tail moderately long.

Twelve mammæ.

Body covered with a thick skin, clothed with stiff and long hairs called bristles.

Stomach membranous and simple.

HABIT.   Omnivorous, feeding principally on roots and fruits, voracious to excess, delighting to wallow in soft, muddy, or marshy places.

Inhabit the ancient continent.

Species.

1. *Sus scrofa*, (Encycl. pl. 37 and 38.) *Sus ferus*, Plin. *Sus aper*, Briss. *Sus scrofa*, Var. *Aper*, Linn. *Le Sanglier*, Buff. Vulgarly " *the Hog.*"

Char. Essent. Tusks robust, triangular, directed laterally, moderately elongated; no protuberance beneath the eyes.

Inhabit the temperate climates of Europe and Asia.

Not indigenous to North America, but many of the domestic varieties exist, some of which have been allowed to run wild, and propagate in the western forests; these have in part regained their native instinct and ferocity, their ears becoming erect in some instances; when attacked by Bears, Panthers, or other enemies, they unite together for common safety, forming themselves into a solid triangle, the strongest males presenting their front to the enemy, the young being in the middle. They feed on acorns, nuts, fruits, roots, &c.

Genus.

Pecari or *Dicotyles*, Cuv. *Sus*, Linn. Erxleb. Bodd. Schreb. Geoff. Illig.

CHARACTERS.

Dental formula.—Teeth 38.
superior 18.
{ Incisor 4.
{ Canine 2.
{ Molar 12.
inferior 20.
{ Incisor 6.
{ Canine 2.
{ Molar 12.

Superior incisors vertical, inferior projecting forwards.

Canines small, triangular, very sharp, nearly similar in their position to those of the Boar, but not projecting out of the mouth.

Molars with tubercular crowns; tubercles rounded, and irregularly disposed.

Head long and pointed; snout straight, terminated by a cartilage.

Ears moderately long, pointed; eyes small, pupil round.

Fore feet with four toes, the two intermediate

the largest, the two lateral are much shorter, and do not rest on the ground; hind feet with three toes, two long like the anterior, and one shorter internally; the external altogether wanting.

A gland situated upon the lumbar region, excreting through a valvular opening an extremely fetid, oily humour.

Tail replaced by a tubercle; body covered with strong, stiff bristles.

The metatarsal and metacarpal bones of the two large toes of all the feet united together to form a canon bone like that of ruminants.

Stomach divided into many pouches by membranous septæ.

Habit.   Analogous to that of the wild Boar.

Species.

1. *Dicotyles torquatus*, Fred. Cuv. Dict. des Sciences Nat. t. 9. p. 518.

Pecari, Buff. Hist. Nat. t. 10. pl. 3.

Pecari ou *tajassou*, Daub. Descrip. Anat.

Taytetou, d'Azara, Essai sur l'Hist. Nat. des Quadr. du Parag. t. 1. p. 31. *Patira de la Guyane*, according to Laborde.

Sus tajassu, Linn. Erxleb. Bodd.

Pecari, F. Cuv. Mamm. Lithogr.   (Encycl. pl. 39. fig. 2.)

Char. Essent.   Hairs annulated by dirty-white and black; a large whitish band, descending obliquely from each shoulder to the sides of the neck.

DIMENSIONS. Total length two feet seven inches; height before, one foot six inches six lines; height behind, one foot seven inches; length of the head, two inches four lines.

DESCRIPTION. General aspect of the common hog—ears straight; body rather contracted, covered with very stiff bristles, alternately annulated throughout their length with dirty-white and black, from whence results the general complexion of deep gray; a whitish band, two inches broad, departing from the top of the shoulder on each side runs towards the lower part of the neck; cheeks of a less deep gray than the rest of the body; hairs of the head short, and very sparse about the eyes and toes; skin, the colour of livid flesh, the humour secreted by the dorsal gland diffusing a smell somewhat similar to that of garlic.

The young animal of a clear brownish-fawn colour, with a blackish dorsal line.

HABIT. In a savage state, the Pecari live in small families, affecting generally elevated situations; when attacked by the Panther, they fight courageously, and never desert each other, so that the Panther is occasionally found dead on the field, surrounded by half a dozen of his slain enemies. In a domestic state they attach themselves to man, and are fond of his caresses.

Inhabit South America, in those countries bordering on the Atlantic, and extend into the United States; are common on Red River, where they were noticed by Mr. Nuttall, who also states that a skull of this animal was found in the Saltpetre cave of Kentucky. Vid. "Travels in Arkansa Territory," p. 155.*

Genus.

Tapirus, Briss. Schreb. Cuv. Geoff.
Tapir, Gmel. Illig.
Hippopotamus, Linn.
Hydrochærus, Erxleb. Storr.

CHARACTERS.

Dental formula.—Teeth 44. {
superior 22. { Incisor 6. Canine 2. Molar 14.
inferior 22. { Incisor 6. Canine 2. Molar 14.
}

---

* Mr. Nuttall probably alludes to the notice by Dr. Samuel Brown, Professor of Practice in the Transylvania University, of a skull found in the Saltpetre caves of Kentucky. (Vid. Barton's Med. and Phys. Journal, vol. ii. part 2. p. 158.) This skull certainly belonged to the recent *Pecari*, and is at present in the cabinet of the American Philosophical Society.

"The very respectable and ingenious Dr. Samuel Brown, informs the editor, that there has recently been discovered in one of the nitrous caves which are so common in Kentucky, the cranium of a *large species of Sus*, or Hog, in a state of excellent preservation. With the exception of the *Mexican Hog* or Peccary, no species of the genus has been discovered native within the limits of North America. The Peccary itself is said to be a pretty common animal in the Trans-Mississippi part of the United States."

Incisors in both jaws opposing after the manner of forceps; the intermediate short, cuneiform, truncated, the lateral nearly in form of canine.

Canines of moderate size, conical, crossing like those of carnivorous animals, an intermediate space between them and the molars.

Molars square, having the crowns marked with two transverse eminences.

Nose prolonged into a moveable trunk, rather short, and not prehensile like that of the elephant.

Eyes small; ears long and moveable.

Anterior extremities provided with four toes, with short and rounded hoofs; the posterior with three toes only; tail very short.

Two inguinal mammæ, those of the male placed on the sheath; skin hard, covered with hair.

HABIT. Similar to that of the hog.

Inhabit South America, Mexico, the peninsula of Malacca, the isle of Sumatra.

The bones of a fossil *Tapir*, of the size of the largest elephants, have been discovered in several localities on the continent of Europe, and are accurately described by M. G. Cuvier, (Recherches sur les Ossem. Foss. 1 edit. tom. 2. chap. 8.)

Hitherto fossil bones of this animal have not been discovered on the continent of America, but among other fossils lately received from the state of Kentucky, (and for which we owe many obligations to *Major Long*, a gentleman whose name has been so frequently connected with the most important discoveries in natural science,) is a molar tooth, which, on being compared with the teeth of the *Tapirs*, both living and fossil, (as well as with those of the *Manatus* and *Kangaroo*, with which alone the *Tapir* could be confounded in this particular,) is recognized as belonging to a very small extinct species of this genus.

Tapirus mastodontoides, (Nobis.)

Character. Less than one third the size of the *Tapirus giganteus*, or nearly the size of the living *Tapir;* crowns of the molars, when worn by detrition, presenting disks resembling those on the teeth of the *Mastodon giganteus.*

DIMENSIONS. (Of the molar tooth.) Length of the crown one inch four tenths; breadth one inch; length of the body projecting above the alveole seven tenths; length of the roots one inch two tenths.

DESCRIPTION. Molar tooth of the upper jaw, left side; crown nearly quadrangular, traversed by two eminences, running obliquely from without, inwards and backwards, united at their external border by a crest of enamel, as in the teeth of the recent *Tapir*; these eminences are about one half worn, and present disks of an irregular form unlike the other fossil, or the recent *Tapirs*, but resembling the disks of a half worn tooth of the *Mastodon giganteus.* On the posterior part of the body of the tooth, near the surface of the crown, projects a sort of spur of enamel, lying in the direction of the transverse oblique eminences. Two strong roots, one anterior, the other posterior, rather flattened in their antero-posterior direction, and slightly divergent at their distal portion, very analogous to those of the small fossil *Tapir* of Cuv. (Anim. Foss. vol. ii. pl. 4.) The whole tooth is completely petrified to its centre, very brittle and tinged with iron.

REMARKS. In size and form, this tooth bears considerable analogy to the teeth of the small fossil *Tapir* of Cuvier, but differs, 1st, in the greater obliquity of the transverse eminences;) (this is less important, as the teeth described by Mr. Cuvier belonged to the lower jaw.) 2nd, In the form of the disks occasioned by detrition it differs from both the fossil and recent *Tapirs*. The transverse eminences or crests of enamel, are straight in the living species, very oblique in this fossil, the disk forming a simple triangle in the former.

Order PECORA.

Ruminating Animals.

Character. Inferior incisors only,* and most frequently eight in number.

Canines sometimes wanting; crõwns of the molars formed of two double crossings of enamel, disposed in pairs, and in inverse directions in the two jaws, the convexity being turned outward in the lower jaw, and inward in the upper; four extremities solely destined for progression; two equal toes furnished with hoofs; a single metacarpal or metatarsal bone for the two toes of each foot.

No clavicles; organs of digestion disposed for rumination; four stomachs, 1. the ventriculus, or paunch; 2. reticulum, bonnet, or honey-comb bag; 3. omasum, or many-plies, which is the smallest; 4. obomasum, ventriculus intestinalis, Caillette, or Red, which has a pyriform appearance, and is next in size to the paunch. Intestines very much developed; mammæ, to the number of two or four, always inguinal. Often with horns, which vary in structure; nourishment, vegetable substances.

Habit. Peaceable; living in forests, where they

* The Camels form the only exception; these having two lateral teeth implanted in the os incisivum of each side; but they have the form and use of canines.

often unite in troops more or less numerous; first swallowing a large quantity of food without chewing, which rests for a time in the first stomach, from whence it is forced into the mouth during repose, to undergo the process of chewing, (their jaws acting laterally,) and then to pass into the second stomach.

Inhabit nearly the whole globe. None have as yet been discovered in New Holland.

Second division; ruminants having either hollow horns, or osseous and deciduous, at least in the male sex.

1. *Tribe.*

Osseous horns, ordinarily branched, deciduous. reproduced every year larger than the year preceding, always existing on the head of males, and occasionally on the head of females.

Genus.

Cervus, Briss. Linn. Erxleb. Bodd. Cuv. Illig.

CHARACTERS.

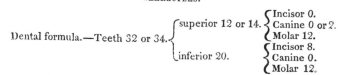

Dental formula.—Teeth 32 or 34.
- superior 12 or 14.
  - Incisor 0.
  - Canine 0 or 2.
  - Molar 12.
- inferior 20.
  - Incisor 8.
  - Canine 0.
  - Molar 12.

Superior canine in the males of several species, commonly compressed, and curved backwards like those of the Musk Deer.

Head long, terminated generally by a muzzle; eyes large, pupil elongated transversely; often cribriform depressions in the bone beneath the inner canthus of the eye.

Eyes large, simple and pointed.

Tongue smooth.

Horns more or less developed, according to the species and age of the individual; at first cartilaginous and clothed with a tender skin, hairy and sensible, afterwards naked and rugous, being placed on two tuberosities of the frontal bone, and composed of a principal trunk, of branches variously directed, of enlarged and flattened parts, or knobs, which surround the bases of the stocks, and which are formed of irregular grains.

Body slender; legs fine and nervous; hairs generally dry and friable, presenting colours which are nearly similarly disposed in all the species; young individuals having often a series of white spots on a fawn base.

Four inguinal mammæ; testicles enclosed in a scrotum, and visible externally; no gall bladder.

Habit. Peaceable, and entirely herbivorous, rather intelligent, living either in troops, or isolated and in pairs, inhabiting large forests or plains; bringing forth one or two young at a birth in spring, in temperate countries, and in all other seasons in warm climates; because, in the first instance, the rut takes place in the fall: in the second instance, these animals are always ready to copulate at all seasons.

Inhabit both continents, and all latitudes.

Species.

1. *Cervus alces*, Linn. Erxleb. *Alces, achlis*, Plin. Aldr. *Alces*, Gesn. Johnst. *Elant*, Perrault, Hist. des Anim. 1. tab. 25. *Original*, Charlevoix. Nouv. Fr. 3. p. 126. *Moose Deer*, Dudley, Phil. Trans. No. 368. p. 155. Dale, Phil. Trans. No. 444. Warden, Descr. des Etats Unis, vol. v. p. 636. *Elan*, Buff. Hist. Nat. tom. 7. pl. 80. *Elk*, Shaw, Gen. Zool. vol. ii. part 2. pl. 174 et 175. *Cervus alce*, Bodd. (Encycl. pl. 57. fig. 2.)

Moose Deer.

Char. Essent. Horns consisting of a simple and very large flattened expansion, (empaumure) furnished with numerous prongs on its external border, with a large, isolated branch on the trunk or principal stock; no muzzle, (or naked part at the extremity of the nose;) snout swollen and cartilaginous; no canines in the males; tail excessively short.

Dimensions. Total length, from the tip of the nose to the base of the tail, six feet ten inches; height before, five feet two inches six lines; height behind, five feet four inches ten lines; length of the head, one foot eleven inches; of the ears, ten inches; of the horns, three feet one inch; breadth between the two horns at their summit, three feet ten inches; length of the neck, one foot six inches, of the tail, one inch six lines; of the fore leg from the elbow to the wrist, one foot five inches; of the metacarpal bone, ten inches; from the wrist to the ground, one foot seven inches; length of the hind leg, from the knee to the os calcis, one foot seven inches; of the metatarsal bone, one foot; from the os calcis to the earth, one foot ten inches; (horns of the male weighing sometimes sixty pounds.)

DESCRIPTION. Head long, narrow before the eyes, enlarged towards the snout, which has much analogy to that of the horse; facial line straight the greater part of its length, and curved above the mouth; upper lip exceedingly developed, and very thick; no muzzle; nostrils, a lateral slit, more open anteriorly than behind; lacrymal pits small; eyes very small, and approaching the base of the horns; the latter are at a very little distance from the ears, which are very long; horns of the male during the first year, resemble those of a stag two years old, then divided during the third and fourth year, and at the fifth year a vast triangular expansion, furnished with from fifteen to twenty-eight points or prongs on its outer border, supported by a peduncle, short and thick, which is itself provided with a large distinct prong directed forwards; female without horns; neck short; a tuft of long hair, like a beard, beneath the throat in both sexes, and a protuberance in the same place in the male; a very marked projection on the withers; back very straight from this point to the tail, which is excessively short; legs very long and thin; metatarsal bone very long in proportion to the metacarpal; feet very long, and placed obliquely upon the soil; hairs coarse and prismatic, very friable, those upon the nucha and withers longer than on other parts, and forming a true mane; general colour fawn-brown on the top of the head, the back and the rump; of a deeper brown beneath the lower jaw and neck, on the shoulders, and arms as far as the wrist, upon the flanks, the thighs, and the top of the hind legs; of much more obscure brown before the anterior legs, above the wrist, and on the anterior portion of the hind feet; ears grayish-brown externally, of a whitish-gray within; the under part of the tail whitish; the young animal of a reddish-brown colour, without spots.

HABIT. The moose live in small troops, in swampy places. Their gait, which is commonly a trot, is much less active than that of other deer. They feed on the buds of trees and on herbs. When they attempt to eat from the ground, they are obliged, from the shortness of their neck, either to kneel, or to separate their fore-legs. The rutting season commences with them about the end of August, and continues during the month of September. The females bring forth from the middle of May to the middle of June: the first time they produce only one young, afterwards two, rarely three. The old moose loose their horns in January and February, and the young in April and May. The first have their new horns by the end of June, and the others in the month of August. Duration of life, fifteen or twenty years.

COUNTRY. The Moose Deer, called Elk, Elg, Œlg, Los, Loos, &c. by the northern inhabitants of the ancient continent, ranges in Europe from the fifty-third to the sixty-third degree of latitude, through part of Prussia, Poland, Sweden, Finland, Russia, and particularly in Livonia, and in Jugrie. In Asia it descends lower, from the forty-fifth to the fifty-first degree of latitude, particularly in Tartary.

In America, where it is named *Monsoll* by the Algonquins, *Moose* or *Moose deer*, by the English, and *Original*, by the French, it is met with in the more northern parts of the United States, and beyond the Great Lakes.

Species.

2. *Cervus tarandus*, Linn. Erxleb. Bodd. *Tarandus*, Plin. Aldr. Ταρανδος, Ælian. *Rangifer*, Gesn. Aldr. *Cervus mirabilis, Cervus palmatus*, Johns. *Reinthier*, Gesn. *Caribou*, Charlev. nouv. tom. 3. p. 192. *Cervus groenlandicus*, Briss. Regn. Anim. p. 88. No. 4. *Karibou*, Ejusd. p. 91. No. 8. *Renne*, Buff. Hist. Nat. tom. 12. pl. 10, 11, and 12. suppl. tom. 3. pl. 18. Bis. *Jeune Renne*, Fred.

Cuv. Mamm. Lithogr. (Encycl. pl. 58. fig. 3 and 4.) *Rein-deer.*

Char. Essent. Horns in both sexes greatly developed, the principal trunks of which are very long, thin and compressed; antlers palmated and indented; no muzzle; no canines; tail short.

DIMENSIONS. Total length five feet six inches; of the tail three inches; length of the head one foot two inches; of the ears three inches six lines; of the horns two feet ten inches; breadth between the horns at their summits two feet two inches; length of the neck ten inches; (size of a common deer, but having the legs thicker in proportion: also the hoofs shorter and thicker.)

DESCRIPTION. Head strong, moderately long; snout rather thin, like other deer, the *Moose* excepted; nostrils oblique, oval, not pierced in a muzzle; lachrymal cavities; ears large; no superior canines in the male; horns in both sexes varying a little in form, but generally composed in the adult males of two very long principal stalks, compressed, cast backwards, having, 1st, near the knob (at the base,) an antler directed forwards, which is terminated by an expansion, rather broad, and bordered by recurved digitations beneath; 2nd, a second antler originating near their middle, directed upwards and forwards, and terminated also by a digitated expansion; 3d, a few other simple antlers above these: and 4th. a terminal expansion, rather small, and furnished with a small number of spiculæ.

Neck very short; legs thick; hoofs rounded and very broad; the small upper hoofs strongly developed; hair of two kinds, the woolly very abundant in winter, the silky like that of the deer, very friable, longer beneath the neck than elsewhere; colour varying according to the seasons, and age of the animal; the young having the superior parts of the body brown, and the inferior red; adult of a deep brown in spring, and passing successively to grayish-brown, to grayish-white, and almost entirely white during the hottest days of summer; lower portions of the legs of a deeper colour than the upper, with a narrow white ring above the hoofs.

HABIT. The Rein-deer is the only animal of this genus which has been enslaved by man; the species, still savage in North America, has been in a great measure tamed in the northern countries of the old continent; the fawns have protuberances on the head at birth, and sprouts two inches long at the end of fifteen days. The male adults and sterile females loose their horns in winter, and the new ones are not entirely finished until the month of August; pregnant females retain theirs until the month of May; castrated individuals often retain their horns one year longer than the others, but they change them at the end of this time. In the month of October, during the rutting season, the males diffuse a very disagreeable odour; they copulate only by night; gestation lasts thirty-three weeks, at the end of which time they bring forth two young in the month of May; the duration of their life is about sixteen years; they feed on herbs in summer, and moss (lichen rangiferinus) in winter, during which season they scratch the snow with their feet in order to obtain this substance; a dipterous insect of the genus *Œstrus* deposits its eggs in the skin of the Rein-deer.

COUNTRY and USAGES. The Laplanders collect large troops of Rein-deer, and travel with them, according to the seasons, in order to procure these animals their favourite nourishment; they castrate the greater part of the males, and harness them to sledges; the females furnish them with milk, the flesh and blood furnish them with food, their skins with clothing, their tendons with sewing threads, &c. In America, these animals abound in the most northern regions, as Spitzbergen, Greenland, Canada, &c. and do not pass the State of Maine towards the United States; nevertheless, they descend to lower latitudes in America than in Europe; they do not occur in Europe lower than the sixtieth degree, though, according to ancient authors, they formerly inhabited the Pyrenees; all the north-east coast of Siberia is inhabited by them; they are found savage in the Uralian mountains along the river Kema.

Species.

3. *Cervus canadensis*, Briss. *Cervus elaphus*, Var. *Canadensis*, Linn. Gmel. *Cerf du Canada*, Perrault, Mem. sur les Anim. tom. 2. pl. 45. *Cerf du Canada, Stag, Red Deer*, Warden, Descrip. des Etats Unis, vol. v. p. 537. *Cervus strongyloceros*, Schreb. Tab. *Stag of America*, Catesby, Carol, app. p. 28. *Cervus major*, Ord. *Wapiti*, Barton, Mitchell, Leach, Warden, vol. v. p. 638. *Elan american*, Berwick, Hist. des Quad. *Le wapiti*, F. Cuvier, Mamm. Lithog. 21st livraison. *Elk* of the Americans, Lewis and Clark's Exped. up the Missouri, vol. ii. p. 167. (Encycl. pl. 38. fig. 2.)

Desmarest, in his Mammalogie, p. 443. has made distinct species of the *Cervus major*, or *Wapiti*, and the *Cervus canadensis*, Briss. though he has admitted the latter with doubt, on the authority of Warden and others, who have named animals without accurately describing them.

Some authors have also confounded the *Cervus canadensis*, with the *Red deer*, (*C. elaphus*, of Europe,) but the European species is smaller and entirely distinct.

By American naturalists, it is well known that the *C. major*, and *C. canadensis*, are one and the same species.

Char. Essent. Branches of the horns cylindrical, very large, with flattened expansions; having the first antler inclined in the direction of the facial line; a very large muzzle; lachrymal depressions; tail very short; superior canines in the male; colour fawn, more or less brown, with a large, and very pale-yellowish spot on the buttocks, comprising the tail.

DIMENSIONS. Height at the withers four feet; height of the horns three feet; length of the first antler one foot; of the second, ten inches; length of the tail two inches.

DESCRIPTION. Head resembling that of the common deer; top of the forehead, occiput, and lower jaw, of a brown colour; a black spot descends from the corner of the mouth on each side of the inferior jaw; parts encircling the eye, brown; neck of a deeper complexion than the sides of the body, of a red mixed with black, with thick and black hairs in form of a dew-lap; body above and flanks of a clear bloody-red; extremities of a deeper brown anteriorly than posteriorly; a very pale-yellowish spot on the buttocks, bordered with a black line on the thighs; tail of the same colour; horns of adults branched, principal stock round; having always three antlers, without counting the subdivisions, more or less numerous, of the crown; first or largest antler somewhat inclined in the direction of the facial line; hair of middle length on the shoulders, flanks, thighs, and top of the head; shorter on the sides and legs, very long on the posterior sides of the head, and on the neck, principally beneath; a brush of yellow hairs, surrounding a corneous substance, of a narrow and elongated form, at the posterior and exterior of the hind leg; interior of the ears white, furnished with tufted hairs, externally of the colour of the surrounding parts; a naked triangular space towards the internal angle of the eye, near the lachrymal depression, which is very large.

Female differing from the male in the absence of horns, and in the less depth of colours.

HABIT. The Elks live in families, the males attaching themselves to the females; the members of each troop are strongly united among themselves; the rutting season commences in September; cast their horns for the most part in the month of March, the leanest Elk retain their horns the longest; the female brings forth in the month of July; when captured young, these animals are easily tamed.

Inhabit Canada, Missouri, and western States. A fine specimen in the Philadelphia Museum, thirteen years old, during nearly the whole of which period it lived in the possession of Mr. Peale; it measures from the tip of the nose to the base of the tail, seven feet seven inches; length of the horns three feet ten inches.

Species.

4. *Cervus virginianus, Virginian Deer,* Pennant. *Fallow-deer,* Lawson, Carol. p. 123. Catesby,

Carol. append. p. 28. *Caricou femelle*, Buff. t. 12. pl. 44.

Cerf de la Louisiane, ou *Cerf du Virginié*, G. Cuvier, Ossem. Foss. tom. iv. p. 34. Ejusd. Reg. Anim. Fred. Cuvier, Mamm. Lithogr. avec quatre figures.

(Encycl. pl. suppl. 13. fig. 2. *Cerf de la Louisiane.*)

Char. Essent. Horns moderate, strongly recurved forwards, having an antler high, placed at the internal face of each stalk, directed inwards, and two or three others at the posterior face directed backwards; lachrymal pits; no canines; a muzzle; colour, a cinnamon-fawn in summer, and a fine gray in winter.

DIMENSIONS. Total length five feet five inches; height before, three feet; behind, three feet three inches; length from beneath the neck to the origin of the tail, two feet nine inches; of the tail, ten inches; the head, one foot; of the horns, following the curvatures, one foot ten inches; weight from ninety to a hundred and twenty pounds.

DESCRIPTION. Form light; head slender; snout pointed; lachrymal pits consisting of a slight fold of the skin; a muzzle partially developed; tail rather long and thin; horns of the fifth year consisting of two cylindrical stalks, whitish, rather smooth, separated at first rather outwards and backwards, and then recurved forcibly forwards

and inwards; an antler, sometimes bifurcated at its
point, originating at the internal face of the stalk,
at some distance above the knob, is directed inwards; others, to the number of two or three,
growing from the last third of the posterior face,
and directed more or less backwards, above and
within; horns of the second year consisting of
simple sprouts, slightly arched backwards and
outwards, so that their points oppose each other;
second horns very little larger, with an additional
antler; third horns, or those of the fourth year,
still larger, and having an additional antler; coat
composed of soft and compact hairs; the colour of
the young animal is of a deep fawn, with little
white spots; that of adults in summer is of a beautiful fawn above; beneath the inferior jaw, within
the ears, the throat, the belly, the interior of the
legs, the posterior borders of the arms, and anterior of the thighs, white; top of the snout bordering on gray; the end of the snout of a deep brown,
with two small white spots on the upper lip; parts
encircling the eyes brown, with a whitish circle
beyond; tail thick and long, white beneath, yellowish above, for the two first thirds, and black
for the remainder; buttocks white only immediately above the tail; no brown or black line on
the back, nor deep oblique line on the buttocks;
a fasciculus of long and hard hairs on the interior
of the tibio-tarsal articulation; in winter the colour
is of a rather deep grayish-brown, resulting from

the hairs disposed in yellowish or blackish rings; above and beneath the eyes, within the ears, beneath the lower jaw, throat, belly, interior of the limbs, beneath the tail, and the corresponding portion of the buttocks, white.

HABIT. They take their winter coat in October; their summer dress in March or April; their horns appear in September, and fall in February; they enter in rut in November or December; gestation lasts nine months; they bring forth in July or August.

Inhabit North America, enjoying the most extensive range.

According to Mr. Say, (Long's Exped. to the Rocky Mountains, vol. i. p. 104.) " the highest northern range of this species, is Canada, in North America; it is also found as far south as the river Oronoco, in South America.

" This species is leanest in February and March, and in best condition in October and November. The rutting season commences in November, and continues about one month, terminating generally about the middle of December. During this season the neck of the male becomes very much dilated.

" The fawn towards autumn looses his spots, and the hair becomes grayish, and lengthens in the winter. In this state the deer is said by the hunters to be *in the gray*.

" This coat is shed in the latter part of May and

31

beginning of June, and is then substituted by the reddish coat; in this state the animal is said to be *in the red*. Towards the last of August, the old bucks begin to change to the dark bluish colour: the doe commences this change a week or two later; in this state they are said to be *in the blue ;* this coat gradually lengthens until it comes to the *gray*. The skin is said to be toughest in the *red*, thickest in the *blue*, and thinnest in the *gray ;* the blue skin is most valuable. The horns are cast in January; they lose the velvet the last of September, and beginning of October. About the middle of March, Mr. Peale shot a large doe, in the matrix of which were three perfectly form-ed young, of the size of a rabbit."

This species displays great enmity towards the *rattlesnake,* which enemy they attack and destroy with singular dexterity and courage; when the deer discover one of these reptiles, they leap into the air to a great distance above it, and descend with their fore feet brought together, forming a solid square, and light on the snake with their whole weight, when they immediately bound away; they return and repeat the same ma-nœuvres until their enemy is completely destroy-ed.

"From May until July, the female of the com-mon deer conceals her young whilst she goes to feed; it is at this time that the hunters take ad-vantage of the maternal feelings of the animal to secure their prey. They conceal themselves and imitate the cry of the fawn; the solicitude of the parent animal for her young, overcomes her usual caution, and believing she hears the cry of her offspring in distress, hurries towards the spot where the hunter lies concealed, and falls an easy prey.

" A variety of this species, three specimens of which occurred at Engineer Cantonment, had all the feet white near the hoofs; this white extremity is divided upon the sides of the foot by the general colour of the leg, which extends down near the hoof, leaving a white triangle in front, of which the point is elevated rather higher than the spurious hoofs. The black mark on the lower lip, rather behind the middle of the sides, is strongly characterized.

" Total length, without the hair at the tip of the tail, five feet four and three-fourths of an inch; length of the ear, six inches and a half; trunk of the tail, nine inches and a half; weight, in February, one hundred and fifteen pounds." (Say.)

Species.

5. *Cervus macrotis*, (*Great Eared Deer*,) Say, Maj. Long's Exped. to the Rocky Mountains, vol. ii. p. 88. *Black Tailed Deer?* Lewis and Clark. vol. i. p. 77. *Mule Deer*, Ejusdem.

Char. Essent. Light reddish-brown above; sides of the nose. and upper portion of the fore part of the nose, dull cinereus; back intermixed with blackish-tipped hairs, which form a distinct line on the neck, near the head tail; reddish-cinereus, black at the tip.

DIMENSIONS. Length from the base of the antlers to the origin of the basal process, two inches; from the basal process to the principal bifurcation, from four and a half to five inches; terminal prongs of the anterior branch, four to four and a half inches; of the posterior branch, two and a half to three inches; from the anterior base of the antlers to the tip of the superior jaw, nine and a quarter inches; of the ears, seven and a half inches; of the trunk of the tail, four inches; of the hair at the tip of the tail, from three to four inches.

DESCRIPTION. Antlers slightly grooved, tuberculated at base, a small branch near the base, corresponding to the situation and direction of that of the *C. virginianus*, the curvature of the anterior line of the antlers is similar in direction, but less in degree, to that of the same deer; near the middle of the entire length of the antlers, they bifurcate equally, and each of these processes again divides near the extremity, the anterior of these smaller processes being somewhat longer than the posterior one. The *ears* are very long, extending to the principal bifurcation, about half the length of the whole antler; the lateral teeth are larger in proportion to the intermediate teeth than those of the *virginianus*; eye-lashes black, the lachrymal aperture larger than in the latter species, the hair also coarser, and undulated and compressed like that of the Elk.

The colour is light reddish-brown above; sides of the head and hair on the fore portion of the nose above, dull cinereus; the back is intermixed with blackish tipped hairs, which form a distinct line on the neck, near the head; the tail is of a pale reddish cinereus colour, and the hair at tip is black; the tip of the trunk of the tail is somewhat compressed, and is almost destitute of hair beneath; the hoofs are shorter and wider than those of the *virginianus*, and more like those of the Elk.

Inhabit the most remote north-western territories of the United States.

Fossil Deer.

1. *Cervus americanus*, (Nob.)
Fossil Elk, of the United States.

In the Transactions of the American Philosophical Society, (vol. i. New Series, p. 375. pl. 10. fig. 4,) there is for the first time, a description of the skull of a fossil animal, by the late Dr. Caspar Wistar, presented by Mr. T. Jefferson to the Society. There can be little doubt, that this skull is the remains of an extinct species of the genus *Cervus*; and is found to possess many characters in common with the Elk, (*Cer-*

vus canadensis Briss.) though it has also many characters which distinguish it from all other species living or fossil, which have hitherto been introduced into the systems. The fossil consists of a skull, but the greater portion of the face, together with both jaws and teeth are destroyed; the posterior portion, together with one side, is in a tolerable state of preservation.

DIMENSIONS. The breadth of the cranium at its narrowest part, which is behind the horns, is 4.65 inches; the greatest breadth, which is immediately above the condyloid processes, is seven inches; greatest depth, from the top of the occipital surface to the posterior margin of the occipital foramen, is 5.25 inches; depth from between the horns, through the sphenoid bone, is 4.7 inches; length of the skull, from the superior margin of the occipital surface to the space between the horns, 6.37 inches; the posterior or occipital surface of the fossil, bears a much closer resemblance to that of the *Cervus canadensis*, than to that of the *Cervus alces*, or to any other species. We shall, therefore, compare it with the Elk.

The whole skull is longer than that of the Elk; the occipital surface proportionably broader; the posterior and inferior base of the horns is concave in the fossil, and the surface for the attachment of muscles beneath the horns on the sides of the occiput, is much more extensive in the latter; the

horns (about four inches only of one remains in the
fossil) proceed in a perfectly straight and lateral
direction, and the portion of the forehead between
the horns is almost straight in the fossil; in the
two last characters it is peculiar; there is also a
much greater distance from the skull to the basal
knob of the horns in the fossil.

A complete set of horns, or jaws containing
teeth, belonging to this animal, have not yet been
discovered; but in a collection of bones disinterred at Big-bone-lick, which we have received a few
weeks since, (and for which we are indebted to
the politeness of Major S. H. Long,) there are frag-
ments of jaws, together with a number of molar
teeth, which I have every reason to believe belonged to the fossil Elk under consideration. On
comparing these teeth with those of the recent
Elk, very little difference is observable, except
that they are longer and more compressed at their
crowns.

Locality. The bones of the American fossil
Elk have hitherto been discovered only in the
morass near the falls of Ohio, called Big-bone-lick,
in company with the bones of the Mastodon, &c. ;
we have lately examined some designs in possession of Dr. Bigsby, which appear to represent the
femur, the humerus, and portions of the horns of
a fossil Elk from Canada.

Third Tribe. Prominences of the os frontis
furnished with a horny sheath, composed of agglu-

tinated fibres, which grow by laminæ, and remain
during life.

Genus.

Antilope, Pallas, Schreb. Gmel. Scopoli, Erxleb.
Bodd. Cuv. Geoff. Illig.
 Tragus, Klein.
 Capra moschus, Linn.
 Gazella, Briss.
 Tragulus, Briss. Klein.
 Antilocapra, Ord.
 Mazama, Rafinesque.

CHARACTERS.

Dental formula.—Teeth 32.
$$\begin{cases} \text{superior 12.} & \begin{cases} \text{Incisor} & 0. \\ \text{Canine} & 0. \\ \text{Molar} & 12. \end{cases} \\ \text{inferior 20.} & \begin{cases} \text{Incisor} & 8. \\ \text{Canine} & 0. \\ \text{Molar} & 12. \end{cases} \end{cases}$$

Incisors generally equal, and contiguous at their
borders; sometimes the two intermediate are very
broad, a little separate from each other, leaning
against the lateral ones by their posterior face.

Horns in both sexes, or in the male only, covering an osseous process of the frontal bone, which
is generally solid and without sinuses, round, variously contorted, often marked with transverse
rings, or with a projecting spiral crest, sometimes
bifurcated.

Facial line more or less straight, often lachrymal depressions or naked sub-orbitar grooves, secreting a peculiar fluid.

A muzzle, or demimuzzle for the most part; none in some species; ears large, pointed and moveable; eyes often very open; tongue smooth; body generally slender, like that of the Deer; legs slender; tail short or moderate; sometimes inguinal pores or deep cuticular folds in the groin.

Brushes or tufts of hairs on the wrists of some species.

Two or four mammæ.

Covering generally sparse, and ornamented with lively colours, agreeably disposed; no beard on the chin.

They possess a gall-bladder.

Habit. Peaceable, and altogether herbivorous; generally uniting in troops; living for the most part beneath the torrid zone; some in temperate climates, and others in northern latitudes, on the summits of mountains covered with snow; rapid in their motions like Deer; bringing forth one or two young at a birth.

Inhabit Africa, India, Tartary, the Alps of Europe, and Rocky Mountains of America.

Eleventh Subgenus, (of authors.)

Antilocapra, Ord, Blainville.

Horns of both sexes moderate, compressed, recurved posteriorly towards the point, in form of a hook, and furnished with an anterior antler; no muzzle; no lachrymal depressions; no tufts on the wrists: general form that of the other Antelopes.

32

Species.

1. *Antilope americana.*

Antilocapra americana. Ord, Journ. de Phys. 1818. *Cervus bifurcatus*, Rafinesque. *Antilope bifurcata*, Smith. *Antilope furcifer*, ejusd. Trans. Linn. Soc. vol. xiii. pl. 2. *Cerf á bois recourbè, Cervus hamatus*, Blainv. Nouv. Bull. Soc. Philom. 1816, p. 80. Schreb. Goldfuss. tab. 264. Desm. Nouv. Dict. d'Hist. Nat. t. 29. p. 542. *Antilope furcifer*, Desm. Mamm. *Prong-horned Antelope.*

Note.—It is somewhat remarkable that so many synonymes should have occurred for an animal so lately discovered as the subject of the present description. The *Prong-horned Antelope*, is now generally admitted to be a true Antelope, and not the type of a distinct subgenus; we know not on what authority Mr. Smith has changed the specific name, (*Americana*,) under which Mr. Ord first described this species.

Char. Essent. Horns rugous, triangular at base, and provided with a very small antler, compressed and turned outwards, terminated superiorly in a recurved point, hooked backwards and rather outwards; colour reddish-fawn above, white beneath; hair rather short, stiff and coarse; a reddish mane upon the neck.

Dimensions. Length of the body, measured from the anterior part of the shoulders to the rump, two feet nine inches; height before, two feet nine inches; length of the tail, four inches; of the horns of the male, one foot; of the antlers, two inches.

DESCRIPTION. Horns slightly marked by transverse wrinkles and rugosities, rather inclined outwards, and turned backwards at their extremity, which is smooth; about two thirds of their height provided with a short antler, directed forwards; eyes large, and placed very high, under the base of the horns; ears pointed, one half the length of the facial line; base of the horns tufted; legs slender; tail short; hairs thick, stiff, coarse, flattened, undulating, and enclosing in their middle a sort of marrow; flanks black; exterior face of the fore legs, and tail above, of a reddish-fawn; breast, belly, interior of the limbs, buttocks, and beneath the tail white; top of the head white, as well as the cheeks and lips; face and nose of a deep chesnut; neck a reddish fawn above, with a white spot near the ear, and marked with white beneath; a reddish tuft of hairs on the back of the head and neck.

Inhabit south-western territories of the United States; (seen on the borders of the Missouri and great plains of Columbia by Lewis and Clark,) a specimen in the Philadelphia Museum.

NOTE.—It is, without doubt, this animal described and badly figured by Hermandez, " Rerum

medicarum Novæ Hispaniæ Thesaurus," &c. p.
324. cap. 15. under the name of *Mazame* seu
Ceruis.

Genus.

Capra, Linn. Pallas, Erxleb. Cuv. Geoff.
Goat.

CHARACTERS.

Dental formula.—Teeth 32.
superior 12. { Incisor 0.
Canine 0.
Molar 12.
inferior 20. { Incisor 8.
Canine 0.
Molar 12.

Incisors of nearly equal dimensions, regularly
arranged and touching at their borders.

Horns directed upwards and outwards, compressed and wrinkled transversely; facial line
straight or even, or somewhat concave; no muzzle; interval of the nostrils naked; no lachrymal
depressions or suborbitar grooves; ears pointed,
straight, and moveable; tongue smooth; body
rather slender; legs rather robust; tail short; no
inguinal pores; no tufts on the wrists; two mammæ.

Coat composed of two sorts of hair; the interior very fine and soft,* more or less abundant;
the exterior long, or very long and smooth; chin
most frequently furnished with a beard; some-

---

* It is this which in some of the Asiatic races, furnishes the
cashmere

times two cuticular appendages, or sorts of glands, hang from beneath the neck.

Testicles contained in a very voluminous scrotum.

HABIT. In the savage state the goats seek the most elevated and inaccessible places, and unite in troops more or less extensive, under the protection of an old male; these animals of all the ruminants display the most vivacity and intelligence; their vision is good; they hear at a distance, and their sense of smell is remarkably acute; they feed on herbs and shrubs; they bring forth two young at a birth.

Inhabit the Granitic chains of Europe and Asia, also the Rocky Mountains of North America.

Species.

1. *Capra montana.*

Ovis montana, Ord, Jour. Philad. Acad. Nat. Sciences, vol. i. part 1. p. 8. 1816. *Rupicapra americana,* Blain. *Antilope americana,* Ejus. Nouv. Bull. Soc. Phil. 1816. p. 80. *Mazama sericea,* Rafin. Amer. Mon. Mag. 1817. p. 44. *Antilope lanigera,* C. H. Smith, Trans. Linn. Soc. p. 38. 1822. Tab. 4. vol. xiii. *Rocky Mountain Goat.*

We have here an animal, described for the first time in 1816, which has already been classed under four distinct genera, with nearly as many specific appellations. This can only be accounted for from the remoteness of the regions inhabited

by these animals, and their consequent scarcity ;
one specimen only of the prepared skin having
reached any cabinet in the world, which is that
at present in the Museum of the Linnean Society
of London, from which the plate is taken accom-
panying Mr. Smith's description of this animal.
Concerning this figure, we must here remark, that
though the drawing from which it has been en-
graved, appears to have been very spirited, nevertheless, as we are assured by Mr. Ord, who repeatedly examined the specimen, the direction of the
tail is not natural, and further, the transverse
wrinkles on the bases of the horns are much too
deep. In the horns of this animal formerly attached to the skin in the Philadelphia Museum, (which
appear to have belonged to an animal in the second
year of its age,) there exists no transverse wrinkles,
only three or four slight undulations on the anterior base of the horns ; they are nearly four inches
in length, slightly recurved, perfectly black, and
obsoletely striated longitudinally, hollow to the
point ; the base of the cavity measures one inch in
diameter. This individual, though young, is by
no means destitute of long hairs, which almost
exclusively occupy the back, from the shoulders
to the tail.

The reasons which have induced us to range
this animal under the genus *Capra*, will be found
detailed below ; the specific name under which

Mr. Ord has described it, having the right of priority, must be retained.

Char. Essent. Horns short, conical, slightly curved backwards, black, and slightly annulated in the old animal; the colour of the animal entirely white, furnished with long silky hairs, and a fine wool beneath the hair; no mane.

DIMENSIONS. In bulk it exceeds the sheep.

DESCRIPTION. Body elongated, but little elevated on the legs; facial line straight; ears rather long and pointed, covered on the inside with long hairs; the neck short; the tail stumpy and directed upwards; the whole structure of the animal robust; the colour is entirely white; the bulk of the animal is considerably increased by a thick coat of long straight hair, of a yellowish tinge; side of the lower jaw, and beneath the throat, furnished with a long beard; beneath the long hair, the skin is covered with a close downy wool, of a clear white colour, and in young animals feeling like unspun cotton; on the face and legs the hair is short and close, similar to that of the sheep and goat; the eye-lashes are white; the horns are about five inches long, above an inch in diameter at base, bending slightly backwards, having two or three annuli, and terminating in a point not always obtuse; the legs exceed in thickness those of a calf; the fetlocks are short and perpendicular.

and the hoofs are of a jet black, high, broad, and with deep grooves in the soles.

REMARKS. Like the Goat, the facial line is nearly straight in the *C. montana*, this line being more or less arched in the Sheep and Antelope. Like the Goat, the *C. montana* is furnished with a long beard; the Sheep and the Antelopes being destitute of this appendage.

In the form and size of the hoofs; in the direction of the tail; in the form of the snout; in the strength and proportion of the limbs in particular, and of the body in general, our animal resembles the Goat, and is unlike the Sheep and Antelopes: the latter animals have, furthermore, never been known to possess a covering consisting of fine long hair, and wool of exceedingly delicate texture, whilst, in this respect, our animal bears a striking analogy to the *Cashmere Goat*. Though the horns are at best uncertain characters, varying as they do in form, in similar species, yet, even in this respect, our animal offers stronger analogy to the Goat than to the nearest allied congenera.

The horns of the young male Goat are very similar to those of the *Capra montana*.

HABIT and COUNTRY. For the following information concerning this highly interesting animal, we are under many obligations to Major S. H. Long, being chiefly the copy of a letter addressed by him to the Philadelphia Agricultural Society.

"The information I am able to furnish, was obtained on the late expedition to the sources of St. Peter's river, &c. and was procured principally from Donald M'Kinzie, Esq. (of the family of Sir Alexander M'Kinzie,) stationed at the junction of the Assiniboin and Red rivers, in the capacity of chief factor for the Hon. H. B. Company on that station; the intelligence furnished by this gentleman was from personal observation.

"The Rocky Mountain sheep inhabit the elevated region comprised in that portion of the mountain range from which its name is derived, situate between the forty-eighth and sixtieth parallels of north latitude.* They are found in great numbers near the head waters of the north fork of Columbia river, where their flesh constitutes the principal food of the natives. The country at the sources of Muddy river, (Marais river of Lewis and Clark,) Saskatchawin and Athabaska rivers are also inhabited by them; but they are said to be less numerous on the eastern slope of the Rocky Mountains than upon the western; they are seldom or never seen at a distance from the mountains, the climate and productions of which appear best adapted to their nature and mode of life. In summer they resort to the peaks and ridges in quest of pasture, but retire to the valleys in win-

* Lewis and Clarke observed this animal as low as forty-five degrees of north latitude.* Vid. Exped. up the Missouri, vol. ii. pp. 35, 42.

ter.   The size of the animal is nearly the same of
the common sheep; their fleece is white, interspersed with long hair, protruding beyond the
wool, and standing erect on the surface of the
body, which gives them a shaggy appearance;
their horns are short, merely projecting beyond
the wool of the head, and slightly arcuated backwards; these, together with their hoofs, are black,
while the other parts of their bodies are uniformly white; their flesh has a musky flavour, and is,
at best, unsavoury.

" They are of easy access to the hunter, who
seldom pursues them unless compelled by hunger.
Their fleece is esteemed of little value by the
traders, and are used only as a covering to the
feet during winter; their skin is of a remarkably
thick and spongy texture. It has been asserted
by good judges, that the silky fineness of the wool
is not surpassed by that of the Cashmere Goat."
(S. H. Long.)

Genus.

Ovis, Linn. Briss. Erxleb. Gmel. Bodd. Cuvier.
Geoff.

Capra, Illig.

Algionomus, Pallas, Ranzam.

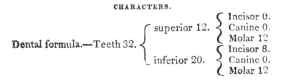

CHARACTERS.

Dental formula.—Teeth 32. { superior 12. { Incisor 0. / Canine 0. / Molar 12 / inferior 20. { Incisor 8. / Canine 0. / Molar 12

Incisors forming an entire arch, regularly approximate at their borders.

Snout without a muzzle; facial line arched.

Horns large, angular, wrinkled transversely, twisted laterally in a spiral form, and enveloping an osseous arch, cellular in structure.

No lachrymal depressions; no beard to the chin; ears moderate, pointed; legs rather slender, without tufts at the wrists; two mammæ; no inguinal pores; tail more or less short, inflected or depending.

HABIT. Analogous to that of the goats.

Inhabit both continents.

Species.

1. *Ovis ammon.*

Mouflon argali, Erxleb. Gmel. Shaw, Gen. Zool. vol. ii. part 2. plate 201. *Ovis argali,* Bodd. *Stepnie baranni,* G. S. Gmel. Voy. in Siberia, tom. i. p. 368. Steller, Kamsh.? p. 127. *Ovis fera sibiricæ, vulgo Argali dicta,* Pallas, Spicilegiæ Zool. fasc. xi. p. tab. 1. *Ovis montana,* Geoff. Ann. du Mus. tom. 2. pl. 60. *Mouflon d'Amerique, Ovis montana,* Desm. Mamm. (Encycl. pl. puppl. 14. fig. 4.) *Big-horn,* Lewis and Clark. *Musimon,* Pliny. *Ophion,* of the Greeks. *Argali* of the Siberians. *Kamennoi barron,* or *sheep of the rocks,* of the Russians. *Taye,* of the Monqui-Indians. *Sheep of California,* Hernandez. *Goadinachtsch,* of the Kamschatkans. *Rikun-donotoh*, of the Kuritians, from its inhabiting the loftier parts of the mountains. *Ibex*, or *Wild Goat*, of Clavigero. *Cul blanc*, of the Canadians. The *Argali*, or *Mountain Sheep*.

The following description is taken from specimens, male and female, in the Philadelphia Museum; on comparing which, with the descriptions and figures of the *Argali* of the old continent, not the slightest specific difference is observable.

Char. Essent. Horns of the male very large, and strong, triangular; flattened before, striated transversely; those of the female compressed and falciform; hair during summer, sparse, grayish-fawn; during winter, thick, hard, reddish-gray, with white about the nose, the throat and beneath the belly; a large yellowish-white space about the tail at all times.

DIMENSIONS. Total length, from the tip of the snout along the back to the base of the tail in the direction of the curvatures of the body, four feet five inches; length of the tail five inches; side of the head from the tip of the nose to the posterior base of the ear, twelve inches; facial line, from the tip of the nose to the occiput, sixteen inches; length of the fore leg, from the brachio-cubital joint to the fetlock joint, nineteen inches; of the fetlock joint three inches; of the hoof, anteriorly, two inches five-tenths; height of the same, laterally, one inch five-tenths; length of the base three inches; length of the posterior leg, from the tibio-femoral joint to the fetlock, twenty-two inches five-tenths; of the fetlock joint two inches; of the hoof two inches three-tenths; length of the horns, following the outer curvature, two feet ten inches; circumference of the base fifteen inches five-tenths; length of the ear three inches five-tenths.

DESCRIPTION. Horns of the male, very large, the bases very near the eyes; curved first backwards, then forwards, with the points curved rather upwards and outwards; deeply wrinkled from their base to one half their length, the rest being more smooth, triangular at base, the largest face anteriorly; horns of the female very slender in comparison with those of the male, nearly straight, almost without wrinkles, and resembling very much those of the domestic he-goat; ears rather broad and pointed, and very straight; neck having some pendulous folds; tail very short; colour of the animal during summer, a grayish-fawn, with a yellowish or reddish line along the back, and a large spot of the same colour surrounding the base of the tail, on the buttocks; internal surface of the extremities, and the belly, of a still more pale-reddish (rather dirty white;) winter colour more reddish above, approaching to white on the snout, on the belly and under the throat.

HABIT. Living in mountainous countries; they are exceedingly active, and are able to ascend precipices inaccessible to other animals; they leap from rock to rock, at great distances, and with incredible velocity; they go in troops of twenty or thirty individuals; they copulate in spring and autumn; the female brings forth one or two at a birth; during the rutting season the males engage in furious combats, and often break off each other's horns.

Inhabit the great Asiatic chain of mountains, particularly those which run north-east into Tartary. According to Gmelin, they inhabit southern Siberia. In North America, they inhabit the Rocky Mountains, about the fiftieth degree of north latitude, and the hundred and fifteenth degree of west longitude, extending south into California.

It is the opinion of eminent naturalists, that the *Argali* of both continents form but one species, having passed originally from one country to the other on the ice. They are supposed also to constitute the original stock of our domestic sheep. A figure of this animal was published by Venegas in 1758, under the name of *Tayè* or *Tage. Noticia de la California*, vol. i. p. 86. printed at Madrid.

In the New York Medical Repository, (vol. vi. p. 238, 1803,) is a description, accompanied with an indifferent figure, of the *Argali* of North America, under the name of " Mountain Ram," by Mr. M'Gillivray, who states, that when travelling

through the plains situated between the Saskatchawin and Missouri rivers, along the Rocky
Mountains, in the fall of 1800, he observed and
killed several of these animals. The dimensions
of the largest male were as follows—length, from
the nose to the root of the tail, five feet; length
of the tail four inches; circumference of the body
four feet; height of the body three feet eight
inches; length of the horn three feet and a half;
girth at the head one foot three inches.

Mr. M'Gillivray says that the Cree Indians, or
Kristianeaux, distinguish this animal by the name
of *My-attic*, or ugly Rein-deer. The slave nations,
comprehending the Blood Indians, Piecans, and
Black-feet Indians, call it *Ema-ki-ca-now*, which
also signifies a kind of deer.

According to professor Pallas, this animal formerly inhabited the regions about the upper Irtish,
and some other parts of Siberia, where it is no
longer seen since colonies have been settled in
these countries. It is common in the Mongalian,
Songarian, and Tartarian Mountains, where it en-
joys its favourite solitude. The *Argali* is found
likewise on the banks of the Lena (in 1794) up as
high as the sixtieth degree of north latitude, and
it propagates its species even in Kamschatka.
From the mountains of Persia there is the stuffed
skin of one in the Museum of the Imperial Academy of Sciences, sent by Gmelin. Dr. Pallas further states, that in the year 1768 he observed

garments made of the hair and wool of this animal, from the islands lying between the continent of America and Kamschatka, which is a further confirmation of the identity of the species inhabiting both continents. Vid. Account of the different kinds of Sheep, &c. by Dr. Pallas, 1794.

Genus.

Ovibos, Blainville.
Bos, Pennant, Gmel. Shaw, Bodd. Illig. Cuvier.

CHARACTERS.

Dental formula.—Teeth 32.
- superior 12.
  - Incisor 0.
  - Canine 0.
  - Molar 12.
- inferior 20.
  - Incisor 8.
  - Canine 0.
  - Molar 12.

Body thick, contracted; legs strong; head short; forehead very elevated; facial line long and abrupt; horns very strong, directed laterally, neither angular or knotty; no muzzle, (in which it particularly differs from the genus *Bos;*) ears short, receding; eyes small; no canal in the upper lip; no lachrymal depressions; tail very short; hairs in tufts and long; no inguinal pores.

Species.

1. *Ovibos moschatus*, (Encycl. pl. suppl. 14. fig. 3.) *Musk Ox*, Penn. Quad. vol. i. p. 31. Ejusd. Arct. Zool. vol. i. p. 8. pl. 7. *Bos moschatus*, Gmel. Bodd. Shaw, Gen. Zool. vol. ii. part 2. p. 407. pl. 212. *Bœuf musquè*, Buff. Hist. Nat. suppl. tom. vi. pl. 5. la tete. *Ovibos*, Blain. Nouv. Bull. de la

Soc. Phil. Juin, 1816. Cuvier, Recherches sur les Ossem. Foss. 1 edit. tom. iv. p. 59. pl. 3. fig. 9. et 10.

Char. Essent. Horns projecting from the summit of the head, very near to each other, very broad at their base, curving first downwards, then elevated laterally at the point; no muzzle; coat composed of long woolly hair, of a deep brown colour.

DIMENSIONS. Size of a heifer two years old.

DESCRIPTION. (Male.) General aspect more resembling a large sheep than an ox; body and head elongated; front very elevated, and furnished with a sort of mane of long hairs diverging from a common centre and covering the roots of the horns; the latter are black, smooth, wide, touching at their base, then curving forwards and rather downwards, applied to the sides of the head, then elevated suddenly upwards and backwards; ears short, receding, entirely covered with soft thick hair; eyes very small and widely separate from each other, and very far from the end of the nose, comprised in the first arch formed by the horns; nose or facial line very much elongated, blunt as in the ram; nostrils lateral and small, placed nearer together than those of the ox, but less near than those of the ram; no muzzle; mouth very small; lips rather thick, the superior offering no medial groove; legs strong and short; hoofs larger on the fore than on the hind feet, of a deep brown colour, and converging towards each other on each foot; tail very short, and concealed by the rump; neck, trunk and origin of the legs, clothed with two kinds of hair, a very thick and long wool, and fine bristles, which traverse it; extremities, from one half of the fore-arm, and the commencement of the hind legs, furnished with short and compact hairs near the skin; beneath the neck and lower jaw furnished with very long hair, of the same nature with those of the back; hairs of the face, shorter the nearer they approach the end of the nose, which is entirely covered with them; general colour, a reddish-brown, with nearly black-brown in some places; around the nostrils, upper lip and extremity of the lower lip, white.

Note.—(Fossil skulls of a species of Bos somewhat similar to the above, have been found in Siberia, figured by Cuvier, Recherches, sur les Ossèm. Foss. vol. iv. pl. 3. fig. 9 and 10.)

Habit. The *Musk buffaloes*, or oxen, go in droves of twenty or thirty; frequent sterile mountains, and seldom visit woody countries. They are fleet, and climb rocks with facility; their flesh is musky.

Inhabit North America; abound between the sixty-sixth and seventy-third degrees of north latitude, on the western side of Hudson's bay.

It is supposed that the fossil skulls found in Siberia, have been carried there on the ice; should they really prove to have belonged to the musk oxen, which is not clearly ascertained, as Cuvier has remarked.

Genus.

Bos, Linn. Briss. Erxleb. Bodd. Cuv. Geoff. Illig.

Taurus, Storr.

The *Ox*.

CHARACTERS.

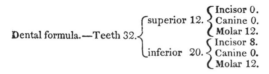

Inferior incisors regularly arranged, broad; body of large size, supported by stout legs; head powerful, facial line straight; ears large, moveable; eyes large; tongue long and smooth; a large muzzle at the end of the snout; no lacrhymal depressions; horns simple, conical, smooth, a transverse section circular, of various curvatures, but often directed laterally, with the point elevated.

A dew-lap, or longitudinal cuticular fold beneath the neck, more or less pendant; tail moderate, or rather long, terminated by a brush of long hairs; four mammæ; no inguinal pores; no tufts of hairs on the wrist

HABIT. Essentially herbivorous; the wild oxen go in troops more or less numerous, according to the species, and frequent woods or plains, where they can find nourishment; the males are more or less brave, and capable of defending themselves against the attacks of wild animals, with their horns.

Inhabit warm and temperate climates; eastern Europe; the mountains of Thibet; India; the southern extremity of Africa; the western territories of the United States, are those places where they exist in a savage state. The domestic cattle, of which the primitive stock appears to be lost, have been introduced into all civilized countries.

Fossil remains prove that four species of this genus formerly inhabited the old continent, and two species the new continent, of which one of the former appears proper to Siberia.

Species.

1. *Bos americanus*, Gmel.

Taurus mexicanus, Hernandez, Mex. p. 587 *Tauri vaccæque quiuiræ regionis*, Fernand: Anim. p. 10. The *Buffalo*, Catesby, Carol. p. 28. tab. 20. *Bœuf sauvage*, Du Pratz, Louisian. t. 2. p. 66. *Bison*, Buffon, suppl. t. 3. pl. 5. *American Bull*, Penn. Quad. tab. 2. fig. 2. *Buffalo*, Shaw, Gen. Zool. pl. 206. *Bos bison*, Erxleb. Linn. *Bos urus*, var. Bodd. *Bison*, Warden, vol. v. p. 643. Long's Expedition to the Rocky Mountains.

Char. Essent. Horns rather small, round, placed on the side of the head, very distant from each other, directed first laterally, then upwards.

Withers very projecting; head, shoulders, and superior parts of the anterior extremities, covered with long woolly hair, very abundant; a beard; tail very short.

DIMENSIONS. Total length seven feet ten inches; of the tail one foot seven inches; of the head one foot seven inches; height at the withers four feet eleven inches; at the rump three feet eleven inches; (some of the largest weigh from 1600 to 2000 pounds.)

DESCRIPTION. Form contracted; head short and thick; horns small, growing horizontally from the sides of the head, and then elevated upwards; eyes rather small; shoulders very much elevated; posterior portions of the body and hind legs very light proportionably; a very thick woolly hair covering the summit of the head, the cheeks, facial line, the neck and the shoulders; long straight hair forming a thick beard, hanging beneath the chin, and broad ruffles towards the upper part of the fore legs; flanks, rump, thighs, and hind legs clothed with very short and compact hair; tail covered with sparse hairs, and terminated with a tuft.

General colour, black on the head, chesnut on the shoulders, and a deep brown on the back, the sides, the belly, and fore parts; hair longer during the winter season, particularly on the posterior parts of the body. The spinous processes of the anterior dorsal vertebræ measure from one foot and a half to two feet in length; the diameter of the bodies of the vertebræ being two inches.

HABIT. The American Bison or Buffalo inhabit the great prairies west of the Mississippi; they often unite in immense troops, supposed in some instances to amount to 10,000. During the rutting season, about the middle of June, the males engage in mortal combats, disputing for the females; generally speaking, they are rather timid, but when wounded, or during the rutting season, they become very fierce.

Inhabit the temperate parts of North America; they were observed in the two Carolinas soon after the arrival of the first colonists. They have long since been exterminated from Pennsylvania, and are not known to exist at present east of the Mississippi river; they were observed in a savage state in Kentucky so late as the year 1766, but have gradually retired before the white settlers, and appear to have concentrated in the plains of Missouri.

For a particular account of the geographical distribution of this animal, Vid. Major Long's Expedition to the sources of the St. Peter's River, &c.

Fossil Ox.

Species.

1. *Bos bombifrons*, (Nobis.)

This species has not heretofore been introduced into the systems, nor even noticed by systematic writers. It was first described from a fossil skull, presented to the American Philosophical Society, by Mr. T. Jefferson. The description was drawn up by the late Caspar Wistar, M. D. and published in the transactions of the society. (Vol. 1st, New Series, p. 379. pl. xi. fig. 10 and 11.)

Character. Top of the head, between the horns strongly arched and projecting; facial line forming rather an acute angle, with the occipital surface; horns first project laterally from the sides of the head, then curve downwards, they are placed on the skull at a considerable distance anterior to the union of the facial and occipital surfaces.

DESCRIPTION. Part of the nose and face of this skull are destroyed, as well as the jaws and teeth; in size and general form it approaches nearest to the skull of the *Bos americanus*, but differs in the following particulars. The space on the top of the head between the horns, is nearly straight in the *Bison*, whereas it is prominently arched in the fossil; in the *Bison*, the horns project from the sides of the head near the union formed by the occipital and facial surfaces, first in a lateral direction, then curve *upwards*, tapering, rather slender and pointed. In the fossil, the horns project from the sides of the head, at a considerable distance anterior to the union of the facial and occipital surfaces, first laterally, then curve *downwards*; which disposition of the horns distinguish this fossil skull from all other skulls of this genus, fossil or recent; the horns are thicker, less tapering, and less pointed than those of the *Bison*. The concavity which exists to a greater or less extent in all animals of this genus, beneath, and posterior to the base of the skull, is much more extensive in the fossil than in the bison skull. The occipital surface is less broad in the fossil skull. From which it is shown, that in former times a species of *Bison* inhabited this country, differing essentially from the *Bison* of the present day.

In the collection of fossils presented by Major Long, from Big-bone-lick, are the fossil teeth of a species of *Bos*, which most probably belonged to the fossil animal now under consideration. On comparing these teeth with those of the recent bison, very little difference is observable, excepting that they are thicker at the crowns, and more deeply grooved on the sides, and altogether more robust.

LOCALITY. From Big-bone-lick, near the falls of Ohio. (State of Kentucky.)

Species.

2. *Bos latifrons*, (nobis.)

Broad headed Fossil Ox.

The specimen, a portion of the skull with a part of one horn attached, is in the Museum of the American Philosophical Society, and is the same figured in Cuvier's Anim. Fossiles, 1st ed. vol. iv. pl. 3. fig. 2. Ann. du Mus. d'Hist. Nat. (Ejusdem.)

DESCRIPTION. This skull differs very little from that of the *Auroch*, (*Bos urus*, Bodd. Pallas, Cuv.) The forehead is arched, broader than high; the horns are attached two inches before the line, formed by the union of the facial and occipital surfaces, which latter form an obtuse angle; the plane of the occiput represents a semicircle; the horn is twenty-eight inches in circumference at its base.

LOCALITY. State of Kentucky. Similar fossil skulls have been found in Europe, on the borders of the Rhine, near to Cracovie in Bohemia, &c

35

Order CETA.

Characters. Body pisciform, terminated by a caudal appendage of a cartilaginous nature, and horizontal.

Two anterior members only, in form of fins; the bones of which are very flat and short.

Head joined to the body by a very short and thick neck, composed of seven cervical vertebræ, very thin, and in part anchylosed with each other.

Two pectoral or abdominal mammæ.

Ears, external meatus very small; skin more or less thick, without any hair; brain large; the hemispheres much developed.

Petrous portion of the temporal bone, which contains the internal organ of hearing, entirely separate from the head, or attached only by ligaments.

Pelvis, and bones of the posterior extremities, represented by two rudimentary bones, lost in the flesh.

Like all other mammalia, they respire with lungs, are warm-blooded, and possess a double circulation, &c.

Habit. The largest animals known; entirely aquatic; for the most part carnivorous; swimming by the aid of their tail, which moves upward and downward, and not from right to left as that of fishes; viviparous; suckling their young as other mammifera, &c.

Inhabit nearly all seas, at least the *whales* properly so called, but they appear to prefer the polar regions to temperate or warm latitudes. The *Herbivorous cetacia* on the contrary, are peculiar to the equatorial regions.

---

1. *Family*, CETACEA Herbivora, Sirenia.

Character. Crowns of the molar teeth flat; furnished with tusks sometimes in the upper jaw.

Two pectoral mammæ; whiskers in some instances large.

Nostrils placed at the end of the snout; nasal apertures in the skull situated superiorly.

Body very massive.

Genus.

Manatus, Rondelet, Linn. Scopoli. Storr, Lacep. Cuv. Geoff. Illig.

Trichechus, Linn. Erxleb. Schreb. Shaw, Gmel.
Manati, Bodd. *Lamantin*, Cuv.
Sea Cow.

CHARACTERS.

Dental formula.—teeth 34 or 38.
superior 18 or 20. Incisor 2. Canine 2. Molar 14 or 16.
inferior 16 or 18. Incisor 0. Canine 0. Molar 16 or 18.

The incisors very small, existing only in the fetus.

Adults have only thirty-two teeth, as four molars fall in early life.

Crowns of the molars present two transverse tubercles, with three points at their summits in the young tooth; the superior teeth square; the inferior oblong.

Head not distinct from the body; eyes very small, placed superiorly, between the end of the nose and meatus auditorius externus, which is scarcely apparent.

Tongue oval; posterior parts of the body very thick, depressed and rounded at the end, without a caudal fin, properly so called.

Vestiges of nails on the borders of the pectoral fins.

Whiskers composed of a fasciculus of enormous hairs, directed downwards, and forming on each side a sort of corneous tusk.

Skin naked, very thick and rugous. Penis of the male terminated in a gland, enlarged in form of a mushroom, as in the horse.

Sixteen pairs of ribs, thick, and solid, the two first only articulating with the sternum.

Stomach divided into many pouches. Cœcum bifurcated. Colon capacious.

Habit. These animals live in societies, and feed on vegetable substances; the male displays much attachment to the female, and she much tenderness towards her offspring, which she carries under one of her fins during the first few days of its existence; they sometimes thrust their bodies out of water in search of food along the shores of rivers.

It is supposed that the females of these animals have given rise to the fabulous reports concerning Mermaids; the form of their head, the position of their mammæ, which become very much enlarged during the period of suckling, together with their anterior extremities, might have considerable effect on the imagination of a mariner.

Species.

1. *Manatus latirostris*,* (nob.) Jour. Phil. Acad. Nat. Sciences, v. iii. part 2. p. 390. pl. 13. fig. 1, 2, 3.

This species is only known as yet by the comparison of the skull with those of the *M. americanus*, (Cuv.) and *M. senegalensis*, (Ejusdem;) the *latirostris* resembles the latter much more closely than the former, but possesses characters distinct from either; and I have accordingly named it provisionally.

HABIT and DISTRIBUTION. They are found in considerable numbers, about the mouths of rivers, near the capes of East Florida, lat. 25°. The Indians kill them with the harpoon during the summer months. One Indian has been able to capture ten or twelve during a season. They measure from eight to ten feet in length, and are about the size of an Ox.

It is probable that this is the species mentioned by Captain Henderson in his account of the British settlement of Honduras, (1809.*)

Fossil Manatus.

The ribs and vertebræ of a gigantic species of Fossil Manatus have been discovered on the western shore of Maryland; the vertical diameter of an atlas vertebra being nine inches; transverse diameter of the same, eleven inches. (Vid. Jour. Phil. Acad. Nat. Sciences, vol. iv. p. 32. Notice of the Plesiosaurus and other fossil reliquiæ, &c. by R. Harlan, M. D.)

Genus.

Rytina, Illig.
Trichecus, Gmel.
Manatus, Steller.
Stellerus, Cuv. Desm.

* " The male and female of this species of animal are usually found together, and whilst sporting on the surface of the different lagoons, are frequently destroyed by the harpoon or dart, in the use of which the slaves of the settlement, and the Indians of the neighbouring Mosquito nation, are wonderfully dexterous. The flesh of this animal is particularly admired, and thought to resemble very closely that of veal; the tail, which forms the most valuable part of the Manati, after laying some days in a pickle prepared for it with spices, &c. and eaten cold, is a discovery of which Apicius might have been proud, and which the discriminating palate of Elagabalus would have thought justly entitled to the most distinguished reward."—*Henderson's account of Honduras,* p. 106.

Dental formula.—Teeth 4.
{
  superior 2. { Incisor 0,
                Canine 0
                Molar 2.
  inferior 2. { Incisor 0.
                Canine 0.
                Molar 2.
}

No implanted teeth, only a molar plate on each side of the jaws, attached by numerous vessels and nerves; triturating surface unequal, and grooved by tortuous canals.

Body ventricose in the middle, and tapering gradually as far as the caudal fin.

Head obtuse, without a distinct neck.

No external ears.

Upper and lower lips double.

Eyes furnished with a cartilaginous membrane in form of a crest, which occasionally covers them. Nostrils placed towards the extremity of the snout.

Anterior extremities in form of palmated fins. like those of the sea turtle.

Caudal fin very broad, not very long, cruciform.

Skin destitute of hair, but clothed with a very solid, thick epidermis, and composed of compact tubes or fibres perpendicular to the skin.

Stomach simple.

Species.

1. *Stellerus borealis*, Cuv. Desm. *Manatus*, Steller. *Trichechus manatus*, Var. *borealis*, Gmel. *Trichechus borealis*, Shaw, Gen. Zool. *Whale-tailed Manati*, Penn. *Grand Lamantin du Kamschatka*, Sonnini, Nouv. Dict. d'Hist. Nat. 1. edit.

Char. Essent.   Head round; no tusks; tail cruciform; skin naked, very thick, corneous and fibrous.

DIMENSIONS.   Total length at least twenty-three feet; greatest circumference nineteen feet; weight about eight thousand pounds.

DESCRIPTION.   Head round, confounded with the neck and body; mouth small, placed beneath the snout, and having the lips double, spongy, thick and swollen, furnished exteriorly with white bristles, recurved, and four or five inches long, forming whiskers; lower jaw projecting beyond the upper; opening of the mouth placed near the extremity of the snout, of equal width and length; eyes without eyebrows, but having at the large angle a cartilaginous membrane, covering them at the will of the animal; no external ear; anterior extremities destitute of toes, phalanges and nails; skin an inch thick, without hair.

Anterior extremity consisting of a scapula. humerus; two bones of the fore arm, a carpus and metacarpus, but no phalanges; pelvis composed of two ossa inominata, resembling the ulna of man. attached by strong ligaments to the twenty-fifth vertebra; a pubis; six cervical vertebræ, nineteen dorsal, and thirty-five caudal; stomach simple; intestines very long, (four hundred and sixty-six feet;) cæcum enormous; colon extensive and divided into great cells.

HABIT.   Residing in brackish water in the

mouths of rivers; they pair in spring, and bring forth one at a birth; feeding on fuci; voice resembling the lowing of an Ox.

Inhabit the most northern parts of the South Sea, and particularly the west coast of North America, and of those islands situated between this continent and Kamschatka.

Otho Fabricius states that a cranium of this species was found in Greenland.

2. *Family*, CETA, or *Whales proper.*

Characters. Sometimes provided with teeth, pointed or blunt, all of one description, on the borders of the jaw; sometimes in place of teeth, transverse corneous plates occupy the arch of the palate.

Two mammæ placed near the vent.

Nostrils situated on the summit of the head, very nearly approximated, serving to expel the water taken into the mouth, and are called *blowers.*

Larynx pyramidal, and penetrating the posterior nares.

Eyes flattened anteriorly, with a thick and solid sclerotica; tongue smooth; neither hair, eyelashes, nor whiskers; skin smooth and glossy, covering a thick layer of fat called blubber.

36

Stomach consisting of five, sometimes seven distinct pouches; spleen divided into several distinct lobes.

First Division.

Small headed whales.

Characters. Head of usual proportion with the body.

Genus.

Delphinus, Linn. Briss. Erxleb. Gmel. Cuvier. Geoff. Illig.

Delphinapterus, Lacep.

Monodon, Fabicius.

Hyperoodon, Lacep.

Anarnacus, Lacep.

Uranodon, Illig.

Ancylodon, Illig.

Balæna, Chemnitz. *Dolphin.*

Characters. Teeth all of one description, in form of canines; sometimes a little compressed, and serrated on their cutting borders; in numbers exceedingly various, from a total absence of teeth to as many as two hundred or not more than two.

Jaws more or less produced, in form of a beak, not provided with tusks; the blowing hole in form of a cross, on the top of the head.

Sometimes an adipose dorsal fin; sometimes a simple longitudinal cuticular fold on the back; tail flattened horizontally, and bifurcated.

No cæcum

Habit. The Whales of this genus are the smallest of the family; they inhabit all seas and under very different latitudes; they swim commonly in small troops; and are of a carnivorous nature.

1. Subgenus. *Delphinorhynchus*, Blain.

Snout prolonged into a long and thin beak, not separated from the forehead by a groove; jaws almost linear, with their borders both above and below furnished with numerous teeth; a single dorsal fin, or only a longitudinal cuticular fold, slightly elevated and placed rather posteriorly.

Species.

1. *Delphinus coronatus*, Freminville, Nouv. Bull. de la Soc. Phil. t. 3. No. 56. p. 71. pl. 1. fig. 2. A. B.

Char. Essent. Snout produced into a very long and pointed beak, the inferior longer than the superior; twenty-four teeth on each side below, and only fifteen above; a small dorsal fin; colour black above and beneath; two large, yellow, concentric circles on the forehead.

Dimensions. Total length from thirty to thirty-six feet; circumference more than fifteen feet.

Description. General form elongated; head small, relative to the body; forehead convex, obtuse; jaws in form of a beak. very long and pointed; the inferior being the longest, and having forty-eight very small, sharp, and conical teeth; the superior jaw having thirty; dorsal fin in form of a small cross, nearer to the tail than head; caudal fin forming an entire cross. The pectoral fins of moderate size; colour, uniform black, both above and beneath; forehead surmounted with two yellow concentric circles, the largest being two feet nine inches in diameter, and the interior nearly two feet one inch.

HABIT. This Dolphin is common in the frozen ocean. They begin to show themselves in the seventy-fourth degree of north latitude; they abound particularly about the islands of Spitzbergen; are not very timid, and often approach the vessels. The water which they propel through their blowers, is expelled with much noise and velocity, appearing like light vapour; they seldom attain more than six feet in length.

2. Subgenus. *Delphinus*, Blain.

Snout prolonged into a moderate sized beak, broad at its base, rounded at the extremity like the bill of a goose, and separated from the forehead by a sort of groove; jaws more broad posteriorly; borders furnished with teeth their entire length; a single dorsal fin.

Species.

1. *Delphinis delphis*, Desm. Mamm. p. 514.

(Encycl. Cetolog. pl. 9 and 10, fig. 2.) Vid. for the synonymes the Cetolog. of Bonn. p. 21.

Char. Essent. Jaws moderately prolonged, both of equal length, having on each side forty-two or forty-five teeth, slender, cylindrical, pointed and rather arched, symmetrically arranged; dorsal fin placed on the posterior half of the body; eyes situated nearly on the same line with the rictus of the mouth; body black above, white beneath, both colours intermixing insensibly on the sides.

Inhabit the coasts of North America and of Europe.

Species.

Delphinus canadensis, White Dolphin of Canada, Duhamel, traité des peches, part 2. sect. x. pl. 10. fig. 4. *Dauphin a bec mince,* Cuv. Reg. Anim.? Vulgo, *Gulf-Porpoise, Herring-Hog.*

Char. Essent. Head ventricose; forehead elevated; snout very pointed, and abruptly separated from the forehead; colour of the body, white.

Inhabit the seas of Canada, coast of New England, Long Island, &c.

4. Subgenus. *Phocæna,* Cuvier.

No beak; snout short, and uniformly ventricose; numerous teeth in both jaws; a dorsal fin.

Species.

1. *Delphinus phocæna*, Briss. Regn. Anim. p. 371. No. 2. Linn. Gmel. Bonnaterre, Cetolog. p. 18. G. Cuv. Menag. Nation. Φωχαινα, Aristot. 3. *Phocæna*, Rondelet. Pisc. p. 473. Artedi, gen. 74. *Dauphin marsouin*, Lacep. Hist. Nat. des Cetacès, p. 284. pl. 13. fig. 2. *Porpoise* of the English. (Encycl. Cetolog. pl. 10. fig. 1.)

Char. Essent. Body and tail elongated; snout rounded; teeth compressed, cutting, cylindrical; from twenty-two to twenty-five on both sides of each jaw; dorsal fin situated near the middle of the back, nearly triangular and rectilinear; colour blackish above, and white beneath.

DIMENSIONS. Total length four or five feet.

These animals inhabit near the mouths of large rivers of both continents.

Species.

2. *Delphinus gladiator.*

Delphinus, Muller, Zool. Dan. Prodrom. p. 8. No. 57. *Poisson à sabre*, Pagè, voy. au pole nord. tom. ii. p. 142. *Delphinus maximus*, Olafsen, voy. en Iceland. *Dauphin épée de mer*, Bonnaterre, Cetolog. p. 23. *Dauphin gladiator*, Lacepede, united to the Grampus by Cuvier, Regn. Anim. vol. i. p. 279.

Char. Essent. Body and tail elongated; top of the head very convex; snout cylindrical and short; jaws of equal length; teeth sharp and recurved;

dorsal fin placed very near the nucha, and in length more than one-fifth the total length of the animal.

DIMENSIONS. Total length twenty-three to twenty-five feet.

Inhabit Spitzbergen, straits of Davis, coast of New England.

Species.

3. *Delphinus grampus*, Hunter, *Epaulard* des Saintongeois, *Orca*, Fred. Muller, Fauna Groenlandica. *Butkopf*, of the Dutch. *Grampus*, of the English. *Delphinus orca*, Linn. Gmel. Shaw, Gen. Zool. vol. ii. part 2. pl. 232. *Dauphin epaulard*, Bonnaterre, Cetolog. p. 22. No. 4. *Grampus*, Cuv. Regn. Anim. vol. i. p. 279. *Dauphin orque*, Lacep. *Cacholot*, of Anderson. Duhamel peches, pl. 9. fig. 1. (Encycl. Cetelog. pl. 12. fig. 1.) Desm. Mamm. p. 517.

Char. Essent. Body and tail elongated; cranium slightly convex; snout cylindrical and very short; superior jaw rather longer than the inferior, the latter broader than the former; teeth unequal, blunt, conical and recurved at top; length of the dorsal fin more than one-tenth the total length of the body, and placed towards the middle of the back; blackish colour of the back distinct from the white colour of the belly. Dimensions nearly twenty-five feet.

Inhabit the Atlantic ocean, as far as the straits of Davis.

5. Subgenus. *Delphinapterus*, Lacep.

Head obtuse; snout not prolonged; furnished with a moderate number of teeth, but no dorsal fins.

Species.

1. *Delphinus leucas*, Gmel. *Whitfish*, Anderson Iceland, p. 251. Oranz, Groenland. p. 150. Muller, Prodr. Zool. Dan. p. 50. *Delphinus albicans*, Otho Fabricius, Faun. Groenl. p. 50. *Delphinus pinna in dorso nulla*, Briss. Regn. Anim. p. 374. No. 5. *Dauphin beluga, Delphinus albicans*, Bonnaterre, Encycl. Cetologie, p. 24. No. 6. *Delphinapterus beluga*, Lacep. *Beluga*, Shaw *Huitfish* or *Epaulard blanc*, of the Danes.

Char. Essent. Head obtuse ; teeth short, blunt, nine in number on each side of both jaws; the superior directed obliquely backwards; a small angular eminence takes the place of the dorsal fin; body, tail and fins, of a uniform yellowish-white colour.

Dimensions, from twelve to eighteen feet.

Inhabit the north seas, but particularly the straits of Davis.

6. Subgenus. *Heterodon*, Blainville.

Monodon, Fabr. Bonnaterre. *Hiperoodon* and *Anarnachus*, Lacep. *Uranodon* and *Ancylodon*, Illig. *Epiodon*, Rafin.

Teeth not numerous, (most frequently two only in one jaw, or none at all;) the lower jaw commonly more voluminous than the upper.

Note.—(The *Narwhal*, of which they have made a particular genus, might, according to Desmarest, be rigorously placed under this subgenus.)

Species.

1. *Delphinus anarnachus*, Desm. Mamm. p. 520. *Anarnak*, of the Greenlanders, Otho Fabric. Fauna Groenlandica, p. 31. *Monodon anarnak*, *Monodon spurius*, Bonnaterre, Cetolog. p. 11, No. 2.

Char. Essent. Body elongated; two small recurved canine teeth in the upper jaw only ; a small blackish coloured dorsal fin.

Dimensions. This is one of the smallest animals of the whole order.

Inhabit the seas of Greenland, and do not approach the shore.

Genus.

Monodon, Linn. Erxleb. Gmel. Bonnat.
Ceratodon, Briss. Illig.
Diodon, Storr.
Narwhalus, Lacep. Dumèril, Teidm. Cuvier.
Narwhal.

Dental formula.—Teeth 2. { superior 2. { Incisor 2. Canine 0. Molar 0. } inferior 0. { Incisor 0. Canine 0. Molar 0. } }

One or two large tusks, implanted in the os incisivum, straight, long and pointed, directed in a line with the axis of the body. No other teeth.

General form analogous to that of the Dolphins.

Orifices of the blowing holes united, and situated at the highest part of the back of the head. A longitudinal crest taking the place of the dorsal fin; fins of the flanks of an oval form.

HABIT. These animals, somewhat similar to the Dolphins in their manners, swim in troops, and feed on fish of the genus *Pleuronectes*, as well as on shells; they attack the Whale, and sometimes inflict mortal wounds with their tusks, when they eat the tongues of their victims.

Species.

1. *Monodon monoceros,* Linn. Erxleb. Gmel. *Monodon,* Artedi, Gen. p. 78. N. 1. *Narwhal, oder einhorn,* Anderson, Island. p. 225. Muller, Zool. Dan. Prodrom. p. 6. No. 44. *Monodon narwhal,* Oth. Fabric. Faun. Groendland. p. 29. *Narwhal,* Bonnaterre, Cetolog. p. 10. *Narwhal vulgaire,* Lacep. Shaw, Gen. Zool. vol. ii. part 2. pl. 225.

Home, Comp. Anat. pl. (Encycl. Cetolog. pl. 5. fig. 1, 2, 3.) Vulgo, *Licorne de mer*, or *Sea Unicorn.*

Common Narwhal.

Char. Essent. General form of the body ovoid; length of the head nearly equal to one-fourth that of the body; tusk on the left side commonly solus, the right being seldom developed, grooved spirally, one-half the length of the body; skin of the young animal of a uniform grayish colour on the back, and blackish and marbled in the old; belly white.

DIMENSIONS. From twenty to twenty-two feet, comprising the tusk.

Inhabit the eightieth degree of north latitude, principally on the coast of Iceland, near Davis' Straits, as well as the shores of North America and Greenland.

Species.

2. *Monodon microcephalus,* Desm. Mamm. p. 523. *Narwhal microcephale, Narwhalus microcephalus,* Lacep. Hist. Nat. des Cetac. 159. pl. 5, fig. 2.

Char. Essent. Body and tail very much elongated; general form nearly conical; length of the head nearly equal to one-tenth the total length; tusk long, straight, grooved spirally; skin white, varied with numerous bluish spots

DIMENSIONS.   Medium length twenty-one or twenty-four feet.

HABIT.   Swimming with more facility than the common Narwhal.

Inhabit the fortieth degree of north latitude. One was captured near Boston.   M. Lacepede thinks that the Narwhals, seen near Davis' Straits, are related to this species.

Species.

* 3. *Monodon andersonianus*, Desm. Mamm. p. 523. *Narwhal d'Anderson*, Lacep. p. 163. *Monodon monoceros*, Var. Bonnaterre, (Encycl. Cetolog. p. 11.)   Willughby, Ichthyol. lib. 2. p. 43.

Char. Essent.   Tusk uniform, and without spiral grooves.

Inhabits the North Sea.

Second Division.

Large headed Whales.

The head forming one-third or one-half the total length.

Genus.

Cachalot, Physeter, Linn. Erxleb. Schreb. Cuv. Lacep. Bonnat.

Cetus, Brisson.

Catodon, Linn. Lacep.

Physalis, Lacep.

Characters. Dental formula. From eighteen to twenty teeth on each side of the lower jaw.

Superior jaw broad, elevated, without corneous laminæ, without teeth, or furnished with small teeth nearly concealed by the gums; inferior jaw elongated, narrow, corresponding to a groove in the upper, and armed with thick and conical teeth entering into corresponding cavities in the opposing jaw.

Blowing holes united, and situated near the end of the upper part of the snout.

A dorsal fin in some species; a mere eminence in others.

Large cavities with cartilaginous septi in the superior region of the head, communicating with various parts of the body by particular canals, and filled with an oil which crystallizes in cooling. (Called commonly adipocere, blanc de baleine, spermaceti.)

The *Cachalots* inhabit principally the Polar Regions, but are found sometimes in temperate regions; they war with the seals and feed also on crustacea.

1. Subgenus, *Catodon*, Lacep.

Blowing holes situated completely at the end of the upper surface of the snout. No dorsal fin

Species.

1. *Physeter macrocephalus*, Desm. Mamm. p. 524. Shaw, Gen. Zool. vol. 2. pl. 2. p. 49. pl. 228. *Cachalot macrocèphale*, Lacep. Hist. Nat. des Cetacèes, pl. 10. fig. 1. *Grand cachalot*, Bonn. Cetolog. p. 12. No. 1. (Encycl. Cetolog. pl. 6. fig. 1. et pl. 7. fig. 2.)

Char. Essent. Inferior teeth to the number of twenty or twenty-three on each side, recurved and rather pointed at the extremity; small conical teeth, concealed beneath the gum of the upper jaw; tail very narrow and conical; a longitudinal eminence or false fin on the back, above the anus; body blackish beneath, or a slate blue, slightly spotted with white; belly whitish.

Dimensions. Total length forty-five or sixty feet.

Description. For description, see Cetologie of Bonnaterre.

Note.—(According to M. Cuvier, the blowing hole is single but not symmetrical, being directed to the left side. It is said that the left eye is much smaller than the right.)

Inhabit the North Sea.

Species.

2. *Physeter trumpo*, Desm. Mamm. p. 524. (Encycl. Cetolog. pl. 8. fig. 1.) *Cetus Novæ An-*

gliæ, Briss. Regn. Anim. p. 360. No. 3. Dudley, Philos. Trans. No. 357. Robertson, Trans. Philos. vol. 60. *Blunt headed*, Penn. Zool. Britan. vol. 3. p. 61. *Physeter macrocephalus*, Var. γ. Linn. Gmel. *Cachalot trumpo*, Bonnaterre, Cetolog. p. 14, No. 3. Lacep. Hist. Nat. des Cetacèes, p. 210, pl. 10. fig. 2.

Char. Essent. Head longer than the body; inferior teeth, straight and pointed, eighteen on each side, penetrating as many alveoles on the opposing jaw; body and tail elongated; a rounded eminence rather beyond the origin of the tail.

Dimensions. This species attains to fifty feet in length; twenty-seven feet in circumference.

(M. Cuvier is of the opinion that this species is the same as the preceding.)

Inhabiting the coasts of Bermuda and North America.

Several other species are noticed by Desmarest, Mamm. p. 525 and 526, as frequenting the northern Atlantic coasts, viz. 1. *Physeter catodon;* 2. *P. cylindricus;* 3. *P. microps;* 4. *P. othodon;* 5. *P. mular;* but as there exists some doubt as to their identity, we have briefly noticed them, and refer to Bonn. Cetolog. Loc. Cit. for further detail.

Genus.

Balæna, Willughby, Rai. Artedi, Linn. Briss. Klein. Erxleb. Gmel. Bonn. Lacep. Cuv. Illig.

Physeter. Willugh.

Balænoptera, Lacep.

Superior jaw carinate, or in form of an inverted roof, furnished on each side with transverse corneous laminæ, thin, serrated and fimbriated at their borders.

Blowing holes separate, and placed towards the middle of the upper part of the head; a dorsal fin in some species; nodosities or dorsal prominences in others; cæcum short.

HABIT. Animals of this genus are the largest of the known inhabitants of the globe, feeding on fish, molusca, worms and zoophites. They have no reservoir filled with adipocere like the Cachalots, and do not like these produce ambergris, but the oil which they furnish in abundance, renders them an object of great value.

Inhabit the northern seas, occasionally visiting more temperate latitudes.

1. Subgenus.   *Balæna,* Lacep.

No dorsal fin.

Species.

1. *Balæna mysticetus,* Linn. Erxleb. Gmel. *Balæna major,* Sibbald.   *Balæna vulgaris groenlandica,* Briss. Regn. Anim. p. 347, N. 1. Oth. Fabr. Faun. Groenland. 32.   *Baleine franche,* Bonnat. Cetolog. p. i. N. 1. Lacep. Hist. Nat. des Cetacées, pl. 1. fig. 1. (Encycl. Cetolog. pl. 2. fig. 1.)

Char. Essent. Body thick and short; tail short; no prominence on the back; upper jaw furnished with about seven hundred transverse corneous plates.

DIMENSIONS. Total length from fifty to ninety feet.

For description see Bonnaterre, loc. cit. The size of this species has been overrated at a hundred feet. Of three hundred and twenty-two individuals measured by Captain Scoresby, not one exceeded sixty feet. The average size is fifty feet.

Inhabit the Atlantic Ocean, particularly the Polar Sea, in the neighbourhood of Greenland. According to Scoresby, feeding on actinia, medusa, snails, crabs, shrimps, &c.

Species.

2. *Balæna glacialis*, Klein, Miss. Pisc. 2. p. 12. *Balæna islandica, bipinnis ex nigro candicans, dorso levi*, Briss. Regn. Anim. p. 350. No. 2. *Nord-caper*, Anderson, Island. p. 219. *Baleine nord-caper*, Bonn. Encycl. Cetolog. p. 3. No. 2.

Balæna mysticetus, var. *β*. Gmel.

Baleine nord-caper, Lacep. p. 103. pl. 2 and 3.

Char. Essent. Inferior jaw rounded, very high and broad; body and tail elongated; no prominence on the back; general colour more or less clear gray; beneath the head a large oval surface, of a shining white appearance, with some blackish and grayish spots around it and in its centre.

38

DESCRIPTION. Vid. Bonnaterre, loc. cit.

HABIT. When this species swims on the surface of the water, all parts of the body are immerged, excepting the top of the back and blowing holes; they are very active and fierce, which renders them very difficult to capture.

Inhabit that part of the northern Atlantic situated between Spitzbergen, Norwegia, and Iceland, the seas of Greenland.

Species.

3. *Balæna nodosa*, Bonnaterre, Cetologie, p. 5 No. 4. Briss. Regn. Anim. p. 351. No. 3. *Plok-fisch*, Anderson, Island. p. 224. Crantz, Groenland. p. 146. Dudley Philos. Trans. No. 387. p. 256. Art. 2. *Balæna gibbosa*, Var. B. (Novæ Angliæ,) Gmel. *Baleine noueuse*, Lacep. Hist. des Cetacèes, p. 3.

Char. Essent. A prominence on the back, slightly inclined backwards, and situated near the tail; pectoral fins white, very long and distant from the end of the snout. Described by Bonnaterre.

Frequent the coast of New England.

Species.

4. *Balæna gibbosa*, Bonnaterre Cetolog. *Balæna gibbis, vel nodis sex. Balæna mæra*, Klein. Miss. pisc. 2. p. 13. ? *Baleine á six bosses*, Briss.

Regn. Anim. p. 351. No. 4. Crantz. Groenl. p.
146. Muller. *Balleine bossue,* Lacep. Erxleb.

Char. Essent. Five or six protuberances on
the back, near the tail; corneous laminæ white.
Described by Bonnaterre, loc. cit.

Frequents the seas in the vicinity of New England.

2. Subgenus. *Balænoptera,* Lacep.

Possessed of corneous plates, and a dorsal fin.

Species.

1. *Balæna gibbar,* Bonnat. Cetolog. *Finfisch,*
Marten's, Spitzb. p. 125. p. 2. *Balæna fistula
duplici in medio capite, tubero pinniformi in ex-
tremo dorso,* Artedi, Gen. 77. Syn. 107. *Baleine
gibbar,* Rondelet, Hist. des poiss. 1. part. liv. 16.
ch. 8. *Blæna tripinnis, ventre levi,* Briss. Regn.
Anim. p. 352. No. 5. *Balæna physalus,* Linn.
Erxleb. Gmel. *Baleinoptère gibbar,* Lacep. Hist.
des Cetacèes, p. 114. pl. 1. fig. 2.

Char. Essent. Jaws pointed and equally prolonged; corneous plates short, of a bluish colour;
no fold beneath the throat or under the belly;
body brown above, white beneath.

DIMENSIONS. Length of the body equal that of
the *B. mysticetus,* circumference much less. Described by Bonnaterre, loc. cit.

Frequent the frozen Arctic ocean, particularly

near to Greenland. They are also found in the
northern Atlantic ocean; they descend even to
the thirtieth degree. Martin observed one of
this species in the straits of Gibraltąr, in 1673.

Species.

2. *Balæna boops*, Linn. Syst. Nat. edit. 10.
Erxleb. Gmel. *Jubartes*, Klein, Miss. pisc. 2. p.
13. *Jupiter-fisch*, Anderson, Island. p. 220. *Baleine à museau pointù, balæna tripinnis ventre ru-
goso, rostro acuto*, Briss. Regn. Anim. p. 355. No.
7. *Baleinoptère jubarte*, Lacep. Hist. Nat. des
Cetacèes. p. 120. pl. 4. fig. 1. (Encycl. Cetolog.
pl. 3. fig. 2.)

Char. Essent. Nucha elevated and rounded;
snout prolonged, broad and rather rounded; longitudinal folds beneath the throat and belly; tuberosities nearly hemispherical, situated anterior
to the blowing holes; dorsal fin curved backwards.

DIMENSIONS. Total length, from fifty-one to
fifty-four feet.

(For description, vid. Bonnaterre, loc. cit.) Its
range is principally about the Greenland seas,
and Iceland. According to Lacepede, they visit
both hemispheres. They pass the winter in the
high seas, and visit the shores during summer.

Species.

3. * *Balæna rostrata*, Hunter. Trans. Philos.

Soc. 1787. Oth. Fred. Muller, Faun. Groenland. p. 40. *Baleine à bec*, Bonn. Cetolog. p. 8. No. 8. *Balænoptera acuto-rostrata*, Lacep. Hist. Nat. des Cetacées, p. 134. pl. 4. fig. 2. (Encycl. Cetolog. pl. 4. fig. 1.)

Char. Essent. Both jaws pointed, the upper shorter and narrower than the lower; longitudinal folds beneath the throat and belly; corneous plates short and whitish; body above of a deep black, beneath whitish, shaded with blackish spots.

DIMENSIONS. Total length twenty-seven or twenty-eight feet.

(For description vid. Bonnaterre.)

M. Cuvier thinks this species is not clearly ascertained to be different from the *B. boops*.

Frequent the northern Atlantic, the shores of both continents.

ADDENDA.

Messrs. Lewis and Clark, in the history of their Expedition up the Missouri, have described, with their usual accuracy, several new animals, which have neither received scientific names nor assumed that station in the systems to which they properly belong. The first of these to which we allude, are three species of the genus *Arctomys*, two of which inhabit the great plains of the Columbia river, from the Rocky Mountains to the Pacific Ocean; the other, the plains of Missouri.

Mr. Rafinesque has attempted an arrangement of these animals, by constructing from them a new genus, which he names "*Anisonyx*,"* and to which he assigns the following characters.—" Teeth like those of Squirrels; *no cheek-pouches*; five clawed toes to all the feet, the two internal of which on the fore feet very short, the *three* others long, with very sharp nails; tail distichous like that of Squirrels. (This genus differs from the Marmots and the Squirrels in the number and form of the fingers.")

In the above description of Mr. Rafinesque,

---

* Vid. American Monthly Magazine, vol. ii. p. 45. 1817

we detect false translation and interpolation, which are noted by italics. On examination of the descriptions of these animals by Messrs. Lewis and Clark, they will be found to be generically allied to the Marmots.

Genus.

Arctomys.

Species.

1. *Arctomys brachyura.*
Anisonyx brachyura, Rafinesque, Amer. Mon. Magaz. vol. ii. p. 45.
Burrowing Squirrel, Lewis and Clark's Exped. up the Missouri, vol. ii. p. 173.
Short tailed Marmot.

Char. Essent. Colour cinereus-brown above, a light brick-red beneath; tail flat, reddish, subdistichous, one-seventh of the total length.

Dimensions. Total length two feet five inches, including the tail, the latter being two inches and a half long.

Description. The neck and legs are short; the ears are likewise short, obtusely pointed, and lie close to the head; the aperture larger than will generally be found among burrowing animals; the eyes are of a moderate size, the pupil black, and the iris of a dark sooty-brown; the whiskers are full, long and black; the teeth, and, indeed, the whole contour, resemble those of the Squirrel;

each foot has five toes; the two inner ones
(thumbs) of the fore feet are remarkably short,
and are equipped with blunt nails; the remaining
toes (nails) on the front feet are long, black, slightly curved, and sharply pointed; the hair of the
tail is thickly inserted on the sides only, which
gives it a flat appearance, and a long oval form;
the tips of the hair forming the outer edges of the
tail are white, the other extremity of a fox-red;
the under part of the tail resembles an iron-gray,
the upper is of a reddish-brown; the lower part
of the jaws, the under part of the neck, legs, and
feet, from the body and belly downwards, are of a
light brick-red; the nose and eyes are of a darker
shade of the same colour; the upper part of the
head, neck and body, are of a curious brown-gray,
with a slight tinge of brick-red; the longer hairs
of these parts are of a reddish-white colour at their
extremities, and falling together, give this animal
a speckled appearance.

HABIT. These animals form in large companies
like those on the Missouri, (*Arctomys ludoviciani*,
Ord,) occupying, with their burrows, sometimes
two hundred acres of land; the burrows are separate, and each possesses, perhaps, ten or twelve
of these inhabitants. There is a little mound in
front of the hole, formed of the earth thrown out
of the burrow, and frequently there are three or
four distinct holes, forming one burrow, with these
entrances around the base of these little mounds.

These mounds, sometimes about two feet in height, and four in diameter, are occupied as watch towers by the inhabitants of these little communities. The Squirrels, one or more, are irregularly distributed on the tract they thus occupy, at the distance of ten, twenty, or sometimes from thirty to forty yards. When any one approaches, they make a shrill whistling sound, somewhat resembling *tweet, tweet, tweet,* the signal for their party to take the alarm, and to retire into their intrenchments. They feed on the roots of grass, &c.

Inhabit the plains of Columbia. (Lewis and Clark.)

Species.

2. *Arctomys latrans,* (nob.)

Barking Squirrel, Lewis and Clark's Exped. up the Missouri, vol. ii. p. 175.

Char. Essent. Colour a uniform brick-red, lighter beneath; cheeks furnished with pouches; a few long hairs are inserted on each jaw, and directly over the eyes.

DIMENSIONS. From the extremity of the nose to the end of the tail, one foot five inches; tail, four inches; weighing about three pounds.

DESCRIPTION. Colour of a uniform brick-red, the former predominating; the under side of the neck and belly are lighter than the other parts of the body; the legs are short, and the breast and shoulders wide: the head is stout and muscular.

and terminates more bluntly, wider, and flatter than that of the common Squirrel; the nose is armed with whiskers on each side, and a few long hairs are inserted on each jaw, and directly over the eyes; the eye is small and black; each foot has five toes, and the two outer ones are much shorter than those in the centre; the two inner toes of the fore feet are long, sharp, and well adapted to digging and scratching.

HABIT. Notwithstanding the clumsiness of his form, he is remarkably active, and he burrows in the ground with great rapidity. These animals burrow and reside in their little subterraneous villages like the burrowing Squirrel. To these apartments, although six or eight usually associate together, there is but one entrance. They are of great depth, and Captain Lewis once pursued one to the depth of ten feet, and did not reach the end of the burrow. They occupy, in this manner, several hundred acres of ground, and when at rest, their position is generally erect on their hinder feet and rump; they sit with much confidence, and bark at the intruder as he approaches, with a fretful and harmless intrepidity. The note resembles that of the little toy-dog; the yelps are quick, in angry succession, attended by rapid and convulsive motions, as if they were determined to sally forth in defence of their freehold. They feed on the grass of their village, the limits of which they never venture to exceed. As soon as the frost commences, they shut themselves up in their caverns, and continue until the spring opens. The flesh of this animal is not unpleasant to the taste.

Inhabit the plains of the Missouri. (Lewis and Clark.)

Species.

3. *Arctomys rufa.**

Sewellel, of the Indians of the western coast. Lewis and Clark's Exped. up the Missouri, vol. ii. p. 176.

Anisonyx rufa, Rafinesque, Amer. Mon. Magaz. who has confounded it with the preceding species.

Char. Essent. General colour reddish-brown; fur short, thick and silky; ears short, thin and pointed, covered with hair.

DIMENSIONS. Total length, from fourteen to eighteen inches (of the dressed skin, from which the tail is always separated by the Indians.)

DESCRIPTION. Ears short, thin, and pointed, and covered with a fine short hair, of a uniform reddish-brown; the bottom or the base of the long hairs, which exceed the fur but little in length, as well as the fur itself, are of a dark colour next the skin for two-thirds the length of this animal; the fur and hair are very fine, short, thickly set, and silky; the ends of the fur and tip of the hair are of a reddish-brown, and that colour predominates in the usual appearance of the animal.

Inhabit the woody plains of Columbia, more abundant in the neighbourhood of the Great Falls and Rapids of the Columbia than on the sea coast.

Captain Lewis offered considerable rewards to the Indians, but was never able to procure one of these animals alive.

Genus.

Meles?

Species.

1. *Meles jeffersonii*, (Nobis.)

Braro, of the French hunters, Lewis and Clark's Exped. up the Missouri, vol. ii. p. 177.

Badger of Columbia.

Char. Essent. Body proportionably long, fore legs large, muscular, formed like those of the turnspit-dog; all the legs short; breast and shoulders broad; neck short; mouth wide; whiskers placed in four points on each side of the nose.

DIMENSIONS. Body long in proportion to its thickness; tail four inches long; the whole animal weighing from fourteen to eighteen pounds.

DESCRIPTION. The fore legs are remarkably large, short, and muscular; neck short; mouth wide, and furnished with straight teeth, both above and below, with four sharp, straight, pointed tusks, two in the upper and two in the lower jaw; the eyes are black and small; whiskers placed in four points on each side near the nose, and on the jaws near the opening of the mouth;

the ears short, wide, and oppressed, as if a part had been amputated; the tail is four inches in length, the hair of which is longest at the point of the junction with the body, and growing shorter until it ends in an acute point; the hairs of the body are much shorter on the sides and rump than those on any other part, which gives the body an apparent flatness, particularly when the animal rests upon his belly; the hair is upwards of three inches in length, especially on the rump, where it extends so far towards the point of the tail that it conceals the shape of that part, and gives to the whole of the hinder parts of the body the appearance of a right angle triangle, of which the point of the tail forms an acute angle; the small quantity of coarse fur intermixed with the hair is of a reddish-pale yellow.

HABIT. They burrow in hard grounds with surprising ease and dexterity, and will cover themselves in a very few moments; they have long fixed nails on each foot, those on the fore feet are much the longest, and one of those on each hind foot is double.

Inhabit the open plains of Columbia, sometimes those of the Missouri, and are sometimes found in the woods.

Genus.

Lepus.

Species.

Lepus virginianus, Var.? (Nobis.)

Varying hare, Lewis and Clark's Expedition up the Missouri, vol. ii. p. 179.

Char. Essent. Colour, plumbeous above, white beneath, during the summer; of a pure white in winter; tips of the ears, black or reddish-brown at all seasons; body covered with fine, close fur; tail round, bluntly pointed.

DIMENSIONS. Body smaller and longer in proportion than that of the common rabbit, (*L. americanus*,) weighing from seven to eleven pounds.

DESCRIPTION. The eye is large and prominent, the pupil of a deep sea-green, occupying one third of the diameter of the eye; the iris is of a bright yellowish and silver colour; the ears are placed far back, and very near each other, which the animal can, with surprising ease and quickness, dilate and throw forwards, or contract and hold upon his back at pleasure; the head, neck, back, shoulders, thighs and outer part of the legs are of a lead colour; the sides as they approach the belly, become gradually more white; the belly, breast, and inner part of the legs and thighs are white, with a light shade of lead colour; the tail is round and bluntly pointed, covered with white, soft, fine fur, not quite so long as on the other parts of the body; the body is covered with deep, fine, soft, close fur.

The colours here described, are those which the animal assumes from the middle of April to

the middle of November; the rest of the year
he is pure white, except the black and reddish-
brown of the ears, which never change. A few
reddish spots are sometimes intermixed with the
white, at this season, (February 26, 1806,) on
their heads and the upper part of their necks and
shoulders; the body of the animal is smaller and
longer in proportion to its height than in the rabbit.
When he runs he conveys his tail straight behind, in the direction of the body; he appears to
run and bound with surprising agility and ease.
He is extremely fleet, and never burrows or takes
shelter in the ground when pursued. His teeth
are like those of the rabbit, as is also his upper
lip, which is divided as high as the nose.

Habit. His food is grass and herbs, and in
winter he feeds much on the bark of several aro-
matic herbs growing on the plains. Captain Lewis
measured the leaps of this animal, and found them
commonly from eighteen to twenty-one feet; they
are generally found separate, and are never seen
to associate in greater numbers than two or three.

Inhabit the plains of Columbia, on the western
side of the Rocky mountains, on the eastward of
these mountains they inhabit the plains of the
Missouri. (Lewis and Clark.)

Genus.

Canis.
The following notice of the North American

Indian dogs, is extracted from the manuscript
notes of the late Mr. William Bartram, one of the
earliest naturalists of this country.

" The *Indian dogs* which I have observed
among the south-western nations, are generally
black, pied-black and white, and some of other
colours, but most commonly black; having sharp
pointed, erect ears; the muzzle long and pointed,
much like the wolf, but their tail is not so bushy,
and they are not so noisy as our dogs; they are
slender and of various sizes, some not larger than
the fox, and resembling them in shape and appearance; probably a spurious race engendered between the wolf and fox; displaying the sly and
subtle look of these animals. They are fierce,
watchful, and faithful to their keepers, but have a
peculiar antipathy to white people.

" The *Newfoundland dog* is undoubtedly native
of North America, and seem to be of the same
race, or derived from the *Greenland dogs*. They
are much larger than the *Indian dog* above noticed, being as large or larger than the wolf or
mastiff, and are remarkably different in shape, being more clumsily formed; their limbs strong and
muscular; their ears not so erect and peaked,
being more like those of the bear, as is also their
muzzle; their lips are not so pendant, infolded, or
tumid, as those of the Spaniel or European dogs.
Their tail is very short, like that of the bear:

they are variously coloured and differently coat-
ed; some being woolly or shagged; others have
fine, short hair, a little curled, which kind are esteemed the best. They are remarkable for their
sagacity, watchfulness, and fidelity."

INDEX.

LIST OF SUBSCRIBERS.

	Copies.
Archer, Joseph	1
Atley, E. A., M. D.	1
Adams, Thomas	1
Bigsby, I. T., M. D. London,	1
Brown, Frederic	1
Betton, Samuel, M. D.	1
Bell, John, M. D.	1
Banker, C. N.	1
Barton, J. R., M. D.	1
Brown, Oris A.	1
Bonaparte, Charles	2
Barton, W. P. C., M. D.	1
Burr, I. H., M. D.	1
Brevoort, H., N. York,	1
Bronson, O., N. York,	1
Barnes, D. H., N. York,	1
Brown, M.	1
Bird, R. M.	1
Coates, B. H., M. D.	1
Chapman, N., M. D.	2
Chancellor, Henry	1
Collin, Nicholas, D. D.	1
Cozzens, I., N. York,	1
Clark, E., N. York,	1
Cooper, W., N. York,	3
Clay, E.	1
Dewees, W. P., M. D.	1
Dietz, R.	1
Dekay, J. E., M. D. N. York,	5
Delafield, J., N. Y.	1
Emerson, G. B., M. D.	1
Eberle, John, M. D.	1
Emlen, Samuel, M. D.	1
Gibson, W., M. D.	1
Gebhard, L. P., M. D.	1
Godman, J. D., M. D.	1
Goodrich, A. T., N. York,	2
Hembel, William	1
Harris, Thomas, M. D.	1
Haxall, R. W.	1
Haines, Reuben	1
Hartshorn, Joseph, M. D.	1
Howell, W. W.	1
Hosack, D., M. D. N. York.	1

	Copies.
Halsey, L. jr. Princeton, N. J.	1
Halsey, A., N. York,	2
Jackson, Samuel, M. D.	1
Knight, Alexander, M. D.	1
King, F., M. D. N. York,	1
La Roche, R., M. D.	1
Leamy, John A.	1
Long, S. H.	1
Library of the Lyceum of Nat. Hist., N. Y.	1
Logan, A. S.	1
Meigs, C. D., M. D.	1
Mitchel, I. K., M. D.	2
Morton, Samuel, M. D.	1
Mease James, M. D.	1
M'Call, W. C.	1
M'Clellan, G., M. D.	1
M'Ewen, Charles	1
Parrish, Joseph, M. D.	1
Price, E. K.	1
Pennock, Caspar	1
Persicoe, G.	1
Richards, B. W.	1
Rotch, I. R., New Bedford,	1
Smith, D. B.	1
Stewart, I., M. D.	1
Smith, I. I.	1
Star, Isaac	1
Spackman, George	1
Snowden, I. C., M. D.	1
Temple, Solomon	1
Ware, N. A.	2
Wetherill, Charles	1
Wetherill, William, M. D.	1
Wetherill, I. P.	1
Wetherill, Samuel	1
Warren, W. C., M. D.	1
Wood, G. B., M. D.	1
Wistar, Caspar, M. D.	1
Walmsly, W. W.	1
Wilder & Campbell, N. Y.	5
Webster, M. H., Albany,	1
Van Rensselaer, M. D.	1
York, E.	1

ERRATA.

In detailing the habits of the American Pole-Cat, (Mephitis, Cuv.) vid. p. 69, we have stated on the authority of Professor *Kalm** and others, that this animal wets its tail with the fetid liquor of the anal glands, in order to sprinkle it on its adversaries; we have since been credibly informed that this is a vulgar error. The Pole-Cat is naturally a very clean animal, and never intentionally soils itself with its own excretions; on the contrary, when pursued, these animals invariably turn their tail over their back, invert the anus in a slight degree, and squirt the offensive liquor to the distance of several yards; this fluid, besides its extremely offensive odour, possesses the property of excoriating the skin, and producing violent inflammation when it strikes the eyes.

Page 201, line 23 et 27, for *Megalonix* read *Megalonyx*.

* Vid. Kalm's Travels in North America, vol. i. p. 274

NATURAL HISTORY
AND
REMARKS ON AN ARTICLE
IN THE NORTH AMERICAN REVIEW

[John Godman]

NATURAL HISTORY.*

Few departments of knowledge, have been more injured by incorrect or prejudiced views of their real character, than Natural History; which some regard as a mere collection of tales for the amusement of children, or idlers; and others, as an aggregation of learned lumber, too heavy for use, and too harsh to be interesting. That such notions are not altogether unwarranted by those who have been called Naturalists, is too true; many of their books being filled with the most incredible nonsense, while a very large number of those claiming to rank as purely scientific, are little better than Dictionaries, in which the authors have tasked their ingenuity, to accumulate all the harsh and barbarous terms they could compound from various living and dead languages. Yet granting thus much, by no means renders it fair to argue against the usefulness of Natural History, from the abuses which have been cloaked under

* Dr. Godman, professor of Natural History in the Institute, has engaged to become a contributor to, and to aid the Editor in conducting this department of the Journal.

its name; a similar mode of reasoning, might lead to the rejection of the most admirable and valuable institutions, since we cannot find one, however excellent, which has not in some degree been abused.

Another prejudice which has tended to retard the diffusion of a proper knowledge of Natural History, is the idea that a great deal of *learning* is necessary to beginners of this study. Hence, many excellent opportunities have been entirely lost of observing and establishing facts, concerning which the world may long remain in doubt; those who have enjoyed such opportunities, have supposed it necessary that they should be very learned, before they would have a right to announce what they had seen. It is most true that preliminary education is of great advantage in all Sciences and Arts; but in Natural History, which is almost exclusively a science of observation, a close attention to facts seen, and an accurate relation of them as they occur, are of more value than the most learned discussion, and would be certainly far more acceptable, than the highest refinements of speculation. All the learning that is necessary for any one to become *practically* (which is, *usefully*) acquainted with Natural History, is a sufficient degree of intellectual cultivation, to save him from seeing incorrectly, or mistaking secondary, for the primary, and really important circumstances. For instance, it was long supposed by observers, that the *Skunk* (or Pole-cat, as it is popularly called,) diffused its powerfully offensive odour by sprinkling a fluid on its disturbers with its bushy tail; and this silly notion has been repeated until very recently, even by grave authors. More accurate observation has shown that the animal raises the tail suddenly, *previous* to the diffusion of the offensive liquor; and in order to prevent this substance from touching it, being peculiarly clean and neat in its own person. Various analogous cases may occur, in which incorrect conclusions might be drawn, without some preparatory knowledge; but with the proper care in making observations, or stating the actual condition of facts, even incorrect conclusions, will be comparatively harmless.

Every man of ordinary capacity, may study Natural History for himself, and advantageously too, if he be really desirous to form an acquaintance with *Nature* through her works, rather than to shine as a framer of systems, or a composer of theories. To study Natural History, it is only necessary for us to use our eyesight—to look upon the multitudes of living beings by which we are surrounded, observe their peculiar construction and adaptation to the places they occupy, their modes of living, and the relations they bear to other animals, and to man himself: this is the study of *Natural History*. The fruitless and wearying discussion of technical phrases, or the propriety of various classico-barbarous appellations, with hair splitting distinctions of genera, sub-genera, species and varieties, is NOT Natural History, but the study of *Nomenclature;* a dry and barren waste! tenanted only by fierce and fruitless jealousies, recriminations and disquiets of every degree!

The study of Natural History is too beneficial in its influence, to allow of its being restricted to the few who are able to approach it through the severe and uninviting method of arbitrary and artificial classification. As its immediate tendency is to enlighten the mind, and warm the heart; to enlarge our feelings of respect for our own race, and enable us more correctly to appreciate the beneficent wisdom of the Creator, we believe that those writers who endeavour to render Natural History generally accessible, confer more benefit on mankind, than if they filled whole libraries with books of the *deepest* learning, too abstruse to be generally read ; therefore but seldom approached, and still more seldom understood.

The difference between *learning*, and *wisdom*, is never more clearly perceived, than when we observe the conduct of those who mistake *Classification* and *Nomenclature*, for Natural History ; and violently object to every effort made to diffuse knowledge, without the shackles they have imposed on themselves. Many such men are truly and deeply *learned*, but they certainly are not *wise*, when they forget that classifying, and naming, are only among the *means* of acquiring knowledge, and are not the *end* we have in view ; that scientific arrangements are mere *instruments* to work withal ; that systems at best serve the purpose of an index ; that they are arbitrary and mutable ; always the productions of Art, and seldom having much affinity with Nature.

Nevertheless, a good machine to work with, is extremely desirable ; and the best system we can find, is an excellent aid in the study of Natural Objects, provided we never once forget, that the *system* at best is but a *tool* with which we are to accomplish a very important work, the collection and arrangement of useful knowledge. Such a system, as far as utility is concerned, has been formed by GEORGE CUVIER, (better, and more emphatically known as CUVIER,) founded on characters furnished by the Anatomy of Animals. Their rank in the scale, is determined by their degree of approach to the construction of the human body ; and their relations to each other, determined by their peculiar regimen or modes of life, and organs of digestion—as indicated by the subsidiary apparatus for the seizure, and mastication of their food.

Our object in thus endeavouring to invite more general attention to this delightful study, is to open a new and most ample source of gratification to many, who have both leisure and opportunities for observation, but are withheld by mistaken notions. There is in fact, a vast deal yet to be observed, before the Natural History, of even our most common animals, can be completed ; and every actual observation, will be of the highest value. Independent of this, as a source of individual gratification, it is not to be excelled ; seeing that the objects of nature are boundless, and the field is open to all. It is not in books that we are to find nature ; though they may aid us in planning our walks, or in guiding our observations ; but it is in the fields and woods, in the plain, and on the mountain, by the side of the rippling brook, or on the sandy beach lashed by ocean's foaming waters, that the student must look, with the fullest certainty, of finding objects capable of rewarding his search; and opening his eyes to perceive, that the works of the Creator, are best to be understood when read from that great book which is accessible to all, and is *unobscured* by gloss or commentary.

TH.

Remarks on an Article in the North American Review.

The last number of the North American Review, (50th) contains a criticism on a work published sometime since in this city, entitled "Fauna Americana." This article contains many judicious and useful remarks, written in a candid and manly style; yet to judge merely from the review itself, one might infer that the writer was not technically familiar with the subject before him; and although he has given numerous proofs of discrimination and judgment, does not *appear* fully to understand the actual condition, "the form and pressure" of scientific Natural History, as it now exists. We say he *appears* to be in this condition, for we have no mode of judging of his standing, except through the review before us. The impression we have received from reading this criticism is, that it is written by one accustomed to close thinking and sound logic; but not practically and technically, a Naturalist; to whom the glaring faults of the book have been pointed out by one familiar with the subject, but in a desultory manner; in short. by a person who is an admirer of Natural History, but not a closely applied, or profound student of the science. Such is our impression; though we well know how easy it is to be mistaken.

The writer of the review, has truly found a very sufficient number of faults in the "Fauna," but a *technical* critic would have attributed these faults to M. DESMAREST in very great part, and not to the American "Author;" since, out of three hundred and fourteen pages, very nearly, if not quite, *two hundred* and *fifty* are verbally and literally translated from the "*Mammalogie*" of the French Naturalist. This a *technical* critic ought to have known. The faults for which the American Author is really responsible, (although he did actually assume the others,) are those parts which are considered as peculiarly *original*, in the "Fauna;" and these are certainly not few. Except these *original* errors, the whole of the rest should be charged to *Desmarest;* he it is, who should be scolded for not introducing the extracts from Bonnaterre's "*Cetologie*," as it is he, who quoted this writer. We believe that the author of the "Fauna" never saw that work; nay, we are almost sure it has not yet reached America.

A technical critic would have known better than to elevate to the rank of an *original* work, such a one as the "Fauna," under whatever guise it might be presented to the world. A reviewer is, with no great impropriety, supposed to know all things relative to the subject on which he writes; or, in other words, the publication of a review, presupposes that the writer has taken pains to acquire all necessary information. Had this been the case in the present instance, the reviewer would have saved much trouble by stating the plagiarism above indicated ; as well as done more ample justice to the science and literature of his own country.

The best part of the review, is that in which it alludes to the confused classification in the "Fauna ;" and the want of dignity exhibited, in bringing personal squabbles, into systematic works. The observations on fossil animals, the distinction of genera and species, and on Cuvier, is the weakest part, as well as the least applicable to the matter in hand. Of the actual faults of the "Fauna," or what we have called the *original* errors, the reviewer has seen and felt (for no technical Naturalist can avoid feeling as well as seeing them,) but few ; and these inaccurately, though he has stated in general terms, that there were too many to be pointed out individually. That the "Author" is competently acquainted with Natural History, the reviewer admits from the evidence before him—this no Naturalist can possibly conclude from the *book*, though we know it to be so, *in fact.* The *book* displays extraordinary ignorance of the first principles of the science ; as in the formation of *species* from variations in dental formulæ ; when if any thing were done, it should have been to form a new genus or sub-genus. A technical critic would not have passed over so slightly, the formation of a new genus of *extinct* quadrupeds, from a *recent* skull found on the banks of the Delaware ; not a "mutilated" one, as the reviewer supposes, but the skull of an animal thrown overboard from some vessel, which probably had been bringing the animal alive, to Peale's Museum. This is a good specimen of the skull of a well known genus ; the Paca of South America, established under the title of Cœlogenus by F. Cuvier in 1810, and accurately figured in the Annals of the French Museum,* of which several copies have long been in Philadelphia. It is moreover described in all the systematic books, and its dental system is accurately figured in the "Dents des Mammiféres" frequently quoted by the "Fauna :" even in Desmarest, there is a full account of it. This skull, the author of the "Fauna" compares with the first animal in the order, the beaver ; instead of discovering by its structure, how much more nearly it is approached by various other genera, which in fact are but slightly removed from it. Were the author judged by his *book* alone, his claims to consideration as a scientific Naturalist, would be reduced to rather worse than nothing.

The great error of the author of the "Fauna," consisted in translating,† and being in haste ; had he relied on his own resources, and exerted his own industry, for which he is laudably conspicuous, he would have made a better book, and been far more useful in his day and generation. As it is, his book has fallen "dead born" from the Press ; and until eventually engulphed in that oblivion, to

* This "original" error was first pointed out by T. Say.

† It is but just to state, that he acknowledges having translated "the *descriptions* of about fifty" *species*, though he is silent concerning all the rest.

which its peculiar character is rapidly hurrying it, will serve as a beacon to future adventurers on the same perilous seas.

On another occasion, it will give us much pleasure to consider some of the propositions advanced by the reviewer, to whom we are indebted for the article in the North American. Whether *technical* or not, we flatter ourselves we could convince him of some inaccurate conclusions, into which he has been led during the course of his well written paper, considering it for the present, rather as an essay on the principles of classification, than as a criticism on a particular book: at the same time, we freely confess, that we shall be happy to receive, at all times, the observations of so well exercised, and judicious a mind. **x.**

[REVIEW OF] FAUNA AMERICANA

[John Godman]

Art. VI.—*Fauna Americana; being a Description of the Mammiferous Animals inhabiting North America.* By Richard Harlan, M. D. Philadelphia. 1825. A. Finley. 8vo. pp. 318.

The object of this work is to present, under a systematic arrangement, a scientific history of all the mammiferous animals of North America, and it is probably the first attempt of the kind. The object, however, which is professed in its title, is not wholly followed up in the body of the work; the animals of Mexico being avowedly excluded from the description and arrangement, although, in the preface, an enumeration is given of those known to exist in that country. The number of animals, described within the region embraced by Dr Harlan's plan, is greater than we should have at first supposed to be now known to naturalists. He has been able to distinguish, he remarks, one hundred and fortyseven species, with considerable accuracy. From his preface we quote the following passage.

' A work, having for its object the illustration of the natural history of our country, cannot fail to prove interesting, and has long been a desideratum to naturalists. However unqualified for the task, I have nevertheless found ample room for additions, alterations, and improvements. On the *utility* of the undertaking it will be unnecessary to insist, when, on referring to the latest authorities who have treated of this subject, we are struck with the confusion, the errors, and the deficiencies, which still prevail. In the very latest work, Desmarest's Mammalogie, published in the year 1820, which professes to describe all the species of Mammalia hitherto known, the number inhabiting North America is limited to one hundred *species.* Of these many are described as uncertain, and his accounts of the manners and habits of most of them are at best deficient.'

What these additions, alterations, and improvements are; in what manner confusion has been reduced to order, errors corrected, and deficiencies supplied, may appear in the sequel. Meantime, to exhibit the author's labors within a small compass, we have prepared, and think proper to insert in this place, a catalogue of the animals described in his work, in their systematic order as marshalled by him. This will serve at once to show the field over which his labors have been spread, and give those, who seldom consult books of this description, an opportunity of taking in, at a single view, the whole of the animals of this class, found in this part of North America.   In order to assist in the discrimination of the names belonging to genera and species, those of genera are printed in small capitals, those of species in the common small type.   Those genera and species introduced by Dr Harlan, as being first noticed, described, or named by him, are in italics, and those which have been only known in the fossil state, have an asterisk prefixed.

CLASS MAMMALIA.
ORDER I. PRIMATES.
HOMO.   1 sapiens.   American Variety.
ORDER III. CARNIVORA.
Family Cheiroptera.   Tribe Vespertilio.
RHINOPOMA.   1 caroliniensis.
VESPERTILIO.   1 caroliniensis, 2 noveboracensis, 3 pruinosus, 4 arquatus.
TAPHOZOUS.   1 rufus.
Family Insectivora.   First Division.
SOREX.   1 constrictus, 2 araneus, 3 parvus, 4 brevicaudatus.
SCALOPS.   1 canadensis, 2 *pennsylvanica.*
CONDYLURA.   1 cristata, 2 longicaudata, 3 *macroura.*
TALPA.   1 europea.
Family Carnivora.   First Tribe, Plantigrada.
URSUS.   1 arctos, 2 cinereus, 3 americanus, 4 maritimus.
PROCYON.   1 (URSUS) lotor.
TAXUS.   1 (MELES) labradoria, 2 jeffersonii.
GULO.   1 arcticus.
MUSTELA.   1 vulgaris, 2 erminea, 3 *lutreocephala*, 4 vison, 5 canadensis, 6 martes.
MEPHITIS.   1 americana.
LUTRA.   1 brasiliensis, 2 marina.
CANIS.   1 familiaris, 2 lupus, 3 lycaon, 4 latrans, 5 nubilus, 6 vulpes, 7 argentatus, 8 decussatus, 9 virginianus, 10 fulvus, 11 cinereo-argenteus, 12 velox, 13 lagopus.
FELIS.   1 concolor, 2 onca, 3 pardalis, 4 canadensis, 5 rufa, 6 fasciata, 7 montana, 8 aurea.
Tribe. Carnivorous Amphibious Animals. (Carnivora pinnipedia.)
PHOCA.   1 cristata, 2 vitulina, 3 groenlandica, 4 fetida, 5 barbata, 6 (OTARIA) ursina.
TRICHECUS.   1 rosmarus.
Family Marsupialia.
DIDELPHIS.   1 virginiana.

ORDER IV. GLIRES.
Section I.

CASTOR. 1 fiber.

*OSTEOPERA. 1 *platycephala.*

FIBER. 1 zibethicus.

ARVICOLA. 1 amphibius, 2 xanthognatha, 3 *palustris*, 4 *hortensis*, 5 floridanus, 6 pennsylvanica.

LEMMUS. 1 hudsonius.

MUS. 1 rattus, 2 sylvaticus.

PSEUDOSTOMA. 1 bursarius.

GERBILLUS. 1 canadensis, 2 labradorius.

ARCTOMYS. 1 monax, 2 empetra, 3 ludoviciani, 4 tridecem-lineata, 5 franklinii, 6 richardsonii, 7 pruinosa, 8 parryii, 9 brachyura, 10 *latrans*, 11 rufa.

SCIURUS. 1 cinereus, 2 capistratus, 3 rufiventer, 4 niger, 5 magnicaudatus, 6 quadrivittatus, 7 lateralis, 8 grammurus, 9 striatus, 10 hudsonius, 11 ludovicianus.

PTEROMYS. 1 volucella.

HYSTRIX. 1 dorsata.

LEPUS. 1 americanus, 2 glacialis, 3 *virginianus.*

ORDER V. EDENTATA.
First Tribe. Tardigrada.

*MEGATHERUIM. 1 *cuvieri.

*MEGALONYX. 1 *jeffersonii.

ORDER VI. PACHYDERMATA.
First Family. Proboscidea.

ELEPHAS. 1 *primogenius.

*MASTODON. 1 *giganteum, 2 *angustidens.

Second Family. Pachydermata, properly so called.

SUS. 1 scrofa.

DICOTYLES. 1 torquatus.

TAPIRUS. 1 *mastodontoides.*

ORDER VII. PECORA.
Second Division. First Tribe.

CERVUS. 1 alces, 2 tarandus, 3 canadensis, 4 virginianus, 5 macrotis, 6 *americanus.*

Third Tribe.

ANTILOPE. 1 americana.

CAPRA. 1 montana.

OVIS. 1 ammon.

OVIBOS. 1 moschatus.

BOS. 1 americanus, 2 *bombifrons, 3 *latifrons.*

ORDER VIII. CETA.
First Family. Cetacea Herbivora, Sirenia.

MANATUS. 1 latirostris.

RYTINA. 1 (STELLEBUS) borealis.

Second Family. Ceta or Whales proper. First Division.
DELPHINUS. 1 coronatus, 2 delphis, 3 canadensis, 4 phocœna,
5 gladiator, 6 grampus, 7 leucas, 8 anarnachus.
MONODON. 1 monoceros, 2 microcephalus, 3 andersonianus.
Second Division.
PHYSETER. 1 macrocephalus, 2 trumpo.
BALÆNA. 1 mysticetus, 2 glacialis, 3 nodosa, 4 gibbosa, 5 gib-
bar, 6 boops, 7 rostrata.

Unless there is some oversight in making out this catalogue,
which we presume there is not, the following table exhibits
the number of species in each order; and, by way of comparison, we place by the side of it, a table given by the author,
in his preface.

Orders.	Number of Species.	Author's Table.
1. Primates,	1	1
3. Carnivora,	62	60
4. Glires,	42	37
5. Edentata,	2	6
6. Pachydermata,	6	2
7. Pecora,	13	13
8. Ceta,	22	28
	148	147

It will be perceived, that, if this enumeration is to be trusted, and great care has been taken to make it accurate, the
author's table is wrong in five orders out of seven. Two of
these errors may, however, be attributed to an accidental
transposition of numbers, viz. orders 5 and 6. For the rest,
there seems to be no such excuse. He speaks, also, in the
preface, of eleven fossil species; only ten are contained in the
above list. He must, therefore, intend to include a fossil
species of Manatus, which is neither named nor numbered,
and which, if admitted, will make the number of the last order
23, and the total of all the orders 149.

In the construction of his orders, Dr Harlan appears to
have followed the *Règne Animal* of Cuvier, and we have
numbered them accordingly. The names, however, are
adopted, partly from that author, and partly from Linnæus.
Thus, for the first order, he retains the Linnæan denomination, Primates; although he excludes from it the bats, and,
we presume, the monkeys also, which originally belonged to
it. To the fourth order he gives the name Glires, instead of

the more modern and expressive one of Rodentia. To the seventh, the proper appellation, Ruminantia, is applied in the preface, but in the body of the work, this is discarded for Pecora ; and so, also, Cetacea in the preface becomes Ceta in the sequel. There does not appear to be any sufficient reason for thus retaining the Linnæan names of a few of the orders, whilst their constitution, and the names also of all the others, are adopted from a different system. Names themselves are not originally of any very great consequence, yet they become so, when they have been employed for a long time to designate particular things. It is not, perhaps, in itself a matter of much importance, whether the first order of Mammalia be denominated Primates, or Bimana ; but since it is generally known that the naturalists, who have severally adopted these names, constituted the order in a manner entirely different ; that Cuvier places in it man alone, whilst Linnæus associated him with monkeys, lemurs, sapajous, and bats; the terms are gradually understood in a specific sense, and bear always the meaning attached to them by those, who first introduced them. At all events, the adoption of any new method of arrangement, or the use of any terms in a sense differing from that generally received, should be premised by some sufficient explanation.

It is stated in the preface, that ' twentyfive species are common to both continents, without including the cetaceous animals.' That is to say, about one fifth part of the quadrupeds, inhabiting North America, are common to it with the Eastern continent. Dr Harlan is too ready to admit the identity of species of the new, with others of the old world, or at least he does it without showing that deliberation, which the decision demands, and without apparently considering the doubts, which rest upon the subject. It certainly admits of a doubt, whether any species of animals is common to the two continents, except where it may have been transported from one to the other, by some accidental mode of conveyance, or unless it resides in the northern regions, and is capable of enduring the rigors of a polar winter, so that it may be supposed to have passed in some way from one continent to the other.

It is a general result of the observations, upon the distribution of both the vegetable and animal creation, that each species appears originally to have inhabited some particular region, from which it has spread more or less extensively, according to its own nature, and the nature of the country in which it was first placed. Buffon remarked, that the animals of the old world were in general different from those of the new, and that the species common to both were such, as are able to endure the extreme cold of the arctic regions, and may therefore be supposed to have found a way from one continent to the other, where they approach very near together, and may have been formerly joined. Of the general truth of this statement, there is abundant proof. Whether there are not many individual exceptions is not so easily determined. All the largest, the most clearly described, and the most easily distinguished animals of the old world, are certainly peculiar to it; and although there may be in the new, animals closely resembling them, corresponding to them, and often mistaken for them, yet they are almost always specifically, and often generically distinct. Thus of the Proboscidean family, the living elephants are peculiar to the eastern continent; and fossil remains indicate the former existence in the western, of a race of animals resembling them in many important particulars, although generically distinct; whilst there is sufficient evidence, that a species of elephant, adapted by its structure to endure the cold of the northern regions, formerly existed in both. Of the celebrated ferocious animals of the feline race, we have not one. It is true we hear of the American tiger, and the American lion, but they are manifestly creatures smaller, less powerful, and less terrible. The wolf, on the contrary, whose constitution is hardy, and able to endure the rigors of a polar winter, is the same in Europe, in Asia, and in America. The two species of camel are confined to Asia and Africa. America has a genus, the Llamas, nearly allied, and not less adapted to the peculiar character of the countries in which it resides. The comparison might be carried farther, and it might be shown, that those species, which have been supposed common, have been small, obscure, imperfectly observed, not easily recognised, and incapable of that precise description, which may be given of the larger.

In confirmation of the same general view, it appears that the successive discovery of new and insulated portions of the globe, as America and New Holland, has brought to light, not only new genera and species, but races of animals of a totally different kind, possessing strange, and before inconceivable characteristics. Thus, on the discovery of America, were first known those singular animals, the sloths, characterised by Buffon as defective monsters, and rude and imperfect attempts of nature; and the marsupial animals, which were then looked upon as strange and anomalous, in their structure and habits. In New Holland an entirely new order of things was opened to the eyes of naturalists. The world of nature, in that remote region, seemed to have been formed upon a new model. The marsupial animals, before considered as exceptions to the general rules of animal conformation, were here found to predominate. Elsewhere regarded as rarities, here there was little else, till, as exceptions to these exceptions, to the infinite disturbance of all quiet and old fashioned naturalists, the monotremous genera, and among them that strange beast, the ornithorhynchus, were brought to light; a tribe of animals, that seem to scorn classification, set rule and order at defiance, and although properly neither flesh, fowl, nor reptile, yet bear such resemblance to each, as to puzzle any one who shall attempt to fix their place in the system of nature.

Another fact to the same purpose is, that of the various animals which inhabit the arctic regions, and whose constitution renders it impossible for them to bear the journey across the tropics, probably not one is found in the antarctic. This is not only true of the land animals, but also of those inhabiting the sea, from the largest, down to the most minute and inconsiderable. It is remarked by MM. Peron and Le Sueur, that upon an examination, not merely of the Dorides, the Aplysias, &c. but carried down to the Holothurias, the Actinias, and the Medusas, or even still farther to the sponges, universally regarded as occupying the lowest rank of animal existence, it is found that out of the whole immense multitude of these antarctic animals, not one is known in the northern seas.

Dr Prichard, a most intelligent English writer, has given the subject a full consideration in his 'Researches into the Physical History of Man,' a work full of learning and ingenuity. After an examination of all the instances in which it

might be supposed, that species were common to the eastern
and western continents, he arrives at the conclusions, that no
animal is common to the warm parts of the two continents;
that no European species is indigenous in both, which is not
a native of countries north of the Baltic in one, and of Canada
in the other; that no Asiatic species is found in America,
except such as inhabit the northern parts of the Russian em-
pire, and most of these in those districts which approximate to
America, whilst some have left proofs of their existence there
in their fossil remains, and some have even been traced
through the intervening islands; and that scarcely any animal
has an extensive range in the northern regions of either continent, which is not common to both. All these considerations point to the general inference, that these tribes are
common to the two continents, because, from their locality
and habits, they have been enabled in some way to effect a
communication from one to the other; but that, originally,
each continent had its peculiar stock of mammiferous animals,
which has continued peculiar in all parts of the continents,
except where such a communication may be conceived, in the
course of ages, to have taken place.

It therefore appears highly probable, that, with the limitations made above, the species aboriginal in each continent
are also peculiar to it. And although this may not be con-
clusively established, the result at least is inevitable, that it
behoves naturalists to be very cautious in admitting the identity of American and foreign species; that it should not be
done except after a thorough examination of both external
and internal characters, and then only by the concurrent
opinion of competent judges.

Dr Harlan is unfortunate in the connexion and arrangement of his species, particularly in the subdivisions of tribes,
families, and subgenera. He in no place directly informs us,
whose system of subdivisions he has adopted. In a work
confined to the animals of a particular country, we can of
course have only parts of a methodical arrangement, but it is
of little use to introduce these parts, when the student has no
clue, by which to discover what and where is the whole to
which they belong. Divisions of this sort have no use or
meaning, except in relation to one another. Class, order,
genus, and species, are terms universally received and au-

thorised by long use ; their extent and meaning are generally understood.   But suborder, family, tribe, and subgenus, not to say section and division, are terms whose signification is by no means accurately defined.   They are too often used in a vague sense, and by different authors in a very different one.   There is a considerable uniformity in the arrangement of the animal kingdom, by naturalists, into the divisions of the first kind ; they have proceeded commonly upon similar principles, and have arrived at results not very unlike.   But with regard to the second kind, much diversity occurs, both in the principles by which authors have been governed in making them, and also in the meaning of the terms used to express them.

A beginner in natural history would be perpetually perplexed, and be liable to constant error, from the want of attention to this point, in the Fauna Americana.   This work may be likely to fall into many such hands, and be taken as a guide in the study of this branch of science.   It should, therefore, have been carefully guarded.   How careless and superficial the author has been in this very particular, we proceed to show by a variety of examples.

The order, Carnivora, he subdivides into families according to Cuvier.   The first family is that of Cheiroptera, containing animals of the bat kind.   This family, as it appears, he subdivides into tribes, and immediately announces, without preparation, ' *Tribe Vespertilio.*'   Under this tribe, after inserting and describing the genus Rhinopoma, he introduces the *genus* Vespertilio, with which he gives the dental formula of Linnæus and Desmarest, marked 1 and 2, implying, as one would imagine, that reference was made to two subdivisions of the genus, but whether this was intended, or whether the formulæ were introduced merely for the purpose of comparison, does not appear, and we are left in doubt what use to make of them.   Then follows the generic description, and one species numbered 1.   Immediately after the description of this species, a new division comes upon us unexpectedly, entitled ' *1st Division,* Vespertilio, *Geoff,*' with a dental formula differing slightly from that of Desmarest, a short description, and an enumeration of the species hitherto observed.   Three species of Vespertilio are then described, which, without reference to that already described, are numbered 1, 2, 3, and among them one which is not of those enumerated, but a page before, as the only ones belonging to this division.

Now it is hard to make anything of this, and yet the author, for aught we know, may have understood himself very well, and had a very clear object in what he has done Still we do not keep up with him in his easy transition from genus to species, from species to division, and from division to species again. This, however, might have been accidental were it the only instance, but it is not so. Proceeding to the next family, Insectivora, we find immediately after the character of the family, a ' 1st *Division*,' intended to include the first *tribe* of this family, according to Cuvier, from whom in fact the description of its character is almost literally translated. Here is an instance of the vague use of terms, concerning which we have spoken. *Tribe* was used under the former family to designate a subdivision of the genera belonging to a family, whilst now the term *division* is used for a similar purpose, which, under the same family, was employed to stand for the parts of a subdivided genus. But although the first division, or, more properly, tribe of this family, is thus noticed and characterised, we look in vain for the second. This is entirely and unaccountably omitted, although there are two genera belonging to it, Condylura and Talpa, which stand thus in the work in a tribe to which they do not belong, and with a character to which they do not correspond.

The family Carnivora follows next, and this is by Cuvier divided into three tribes, Plantigrada, Digitigrada, and Amphibia. Genera belonging to all these tribes are contained in Dr Harlan's book, but he announces only two. The plantigrade animals are defined, (p. 45,) and called ' 1st *tribe*,' but we hear no more of tribes, till fifty pages farther onward we encounter the third tribe, Amphibia, which, however, is not called third, but is introduced simply thus, ' *Tribe*. CARNIVOROUS AMPHIBIOUS ANIMALS (*carnivora pinnipedia*).' This method of arrangement, taken in good earnest, would actually include all the digitigrade animals, such as the weasel, fox, wolf, and cat, under the first tribe.

In the next order, Glires, a similar negligence occurs. This order is generally divided into two families, the charac-

ter of which is founded upon the clavicle, which is strong
and powerful in one, and only rudimentary and imperfect in
the other. The first of these is announced in its proper
place, but is styled *section;* another term to express a division
corresponding to those, which had been before introduced
under a different name. Of the second we discover no
intimation, although two genera are described, which are properly comprehended under it.

These are instances of carelessness, which ought not to
have been suffered to appear in a scientific work, professing
to remove confusion, correct errors, and supply deficiencies.
They are so palpable, indeed, that were they not so numerous, one would have attributed them to inaccuracy of the
press. There are others relating to the more minute details
of this book, a few of which only can be noticed. The
genus Phoca affords a memorable example of the loose and
incomplete manner, in which the author treats his subject.
This genus, it may be proper to premise, has been subdivided by Peron into two subgenera, one of which retains
the denomination Phoca, the other has received that of
Otaria. Dr Harlan gives in the first place five dental formulæ, but without the smallest intimation of the purpose for
which they are introduced ; no use is made of them, no
subdivision founded upon them, they have nothing to do
with the two subgenera ; they correspond to nothing which
he has given us with regard to any other genus, except perhaps Vespertilio, which, as we have seen, is far from being
so full of light, as to be able to impart any. Having
described the genus, the subgenus Phoca is announced,
which is numbered 1, and its character given. Then follow
six species numbered from one to six, the sixth of which belongs to the subgenus Otaria, and is named Otaria with
Phoca as a synonym, whilst the notice and character of
subgenus 2, which should precede it, are omitted. What
makes the matter worse is, that in the next sheet, into which
the account of this genus extends for a few lines, a note is
appended, containing the notice and character of Otaria,
omitted in its proper place, a notice which no one would
comprehend, who was not already acquainted with the history of the genus. The perspicuity, moreover, of a work of
science should not depend upon the contingency of the au-

thor's perceiving his errors and omissions, in season to correct them in the next proof.

Several errors occur in the arrangement of the names and synonyms of genera and species, which render it uncertain, what the name of the genus or species in question is really intended to be. Thus, under the genus *Procyon*, we find the species *Ursus* lotor; under *Taxus*, *Meles* labradorius; under *Rytina*, *Stellerus* borealis. This is explained by stating, that, in the first case the synonym of the species is placed instead of the name, the name being among the synonyms, whilst in the second and third the same mistake occurs with regard to the synonym of the genus. This at least appears to be the explanation. There are errors of a different kind in the names. Thus, we have a genus called *Taphozous taphiens*, the French name, (les Taphiens) or the name of another genus having crept in by accident. The genus Felis is styled, 'Cat or Felis;' and in the same way we have 'Pecari or Dicotyles,' and 'Cachalot, Physeter.'

The style of Dr Harlan's work is loose, and indicative of haste and want of revision. Two or three examples will explain our meaning.

'The above *description*,' says the author, 'is taken principally from a prepared specimen in the possession of Mr C. Bonaparte, and *was killed* on the Blue Mountains, in the state of Pennsylvania.' p. 198. 'The *plane* of the occiput represents a *semicircle*.' p. 273. 'We are credibly informed by an *eyewitness of the fact*, that the Norwegian rat *did not make its appearance* in the United States, any length of time previous to the year 1775.' p. 149.

We intended to make a variety of other criticisms, both in matters of science, and language, which are omitted, because, as it is impossible to notice them all, it is sufficient to have introduced enough to justify the opinions we have expressed. The work is, in fact, so constantly disfigured by instances of looseness, carelessness, and inaccuracy, as to destroy confidence in the fidelity of its execution. The author is evidently not deficient in knowledge of natural history; his errors have mainly arisen, as it appears to us, from the inconsiderate haste with which his work has been written, and hurried through the press. As further proofs of this haste, it may be stated, that Dr Harlan has inserted in his *Addenda,* the description of a number of species, discovered by Messrs Lewis and Clarke, and described in the account of their Expedition up the Missouri many years since, a work to which he repeatedly refers in the body of his book ; and that, for the descriptions of nearly all the species of the last genus in the volume, Balæna, he refers us to *Bonnaterre's Cetologie*, instead of translating or abridging these descriptions, a task of which he has not been in other places very sparing.

There is almost a total want in this work of that mechanical assistance, which may be derived from a skilful application of the mode of printing, to the illustration of the details of natural history, Of the advantages which proceed from this source, even Cuvier has not disdained to avail himself in his great work, upon the classification of the animal kingdom ; and whoever has had occasion to consult it must have perceived the immense facility, which is thus afforded to the student. It is only to appropriate a particular type to the names, and to the descriptions appertaining to each division and subdivision, and the eye catches at once the relative importance and extent of what relates to each. This mechanical aid should never be forgotten ; it is of no trifling assistance even to the most experienced naturalist. But in the Fauna Americana, with a few exceptions, both titles and text are in the same dead unvaried type ; the former in italics, the latter in roman ; so that the clumsy expedient is adopted, of repeating the words genus, subgenus, and species, whenever these divisions occur.

It will be observed upon reference to the catalogue, on a preceding page of this article, that among the animals of North America, Dr Harlan has inserted a considerable number of fossil species. In fact, the whole of those of the order Edentata, and all but one of the indigenous animals of the order Pachydermata, are fossil. The results which have been obtained, by the investigations of some European naturalists into the characters of fossil bones, have something in them grand and imposing. With regard more particularly to those of Cuvier, there seems to be no reason to doubt that the conclusions, at which he has arrived, possess all the certainty of which the subject is capable. The facilities afforded by his situation for the pursuit of this branch of study, the extent of his attainments in the comparative anatomy of living animals, and, with all this previous qualification, the slow, cautious, and deliberate manner in which he comes to results, give him strong claims to our confidence.   Yet it is hard to go along with him when he expresses his belief, that from the smallest remaining bone of any animal, it is possible to determine not only its order, but its genus and species; in short, to reconstruct its whole anatomy ; just as it is possible for the mathematician, from any given equation of a curve, to demonstrate all its properties.   That there is such a relation between the parts of the body of every animal, as is asserted by this distinguished anatomist, and that the peculiarity, which every species exhibits as a whole, is also impressed upon even the most minute part of its fabric, may be readily admitted, but that this character is cognisable in the fang of a cuspidatus, the smallest bone of the tarsus, or one of the extreme phalanges, exceeds our belief.   We cannot forget, in expressing this opinion, the mistake of a European anatomist, second to but few of his time, who, in examining some fossil bones, placed an important fragment of the head in a reversed position, and thus gave an entirely new face to the animal.   It would not be passing strange, could these antediluvian quadrupeds rise up in judgment against the philosophical disturbers of their remains, if they should exhibit metamorphoses, wrought by the hand of science, extremely inconvenient, and somewhat inconsistent with their former habits.   The mammoth, perhaps, might not be sufficiently grateful to anatomists for the elephantine proboscis, so generously bestowed upon him ; and the megalonyx might very reasonably prefer ranging the woods, a ferocious and majestic beast of prey, as Mr Jefferson describes him, to a life of idleness and inactivity, under the very different character of the three toed sloth of the antediluvian world, according to the award of Cuvier.

Seriously, we think that the splendid discoveries, which have resulted from the extraordinary attainments of the French anatomist, and we would not speak of them except with respect and confidence, are likely to lead others into very imperfect and crude speculations upon fossil bones. We do not object to the description of all such remains fully and accurately, in connexion with the description of the living animals of the country where they are found.   This is proper, and indeed highly important and interesting.   But we do strenuously object to their erection into genera and species, except upon the most undoubted authority, and to their being thus unceremoniously embodied in the natural history of a country. Too much doubt must hang over the conclusions at which most naturalists arrive, on such points, to admit of so decided a step as this. Dr Harlan has thought otherwise. He has seen fit, upon the authority of a mutilated skull, found on the shore of the river Delaware, to erect a new genus, *osteopera;* and upon no better foundation, than a single molar tooth, exhumed in the western part of our country, has built a new extinct species of Tapir, which he has had the satisfaction of christening with his own hand. Farther than this; Dr Wistar, in a paper read to the American Philosophical Society, described certain fossil bones, presented by Mr Jefferson, which he believed to belong to species of the genera Cervus and Bos, but modestly forbears to systematise them. Our author has done this office for these neglected reliquiæ, and they accordingly figure among the mammalia of the United States, as the *Cervus Americanus, Bos bombifrons,* and *Bos latifrons,* all ' *nobis,*' which last term, as some of our readers may need to be informed, signifies that the genus, or species, after which it is inserted, has been constituted and named by the naturalist in whose work it appears.

The consideration of this subject suggests another, which is of importance to the accuracy and soundness of American natural history. We mean the growing propensity of naturalists to construct new genera and species. This disposition is unphilosophical and productive of confusion. It is a departure from the true spirit of scientific investigation. It is not so easy a matter for men, of even good attainments in natural history, to determine whether a species has been before described and named, or not. So imperfect are the short descriptions which are often given, so loose and vague is the language of too many naturalists, so extremely difficult indeed is the task of clear description, and so few are there who perform it well, that the identification of a specimen with any known species or genus, is frequently a difficult task, and we should be very cautious in concluding because we cannot identify it, that it is therefore something new. The creation of a new genus in natural history is a weighty matter; it should not be lightly done, it should not be soon done; the subject should be left for repeated consideration and consultation, and should not be ventured, except with the concurrence of more than one skilful naturalist, unless it be by some one whose attainments in science give his opinion weight and authority.

Much less importance is to be attached to the introduction of a new species, and still this requires far more hesitation, than most naturalists seem to feel. At any rate, it is not a matter which demands extraordinary haste. No particular evil results, if the animal in question goes without a legitimate name for a few short months. It is certainly a less evil, than that it should be taken for a new species, when it is in reality an old one, and be thus made to undergo the process of nomenclature a second time. Every new name, it must be recollected, contributes to swell the list of synonyms, already the burden of natural history. But it is the foible of scientific men, at the present day, that they are more anxious to make and promulgate discoveries, than to search out the truth. Some naturalists pride themselves vastly more upon having been the authors of new genera and species, than upon describing with accuracy those already known, ascertaining more exact marks of discrimination between them, or illustrating their character and habits; and yet he performs a far less useful service to science. We repeat, that the task of determining the character of an animal is by no means an easy one, and can be performed by few men with certainty.

Naturalists, of no mean celebrity, do indeed differ essentially in the conclusions at which they arrive, with regard to the same animal, even when possessed of equal means of judging, and equal qualifications. The simple inspection of any work of natural history is sufficient to show us, what confusion and uncertainty are introduced, by this proneness to making discoveries, and this overweening love of the fascinating pronoun *nobis*. The existence of this difficulty, and the obscurity consequent upon it, are admitted by the most eminent naturalists. It is remarked by Cuvier, that in the course of his investigations, he has sometimes found a single species, representing, by means of synonyms, several animals, so different frequently, that they did not even belong to the same genus; and sometimes, on the other hand, the same animal, reappearing in several subgenera and genera, and even in different orders, as a distinct one. 'We have here an animal,' says Dr Harlan, speaking of the Rocky Mountain sheep, 'described for the first time in 1816, which has already been classed under four distinct genera, with nearly as many specific appellations.' To mend the matter, Dr Harlan places it under a fifth genus. For the pronghorned antelope, an animal of recent discovery, we have no less than half a dozen different names.

We cannot close this article, without expressing regret and strong disapprobation, at the manner in which are written two long notes in Dr Harlan's book, (pp. 140, 143,) concerning certain differences into which he has unluckily fallen with other naturalists, in describing and naming some species of the genus Arvicola. The contest maintained in these notes is quite below the dignity of science. With whom the fault rests, it is not for us to inquire, but we feel justified in saying, that, when personal jealousy is allowed to have an influence in constructing new genera and species, and when *nobis* is arrayed against *nobis* with an air of triumph, no good hope remains for the accuracy of investigations thus pursued, nor for the aid they will lend to the progress of genuine science.

REFUTATION

OF

CERTAIN MISREPRESENTATIONS

ISSUED AGAINST THE AUTHOR OF THE

"FAUNA AMERICANA,"

IN

THE PHILADELPHIA FRANKLIN JOURNAL,

No. 1, 1826.

AND IN

THE NORTH AMERICAN REVIEW,

No. 50.

PHILADELPHIA :

Printed by William Stavely, No. 70, South Third Street.
....
1826.

TO THE

PATRONS OF SCIENCE,

AND

THE FRIENDS OF TRUTH,

THESE PAGES

ARE RESPECTFULLY DEDICATED.

REFUTATION, &c.

CRITICISM, when conducted on just principles, inspired by liberal motives, and confined within proper limits, cannot fail of proving beneficial to the advancement of science and to the progress of real knowledge. But when made the vehicle of bitter invective, when personal animosity, envy, and jealousy, behind this mask endeavour to vent their spleen, criticism loses all its dignity, and is debased to a level with anonymous letter writing.

Exposed to the insidious attacks of individuals to whom neither the feelings of shame, the reproaches of conscience, nor the fear of punishment, form any bar to the baseness of their designs, authors would have much reason to lament the dangers of their situation. did they not find some resource in the common consent of the well educated portion of the community to receive with distrust, or to treat with merited contempt, any effort of detraction, however specious, appearing in a form so despicable.

In the weakness of the understanding, which is generally the concomitant of malignant principles, we are happily provided with a further immunity. "We owe it to the bounty of Providence, that the completest depravity of heart is sometimes strangely united with a confusion of the mind, and makes the same man *treacherous* without art, and a *hypocrite* without deceiving."

Assertions, dogmatical and gratuitous, false accusations, wilful misrepresentations, and flat contradictions, are weapons unworthy the dignity of criticism: they are not congenial to the true spirit of science, nor are they ever necessary to the correction of error. The mouth of calumny breathing its pestilence over the promise of growing reputation, may, for the moment, damp the ardour of scientific pursuit, but sooner or later, the *calumniator* must experience the effects of a rebound, and like the envenomed asp that has missed its aim, hide his head in his hateful coil.

Such are the reflections which very naturally arose from the perusal of Dr. Godman's review of the "Fauna Americana," in a recently published number of the "Franklin Journal." (Vid. vol. I. No. I. p. 19, Jan. 1826.) Had Dr. G. confined his animadversions to the scientific circle, or published his observations in a journal dedicated to natural history, no exceptions would have been taken to his review, by the author of the "Fauna;" nor would any notice have been necessary. Those who are capable of distinguishing the *true* from the *false*, such as are in the least degree acquainted with the science, would have detected at first glance, the total incapacity of the author of the review ; (whose ideas, indeed, of this subject, have never soared above "Goldsmith's Animated Nature,") they would further have perceived, that personal animosity alone could have hurried him into the commission of so much misrepresentation and error.

Dealing profusely in gratuitous assertions, misrepresentation, and contradiction, to the almost utter exclusion of any remarks on the *scientific* matter of the "Fauna," the reviewer has no doubt thought his object most certainly attainable by publishing his remarks in a journal that will scarcely meet the eye of the scientific naturalist.

Avoiding, for the present, any observations that might arise from the notice taken of the writer in the North American Review, we proceed in as regular order as the subject will admit, to refute the *assertions* made by Dr. G. in the Franklin Journal, or Mechanics' Magazine.

"The writer of the review, (North American, No. 50,) has truly found a very sufficient number of faults in the 'Fauna;' but a *technical* critic would have attributed these faults to *M. Desmarest* in very great part, and not to the American 'author;' since, out of three hundred and fourteen pages, very nearly, if not quite, *two hundred and fifty* are verbally and literally translated from the '*Mammalogie*' of the French naturalist. This a *technical* critic ought to have known."

Now to all this formidable charge of plagiarism, we might answer the "*technical* critic" in his own coin, by the simple declaration that the whole statement is absolutely, "verbally and literally" false—without any shadow of a foundation—and on the part of the critic, a *wilful* misrepresentation, in as much as he had it in his power to know better, had he taken the pains to make the necessary comparisons: for we do know that he has seen "Desmarest's" work, but that he has never *studied* it, he himself has displayed sufficient evidence.

In the above extract, he offers an unwarrantable contradiction to the plain and candid statement we have made in our introduction to the "Fauna," (vid. p. 4, note) to the following effect:

"Mr. Desmarest, in his advertisement to the second part of his 'Mammalogie,' limits the number of mammalia inhabiting North America, to fifty-four species: as this statement does not in any degree correspond with his descriptions, we presume he has permitted a typographical error, of great importance, to escape his notice. We have enumerated from his work one hundred species, as inhabiting North America; the description of about fifty of these having been found very accurate, are accordingly translated, with very little alteration."

Having thus given credit to Desmarest for fifty species, we honestly thought that we had attributed to him more than was justly his due. It must be recollected that M. Desmarest, in his Mammalogie, professes to give a description of all the mammalia throughout the known world, a field sufficiently extensive for the display of his vast genius; yet, throughout his extensive work, we do not recollect that the author has given the description of a single species not *previously described* in other works :—the chief merit of the "Mammalogie," consisting in an attempt (to a considerable degree successful) at improvement in the scientific arrangement, and in endeavouring to restore order to a subject heretofore disfigured by confusion. Yet was this author's book considered not the less *original, useful,* and *meritorious.*

The Fauna Americana bears the same relation to the mammalia of the *United States,* as does the work of Desmarest to the mammalia of the four quarters of the globe; with this difference, however, that, in addition to order and scientific classification, together with original observations more or less extensive on most of those species previously described, the "Fauna" contains the descriptions of ten new species, seven of which were previously entirely unknown.

The work of M. Desmarest being the most recent, as well as the most correct, was necessarily adopted as a model. We believe that none of his *errors,* relative to North American animals, were left uncorrected ; at least none have been pointed out as yet, not even by the "*technical* critic."

If copying from any author the descriptions of such species as have been well known, and accurately described since the days of Linneus, can be construed into plagiarism, then all modern naturalists are plagiarists. *

* What renders the charges of the " critic" still more presumptuous, is the fact, that he himself stands publicly convicted of plagiarism ; for the proofs of which we need only refer to an able review by Dr. N. R. Smith, in the Philadel. Medical and Surgical Review, No. 2, vol. 2d,

If such a construction be admissible, what must necessarily be the fate of that beautiful volume recently published by Mr. C. Bonaparte, ("American Ornithology,") which contains the description of but one single species of bird not previously known, named, and described. Yet, our "technical critic" does not hesitate, on all occasions, "to elevate to the rank of an *original* work," this production of his patron. We certainly do not intend, that any observation of our own should detract from its merits.

We deny that in any instance we *blindly* copied descriptions; these were compared with specimens of the animals in all cases where this was practicable, and always with the descriptions of preceding authors, when their works could be obtained either in the numerous and extensive libraries of this city or in those of New York. In short, we have followed the method well known to all who possess a real knowledge of natural history, to be that employed by all naturalists in the preparation of systematic works.

We confess that we never enumerated the precise number of *pages* occupied in the "Fauna," by the descriptions of the fifty species attributed to Desmarest, nor do we possess the means at present of obtain-

---

of a work entitled, "Anatomical Investigations, by John D. Godman, M. D." In this paper are examined certain claims set forth in the "Investigations" to a few of those raræ aves, Anatomical discoveries. See further proofs in the Medical Recorder, vol. 8, p. 825. It is not to be presumed that he will attempt to escape from this stigma, by pleading ignorance of Anatomical works so well known, and so justly esteemed, as are those of Bell and Biçhat.

ing accurate information on that subject,* supposing it
in the least degree important ; but as the whole number of *species* described in the " Fauna," amounts to
rather more than one hundred and fifty, occupying
three hundred and fourteen pages, by the fairest
mathematical computation, the fifty species attributed
to Desmarest cannot occupy more than one third, that
is to say, *one hundred* pages, in place of *two hundred*
and *fifty*, agreeably to the unqualified assertion of Dr.
G.† But to proceed with the criticism :

"The faults for which the American author is really responsible (although he did actually assume the others,) are those
parts which are considered as peculiarly *original* in the ' Fauna,' and these are certainly not few."

What these *assumed* faults are, the " critic" has
not informed us : if any really exist, we want some
other proof than his "ipse dixit," especially after
the sample of *veracity* with which he has just furnished us. As relates to the " numerous *original* faults,"
we shall not fail to answer when he is pleased to detail
them.

"Except these original errors," he continues, "the whole
of the rest should be charged to *Desmarest ;* he it is, who should
be scolded for not introducing the extracts from Bonnaterre's
' Cetologie,' as it is he who quoted this writer. We believe

---

* We have returned the work of Desmarest to a distant friend, from whom we borrowed the
only copy in this country, at the time the " Fauna" was preparing. We believe there is, as yet,
no copy in our public libraries.

† In addition to the acknowledgment made in the preface of the Fauna, we have quoted, at
the head of the description of each individual species, the names of the different authors who
have previously described the animal.

that the author of the 'Fauna' never saw that work ; nay, we are almost sure it has not yet reached America."

He " *believes*" we never saw Bonnaterre's work, and would venture the accusation of plagiarism on *his* principle of faith. " There are more *strange things* in heaven and earth, Horatio, than are dreamed of in our philosophy." Nay, he is almost sure the work has not *yet* reached America ; this is the more to be regretted, as the work has been published more than thirty years. We can further assure the " critic" that a work in French, entitled " Cetologie par M. l'Abbé Bonnaterre," has lain on our table for many weeks in succession : and what may prove of more consequence to one who has announced himself as the author of " a forth-coming work on American Natural History," we will freely place it in his power to peruse " Bonnaterre" at his leisure ; for we have not the least objection to assist him in the prosecution of his studies, provided he be really desirous of obtaining information; and must do ourselves the justice to acknowledge, that we notice his blunders, " more in sorrow than in anger," and regret that he has imposed upon us the disagreeable task of exposing his ignorance. The reviewer continues :

" A *technical critic* would have known better than to elevate to the rank of an *original* work, such a one as the ' Fauna,' under whatever guise it might be presented to the world. A reviewer is, with no great impropriety, supposed to know all things relative to the subject on which he writes; or, in other

words, the publication of a review, presupposes that the wri
ter has taken pains to acquire all necessary information. Had
this been the case in the present instance, the reviewer would
have saved much trouble by stating the plagiarism above indicated, as well as done more ample justice to the science and
literature of his own country."

The degree of impudence and arrogance, contained
in this little extract, can only be fully estimated by those
who possess an intimate acquaintance with the real
character of the writer. Previous to taking our leave
of him we trust we shall make it appear, to what extent *he* is acquainted with " all things relative to the
subject on which he writes," or how far the writer
" has taken pains to acquire all necessary information." The. writer in the " North American,"
though unacquainted with natural history, at least
possesses honesty sufficient to avoid accusing an author
of " plagiarism" without cause.

" The best part of the review, (in the North American,) is
that in which it alludes to the confused classification in the
' Fauna ;' and the want of dignity exhibited, in bringing personal squabbles into systematic works."

The classification adopted in the " Fauna," with
very few exceptions, is that of Baron Cuvier ; consequently, the confusion can have no existence but in the
reviewer's muddy intellect : indeed it was never expected that an individual, destitute of first principles,
should be able to comprehend any classification. The
expectation and disappointment of Dr. G. resemble

those of the clown who truly believed he would be able to read by merely placing spectacles before his eyes, though he had never learned his alphabet. If our " critic" really entertains the opinion he has expressed relative to *nomenclature,* he never can obtain a knowledge of natural history: viz. " hair splitting distinctions of genera, sub-genera, species and varieties, is *not* natural history, but the study of *nomenclature,* a dry and barren waste! tenanted only by fierce and fruitless jealousies, recriminations, and disquiets of every degree!" (Vid. Franklin Journal, p. 17.) This we may remark by the way is a pregnant sort of " barrenness."

We believe that nomenclature and classification will still be considered as the foundation of all natural science, at least, so say *Bonnaterre,* Cuvier, &c.*

As regards the " want of dignity in introducing private squabbles," we presume, if he intends any meaning, he refers to two notes inserted in the " Fauna" claiming priority in the description of a new species of quadruped, &c.†

† [We insert the notes for the convenience of general readers.]

Note 1.—*Some weeks after the above description [of the Arvicola hortensis] had been drawn up, and read before the Philadelphia Academy of Natural Sciences,* Messrs. Say and Ord thought it necessary to describe the same animal, and to con-

* " L' histoire de chaque animal en particulier ne pourra recevoir quelques accroissemens, qu' autant qu' on sera d' accord sur la nomenclature ; c'est la base de l'histoire naturelle."
[Vid. Bonnaterre, Cetologie, Avertissement, p. 6.

Whether or not it display a want of dignity, for an author to claim his own property by a candid statement of the facts as they occurred, we leave to public decision. In inserting these notes, we did not as-

struct from it a new genus, which they name " *Sigmodon.*" For this distinction they have no other foundation than a slight and unimportant variation in the form and direction of the plates of enamel, which traverse the crowns of the molars, and the partial division of the root into rudimentary radicles. On similar distinctions, F. Cuvier has founded his *divisions* of the genus *Arvicola,* which " differ from each other in the number of parts of which the teeth are composed."

It could be shown, if necessary, in a number of instances, that greater differences are observable in the different teeth of the same individual, than have served those gentlemen, in the present instance, to construct a new genus; who, in their description of the animal, have entirely neglected to point out any generic distinctions in the *external characters,* (which, in reality, correspond with the genus *Arvicola.*) This neglect is the more extraordinary, as in their former descriptions they have dwelt upon the *external* characters of animals, and, in some cases, to the exclusion of any observations on the structure of the teeth, as was instanced in the " *Mus floridanus.*" The slight variations in the teeth noticed above, provided they be accompanied with well marked differences in the external characters of the animal, may form good grounds for *specific* distinctions, but surely cannot be received as sufficient reason for the construction of a new genus, according to the established laws which regulate naturalists in similar instances; particularly as nature acknowledges no such distinction, inasmuch as the food, the manners, the habits, and we may add, the external characters of this animal, correspond with those of other species of the genus *Arvicola.*

suredly expect to please our opponents or their immediate friends; we can readily believe they would rejoice could the facts they contain be buried in oblivion. This would afford our "critic" especially, another opportunity for the accusation of plagiarism.

We have dwelt the longer on the principles involved in this dispute, believing that, if the precedent be established, it might prove fatal to the best interests of science. The description of the present species is drawn from one of three individuals presented to the Museum by Mr. Ord.—(Vid. Fauna Americana, p. 140.)

NOTE 2.—Since this work went to press, (the "Fauna,") we have received No. 11 of the Journal of the Academy of Natural Sciences, in time to follow up the eventful history of this animal.* In vol. 4, p. 345, of the work above quoted, there is an essay entitled "A New Genus of *Mammalia*, &c. proposed by T. Say, and G. Ord; read March 8, 1825." The name of the proposed genus is "*Neotoma.*" There appears to have been some mistake relative to the date, wherein it is stated that the new genus "*Neotoma*" was proposed; at any rate, it is very certain that on the evening of the 8th of March, the identical animal on which this new genus is founded, was described by those gentlemen as an "*Arvicola*," and this after an attentive examination of the teeth. It was not until this description of the "*Arvicola floridanus*" had passed through the press, that it was recalled by the authors, and the new name substituted. In order to avoid confusion, it will be necessary for naturalists to remember that the animal under notice, is at present described as pertaining to three or four distinct genera. The first notice of this animal, is an imperfect

The notes in question were read by many capable individuals, some of them friends of the parties concerned : all considered them just, and authorized by the nature of the case.

description by Mr. Ord, in the Bull. de la Soc. Philom. 1818, who named it " *Mus floridanus*," (its identity with the genus *Mus*, was doubted from the first, by the French naturalists.)

A more complete description occurs in Maj. Long's exped. to the Rocky Mountains, vol. 1, p. 54, 1819—20, where Mr. Say has adopted in an unqualified manner the name given by Mr. Ord. Thus it remained until the attention of these gentlemen was particularly directed to the dentition of this animal, by the observations of M Desmarest, in his " *Mammalogie.*" They now described the animal as an *Arvicola*, (to which, in reality, it belongs.) Finally, observing that the molar teeth of the animal were furnished with " *roots*," they have constructed the new genus " *Neotoma.*" (The *division* is sufficiently *novel*, it must be confessed, and if adopted, would destroy the whole fabric of classification.)

F. Cuvier has not mentioned the *roots* of the molar teeth of those species from which he has drawn the characters of the genus *Arvicola ;* a circumstance so apt to vary even in the teeth of the same animal, this able naturalist considered as beneath his notice in a work which has for its object *a description of the teeth considered as zoological characters.* (" Dents des mam mifères considerées comme charactères zoologiques.") Notwithstanding this, Messrs. Say and Ord, consider the "roots" of the teeth as of sufficient importance to establish generic distinctions. In the present instance, at least, they admit, that in the softness of the fur, and in the tail being clothed with hair, the " *Neotoma*" resembles the *Arvicola ;* to which I would add, that in all other external characters, this species resem-

" That the ' author' [of the Fauna] is competently acquainted
with natural history, the reviewer [in the North American] admits from the evidence before him. This no naturalist can
possibly conclude from the *book*, though we know it to be so,
in fact."

We must decline accepting this compliment, for
two reasons, viz : in the first place, we know him to
be no judge of an authors merit ;—and secondly, we
fear we shall never be able to return the compliment.
But we claim the particular attention of our readers to
the extract which immediately follows, in which the
" *technical critic,*" has displayed his arrogance and
ignorance in bold colours.

" The *book* displays extraordinary ignorance of the first
principles of the science ; as in the formation of *species* from
variations of dental formulæ ; when if any thing were done, it
should have been to form a new genus or sub-genus."

We would not, certainly, offer a serious refutation
of this absurd error in which the " critic" has involved himself, were it not that his remarks are published
expressly for the purpose of being read by persons

bles the *Arvicola*, as closely as the different species of that
genus resemble each other.

The description which Messrs. Say and Ord have given of
the *teeth* of the " *Neotoma*," (always excepting the roots,) so
exactly corresponds with M. Cuvier's description of the teeth
of the genus Arvicola, that we are tempted to believe the former to be a literal translation. (Vid. Dents des mammifères.
&c. F. Cuvier; first division, page 155.)—Vid. Fauna, p. 143

as unacquainted as himself with the subject he has attempted to review. He does not appear to be aware
that distinctions of species *founded on variations in
the structure of the teeth,** are a common occurrence,
and to be met with in all modern authors ; though we
are far from being of opinion that a difference of
structure in teeth *alone,* unless strongly marked, any
more than any other character taken *singly,* should
be considered, in all instances, as sufficient to establish
a distinction of species. Nevertheless, this difference in the structure of the teeth, in a great number

---

* If the "critic's" remarks concerning dental formulæ, have any meaning
whatever, they must refer to the *structure* of teeth, and not to number and
arrangement; inasmuch as we have, in no instance, formed our species
from variations in dental formulæ. In the case of the " *Scalops Pensylvani-
ca,*" we have detailed the dental formula, in order to prove that the new
animal did actually belong to the *genus* Scalops, and we have minutely described the structure of the teeth, to prove that it did *not* belong to any
species of that genus previously described. In the present instance, this
particular mode of proceeding was rendered necessary, by the fact that
Desmarest and Cuvier have described *differently* the dental formula of the
Scalops. " This a technical critic ought to have known," especially with
the following note before his eyes ; (which is appended to the description
of the animal referred to.) " This species corresponds in the number and
arrangement of its teeth, with the *genus* Scalops of F. Cuvier, but the
structure of the molars, is different from this genus, as described both by
Desmarest and Cuvier."—(Vid. Fauna Americana, p. 34.) The same remarks will apply " a fortiori" to the "Condylura Macroura," four different
dental formulæ having been attributed to this genus. Where no such
difficulties existed, we have not given the *dental formula,* in our descriptions of new species. Mr. T. Say, has occasionally given the variations of
dental formula, in his descriptions of new species, where no such confusion as above, existed.—See his description of the " Sorex Brevicaudus,"
Long's Exped. vol. 1, p. 164. We would not by any means, on this account, accuse Mr. Say of displaying " extraordinary ignorance of the first
principles of the science."

of instances, does constitute the *principal* character of *specific* distinction.

In reconstructing lost animals, and in classifying fossil quadrupeds, we are frequently possessed of no other characters.

The systematic work of Baron Cuvier, (an author who appears to be a great favourite of the "critic," to judge from the great familiarity with which he quotes him, and who can not assuredly be accused of "extraordinary ignorance of the first principles of the science,") has furnished us with numerous examples of cases in point.* We observe here, (as will always be found to be the case,) that a peculiarity of internal organization is accompanied with a corresponding modification of the exterior; by referring back to the "notes" it will be seen that Mr. Say has founded a *generic* distinction on an unimportant variation of the teeth alone, without referring to any external difference.† This we have stated is sometimes necessary in the classification of *fossil* quadrupeds. From the

---

* We quote an example for the benefit of general readers : it is Cuvier's distinctive and *specific* characters of the Indian and African Elephants.

"*Elephas Indicus.—Cuv.*

"Head oblong, forehead concave, with the *crowns of the jaw-teeth presenting transverse, waving ribbands, which are the layers of bone composing the teeth worn by trituration.*"

"*Elephas Africanus.—Cuv.*

"Head round, forehead convex, *jaw-teeth presenting lozenges on their crowns.*—(Vid. Régne Animal, vol. 1, p. 229.)

† There are some peculiarities of dental structure and form, which denote *generic* distinctions, whilst other variations *of less note*, are considered as *specific* characters.

specific characters afforded principally by the teeth. M. Cuvier succeeded in establishing, of the fossil genus Mastodon, (Mammoth,) six species; of the Rhinoceros, four species ; of the Anoplotherium, five species ; of the Palæotherium, twelve species ; of the Tapir, two species; there are numerous other instances, in the work of Cuvier above quoted, and more particularly in his great work on fossil animals. We trust it is now fully ascertained who it is, that " displays extraordinary ignorance of the first principles of the science." A " *technical critic,* ought to have known better !"

We come at length to his notice of an " *original error,*" though, as he himself informs us, we are not indebted to *him* for the discovery.

" A technical critic, would not have passed over so slightly, the formation of a new genus of *extinct* quadrupeds, from a *recent* skull, found on the banks of the Delaware, not a 'mutilated' one, as the reviewer supposes," &c.

We regret to see that the " technical reviewer" cannot make a single statement of even the most simple facts, without misrepresentation.

The animal to which we supposed this skull to have belonged was never affirmed to be *extinct,* and we clearly stated in the Fauna, that " this skull is not in the least degree fossilized."—(Vid. p. 130.)

He positively states that the skull is *not* mutilated. When we first examined it, the os incisivum, the greater portion of the ossa nasi, together with part of the occiput, were *entirely destroyed.* The specimen may be seen among the collection of Comparative Anatomy in Peale's Museum. As regards the commission of an error in describing as new, an animal previously known, we have never attempted to conceal it, and are free to confess having been anticipated in one genus out of the seven which we have constructed in the space of two years.* In justice to ourselves, we may be permitted to state, that we frequently examined that skull with the assistance of Mr. Say, who always declared his ignorance to what animal it belonged : it was too great confidence in his knowledge of such matters that led to the commission of that error, which never was calculated to do harm, and proves only too great haste in the author.

In his concluding paragraph, the " critic" asserts,

" His book [the Fauna] has fallen ' dead born' from the press ; and until eventually engulphed in that oblivion, to which its peculiar character is rapidly hurrying it, will serve as a beacon to future adventurers on the same perilous seas. "

* From February, 1823, to the present time, the author of the " Fauna" has *established* 37 new species of vertebral animals, and 6 new genera. The descriptions of the specimens were originally published in the Philadelphia Journal of the Academy of Natural Sciences, in the Annals of the New York Lyceum of Natural History, and in Silliman's American Journal of Science and Arts. Most of these papers have been republished, or honourably noticed, in the French and British Scientific Journals. Did we feel, in the least degree, shocked at the notice of the "critic," of our " original error," we might refer to an original error, of a nature more glaring, which recently occurred to one of his favourite authors,—in describing a bird as new which had been previously named, described, and correctly figured in " Vieillot," a standard work, to be had in most of the libraries.

It has been well said, that the praise of the *envious*, is far less creditable than their *censure;* they praise only that which they can surpass, but that which surpasses them, they censure. That the "critic" *wishes* the book " dead born," there is no room to doubt; but, that he seriously believes it to be so, is by no means so certain: it is not usual to display so much earnestness and parade, in hurrying the *dead born* to oblivion.

He is the more unfortunate in his predictions, as the Fauna is now preparing for a second edition, which is to include the descriptions of all the *Reptilia* known to inhabit the United States. In order to display his presumption, and render his opinion of the Fauna ridiculous, we have it in our power, (were we disposed to make a parade of science,) to oppose to that opinion, the sentiments of many eminent men, both at home and abroad. From among these documents, we select an extract of one of the letters, with which we have been honoured by the Baron Cuvier, (dated two months after the receipt of the Fauna.)

Paris, 24th October, 1825.

" Veuillez recevoir aussi tous mes remercimens pour l'exemplaire de cet ouvrage interessant que vous avez eu le bonté de m'addresser; il me sera tres utile dans mes travaux ulterieur,

Agrées, Monsieur, l'assurance de ma considération distinguée."

(Signed B. G. CUVIER.

So much for the acumen of the "*technical re-viewer.*" We have noticed separately each paragraph in which there appears any reference to ourselves. Considering that the whole of his criticisms occupy only two pages of the Franklin Journal, they must be acknowledged to be unusually pregnant.

We would now request permission to change provinces, and in our turn claim the privilege of making a few remarks on the papers published by Dr. G. in natural history. How far they may prove the successful prosecution of his studies, and to what extent they add to his own reputation and the dignity of science, will soon appear. In the mean time we may observe, that Dr. G. has *assumed* the highest station among the most successful votaries of science, that of a critical reviewer; he styles himself "Professor of Natural History;" and has announced himself as the author of a "forth-coming work on American Natural History." An individual who thrusts himself before the public with such high titles, should be enabled to present, at least, some proof of his capacity as a naturalist. His great "*book,*" so long promised to the public, will teem (as a matter of course) with abundant original and interesting observations, as well as contain the descriptions of many unknown animals:—the field he has chosen for the display of his powers, is of immense extent, and presents an endless variety—including nothing less (as relates to North America) than all the beasts of the earth, birds of the air, and fish of the waters! *When* this treat will appear, time only can determine. We regret its delay, and in the mean while are compelled to notice such of his essays as are actually before the public. Unfortunately for the parent, his immature productions were not "dead born" from the press; but will descend to posterity, like flies in amber, preserved by the medium which surrounds them. They are in reality far beneath the dignity of criticism, and never would have been dragged from neglect and oblivion, but for the arrogance and effrontery of their author. We would wish to avoid falling into one of Dr. G.'s greatest errors, that of making unqualified assertions ; " Felix quem faciunt aliena pericula cautum ;" and we shall endeavour to profit by his complete failure in scientific criticism, which should *"serve as a beacon to future adventurers on the same perilous seas!"*

The attempts of Dr. G. in the way of Natural History, to which we have referred, consist 1st. in his observations published in the "Philadelphia Museum, or Register of Natural History and the Arts," a new periodical work, No. 1, Jan. 1824, edited by J. D. Godman, M. D. 2d. in a description of the Os hyoides of "the mastodon," (mammoth,) published in the 4th vol. of the Philadelphia Journal of the Academy of Natural Sciences, p. 67, June, 1824. 3d. In an essay, entitled, " Note on the genus Condylura of Illiger ; by J. D. Godman, M. D. July, 1825."*

Concerning the first, or " Philadelphia Museum,"

our notice must necessarily be very brief, as the number contains nothing but extracts from other authors; with the exception, if we rightly remember, of one *original* paper by Mr. Rembrandt Peale, entitled, "Interesting facts relative to the Opossum." Though this paper was not written by the editor, he becomes personally responsible for its errors, in believing in it, and publishing the same without comment. We quote that part of the paper, only, which immediately concerns us.

"In the year 1815, while proprietor of the Baltimore museum, I received an Opossum having nine young ones, larger than mice, which were carefully kept until the young ones grew to be as large as rats, and no longer sought refuge in the maternal pouch. Being desirous of preserving the animal with some of the young ones peeping out of the pouch, they were immediately killed; in skinning the old one, we discovered that *the whole of the pouch and teats* were separated from the animal, and in a day or two would have dropped off, leaving the female opossum as they are often observed, without a vestige of the pouch or false belly. From these facts we are unavoidably led to conclude, that the young do not, of themselves, at first enter the pouch, nor are they introduced subsequent to birth by the parent; but they grow with the growth of the pouch, which is at last capable of containing nine or ten young ones, as large as rats, and that the pouch is formed, and thrown off, with every litter of young.

REMBRANDT PEALE."

The whole of the article, of which the above is an extract, appeared in one of the public newspapers of the day. Among other remarks of the newspaper editor, we noticed the following :—

" We presume the work to be entirely under the control and management of the Messrs. Peale's and the *Professors*."

Which remarks occasioned the following " communication."

" *Feb. 4th,* 1824.

" Messrs. Editors—In your paper of yesterday you were pleased to take honourable notice of a new periodical work, entitled Philadelphia Museum, or Register of Natural History and the Arts. Allow me, sir, through the same medium, to correct an important error you have stated. ' We presume the work to be entirely under the management and control of the Messrs. Peale's and the *professors*.' So far from this being the fact the professors [of the Natural History departments] have not even been consulted on the subject ; and while we are compelled to acknowledge the present number to be beyond the grasp of *scientific criticism,* nevertheless, we can assert without fear of contradiction, that the remarks on the *opossum,* are such as any one, the least informed in Natural History, ought to be ashamed of ; the more especially as correct information is within the reach of every one. Consult *Home's* Comparative Anatomy, (on the generation of the Kangaroo,) Cuvier, Leçons d'Anat. Comp. Dict. d' Hist. Nat. Blainville, Blumenbach, Fife, Lawrence, with a host of European writers ; also, a pamphlet on the subject, by the late Dr. B. S. Barton. We wish the present editor success as long as he can fulfil his duty with impartiality, and not be the means of promulgating error. "

Those who are acquainted with the laws of the animal economy which preside over organic structure, can alone estimate the enormous grossness of the several errors contained in the above extract from the *" interesting facts relative to the opossum."* The first number of the " Philadelphia Museum" proved a " quantum sufficit;" accordingly a second number never appeared. In Dr. G.'s literary bill of mortality, we presume, this production is set down as *" dead born from the press!"*

The next attempt, in order, is the description of a bone taken from among other osteological remnants in the Philadelphia Museum. This specimen, he was assured, belonged to the mastodon. Without hesitating to inquire into the certainty of the fact, without comparing the remnant with the same part in those animals most nearly allied to the mammoth, he immediately proceeded to the description of an isolated specimen, without any reference to its distinctive characters. With these facts before us, we can not be surprised that, in his description, he should completely reverse the order of nature—turn the bone up-side down, and the hind part before, &c. &c. Some notion may be formed of the confusion that must necessarily arise from an occurrence of this nature, by supposing an individual, ignorant of anatomy, attempting the description of an isolated part of the skeleton—of the os humeri, for example ; reversing the bone and attaching its condyles to the scapula! &c.

Dr. G.'s description occupies six pages of the Journal of the Academy of Natural Sciences, and includes

more than thirty errors! when all useful information, connected with the specimen, might have been
stated in one sentence : viz.

*The os hyoide of the mastodon, in all essential
particulars, resembles that of the Elephant.* *

In fine, if the specimen he has described be really
the os hyoide of the mastodon, we are not indebted
to his *elucidations* for the fact.

We had no sooner read his paper, and detected its
errors, than we took the earliest opportunity of in-
forming their author of the fact; and hinted to him
the necessity of an immediate correction of them by
his own hand, offering him our assistance, which he
thankfully accepted; pleading, at the same time, in
extenuation of his errors, his entire ignorance of the
subject which he had attempted to elucidate, promis-
ing in future, that this should prove a caution to him
not to meddle with subjects he did not understand.†

* Dans tous les autres *mammifères,* l'os hyoide présente á peu prés les
mêmes rapports ; seulement il faut observer, pour l' intelligence des descriptions que nous en allons donner, que sa position absolute change
avec celle de l' animal, et que tout ce que est antérieur chez l' homme
devient inferieur dans les mammiféres; et ainsi de suite."—(Cuvier Leçons
d' Anatomie Comp. v. 3, p. 227.)

"Dans l' *Elephant,* le corps est soudé avec les cornes postérieures ; il á
la forme d' une lame applatie, un peu arquée de bas en haut. Ces der-
niéres forment deux branches également applaties, qui remontent obli-
quement en arrière et se recourbent légérement en dedans. L' os styloide
et bifurqué : la branche postérieure est arquée, longue et terminée en
pointe ; l' antérieure, moins longue et droite, s' articule avec les cornes
antérieures."—(Cuv. ut supra, p. 234.)

† He never dreamed at this time, that he should be called in a few
months to teach Natural History. It was a very short period previous to
the appointment here alluded to, that Dr. G. publicly declared, at a meeting of the Academy of Natural Sciences, that he *knew nothing about Natu-*

We regret he has so soon forgot the lesson. We possess a copy of this essay corrected with his own pencil-marks, and offer a few extracts without further comment. The corrections are placed in brackets.

" The specimen from which this description is made, con sists of the whole of the basis, with the *appendix* [styloid bone] and *cornu* of the left [right] side. The appendix [styloid bone] and cornu of the left [right] side, were either not found originally, or have been lost, &c. The basis or anterior [inferior] portion is thick. At the upper [anterior] and anterior [superior] part, the rough bone rises in the centre. The thickness increases until within half an inch of the lower [posterior] edge: when the basis is placed fairly on a plane, it rests on one oblique flattened inferior [superior] surface, and we may form some idea of the obliquity of the direction of the whole os hyoides, supposing the appendix [styloid bone] and cornu to be properly attached. The articulating surfaces are rough, both are obliquely curved inwards towards the upper [anterior] edge of the bone."

He next describes a separate portion of the bone, which he has mistaken for the " *appendix*"* of the hyoide, which is in fact the *styloid bone,* and instead of articulating the anterior extremity of this to the styloid *process* of the temporal bone, he has transferred it to the *posterior* and *superior* end of the cornu, which *nature* intended for articulation with the cornu of the *thyroid* cartilage !—producing a confusion in

ral History. We believe the specimens he has since afforded us, will bear him out in this confession, and offer miserable prospects of his progressive improvement.

* The *appendix* in man, is called *anterior cornu* in brutes, and was lost in the present instance.

his description which we are sure no one would attempt to trace, were we to attempt to unravel it. In the description of this simple styloid bone alone, we enumerate *twenty* errors, in his own pencil-marks. We believe it unnecessary to examine this essay further: its errors "are too many to be pointed out individually."

The third and last essay, entitled "Note on the Genus Condylura," &c. is particularly worthy of our notice; it affords us a specimen of his *originality*, and contains contradictions of some statements in the "Fauna." What was said by Blumenbach of a great work, is peculiarly applicable to the modest little essay now under consideration: viz. "The *new* things are not *true*, and the *true* things are not *new*." We took an early opportunity, at a large meeting of the members of the Academy of Natural Sciences to read an answer to the observations contained in this essay, but as criticisms are not admitted in the pages of the Journal of the Academy, this answer was not then intended for publication, and it will serve us on the present occasion. All the *original* matter, contained in Dr. G.'s essay, will befound comprised in the following extracts : viz.

1st. "The Condylura *cristata* is destitute of an auricle projecting above the *level of the skin*, but is, nevertheless, provided with an *extremely large external ear*."

In speaking of the situation of the meatus externus, he continues :

"It may very easily be missed by those who merely examine *stuffed skins, or specimens preserved in spirits*."

2d. "By comparing the *Condylura* with the *Scalops* we are led to several *interesting* observations. We have seen that the Condylura has a remarkable and large external ear, though it is destitute of a projecting auricle. The Scalops has neither auricle nor meatus externus opening on the side of the head, as the skin of the head extends over the cartilaginous tube, which is small and a simple funnel. The situation of the ear is to be discovered externally, only by a very small spot, not larger than the circumference of an ordinary pin-head."

3d. "That a difference in the *length* of the tail, observed in one species, is not a *specific* difference."

4th. "That the Talpa Europæa does not exist in North America."

Concerning these "original" absurdities, we would now remark, 1st. When naturalists or anatomists are informed of an animal possessing "an *extremely large external ear*," they would assuredly expect to find an "*auricle projecting above the level of the skin*." Cuvier when treating of the organ of hearing of the *Moles*, (in which family he includes the Condylura cristata,) says, "the sense of hearing is very delicate, and the tympanum very large, although the animal is *destitute of an external ear*." (Vid. Regne Animal, vol. I. p. 137.)

2d. When we observe the minute and apparent accuracy with which the author describes the anatomy of the organ of hearing in the *Scalops*, from which he draws so many *interesting* observations, we would naturally be led to suppose that he had dissected, or at least examined the organization of that part; on the contrary, it appears that he trusted to his imagination : otherwise we cannot account for his total misunderstanding of an organization so simple, and at the same time so similar to that of the Condylura.

The fact is, that when we understand the anatomy of the Talpa Europæa, which is sufficiently detailed in the *Dict. d'His. Nat.*, we are acquainted, in all essential particulars, with the anatomy of the organs of sense and motion in all this tribe of animals : indeed, when we consider the similarity of habits, more or less characteristic of the moles, and are aware of the laws which regulate organic structure, this analogy will be readily anticipated.

In our dissections of the Condylura and Scalops, we have observed nothing peculiarly *different*, in the anatomy of either the eye or the ear, and can assure the author of the existence of a slightly elevated, circular meatus externus in the Scalops; though, to use his own expression, " it may be very easily missed by those who merely examine stuffed skins, or specimens preserved in spirits."*

3d. A considerable difference in the length of the tail in any quadruped, we presume, presupposes a difference in the number of vertebræ; which, if a *constant,* is always to be considered a *specific* character.

---

* By reference to the minutes of the Academy of Natural Sciences, it will be found that we read a communication on the anatomy of the Scalops, six years ago.

4th. The only proof he offers of the non-existence of the *Talpa Europæa* in this country, is that he has been unable to find it; but it will be remembered, that we have the same evidence of the non-existence of the *meatus externus* of the Scalops.*

We thought it no more than just, that the author of the " *Note on the genus Condylura*" should have the benefit of these hints, which we hope he will turn to his profit in his " forthcoming work on American Natural History," and conclude by testifying our most perfect conviction, in his own language,

"That it is a great advantage towards true knowledge to disencumber ourselves of error."†

For the present, we take our leave of Dr. Godman as an *author*, and as an *individual* we have long ceased to regard him. Circumstances, which it would be improper here to detail, render it impossible for us to notice him in this light, and place him beyond the pale of *personal* responsibility. It is to the public, who are deceived, and not to the *deceiver* that we address ourselves. A true votary of science, a man of honourable principles, would not have introduced " *personal squabbles*" into a " *critical review.*"

---

* We have heard of a surgeon, who, having performed the operation of lithotomy, on the living subject, was unable to *find* the stone. The bladder contained a stone notwithstanding ; which was subsequently removed by more skilful hands.

† It may appear a matter of curiosity to some, how it happens, that essays so replete with errors and absurdities, occupy a place in a Journal so respectable as that of the Academy of Natural Sciences. This is to be attributed in part to favouritism, and in great measure to the small number of the individuals of that enlightened body who have devoted their attention to zoology and comparative anatomy.

Should any of our readers be inclined to think that we have dealt severely with the "critic" in the Franklin Journal, we conjure them to bear in mind the nature of the provocation we have received, in being dragged before the bar of public opinion, and maliciously and falsely charged with the highest crimes which could be imputed to an author—viz : literary theft ; ignorance of first principles ; quoting authors largely whose works we have never seen ; want of dignity in the mode of treating scientific subjects, &c.: to say nothing of the disgraceful language applied to the work itself. We appeal to all who have reputation to lose, to say what *they* would have done under similar circumstances—to have said less, or that with more suavity, would have been to display an indifference to reputation, and a contempt of public opinion, such as we hope never to entertain. To say more would be no difficult task, but we wished to confine our observations to facts, and to make no assertion unaccompanied with proof.

We shall now close these observations with a few remarks on the review of the " Fauna," contained in the 50th No. of the North American Review.

The author, whoever he may be, has laboured under strong prejudices, and has proved himself very ignorant of the subject he pretends to review. He has accordingly had good sense sufficient to leave the scientific matter of the work almost untouched, and has confined himself to unprofitable remarks and trivial animadversions on the *style* and *manner,* as well as the enumeration of typographical errors. In the language of a distant, and scientific friend (contained in a communication recently received,)

"The reviewer has attacked the shadow, not the substance; he has adverted to errors he could not discover, and questioned facts of which he had no knowledge ; he has shown himself *profoundly arrogant,* and will be tolerated only because his readers, in this country, are generally more ignorant than himself of the subject he has attempted to discuss. He has the vanity to suppose that he has vanquished a fortress, whereas he has only captured a few unarmed stragglers. He is not aware that, while he has been zealously playing with his *brazen* battery, his pieces have only *burnt priming.*"

In presenting to the public a *scientific work,* we most assuredly were not vain enough to suppose it would be free from error. This is an immunity not to be hoped for in the works of even *veteran* authors. While we are sensible that the manner, the style, and even the typographical execution, are by no means unimportant considerations, in a work of any description, yet is there something both trifling and ridiculous, in the disposition of a reviewer to dwell upon them, to the exclusion of more essential matter.

Though we are by no means prepared to plead guilty to all his charges of omission and commission, the reviewer has detected quite too many errors, both in manner and style. Some of them we could not have anticipated after the labour bestowed on the proof-sheets, the corrections of which, was to us, indeed, an employment to which we were altogether unaccustomed. In our next edition we shall certainly profit by the reviewer's correction of style and manner, though not of *matter*.

The reviewer sets out with the ungenerous insinuation, that neither additions, alterations, nor improvements, are to be discovered in the " Fauna." We say *ungenerous*, inasmuch as the reviewer must have been convinced to the contrary; *science* not being requisite to ascertain this fact. He must have known, that a considerable number of the species were new, and never previously described—that at least fifty species had never been acknowledged by even the most recent systematic writers. He could not have been ignorant that many known species were before imperfectly noticed, erroneously described, or merely indicated ; nor will he attempt to deny that in several instances, *species*, and in three or four cases *genera*, had been confounded.

These elucidations, corrections and additions, the reviewer would have noticed, as in honour bound to do, had he not been prejudiced, and determined to find us in the wrong at all hazards.

In a table we have given for the purpose of elucidat ing the distribution of the North American mammalia, the reviewer thinks he has discovered many errors :

while in fact the mistake lies in his mis-comprehension of the subject, and ignorance of zoology—at least, with the exception of one typographical transposition.

" It will be perceived," says the reviewer, "that, if this enumeration [his own table] is to be trusted, and great care has been taken to make it accurate, the author's table is wrong in five orders out of seven."

The enumeration of the reviewer affords sixty-two species for the order carnivora; whilst our table offers sixty as the whole number. By referring to the " Fauna" it will be perceived that two species—viz : " Felis fasciata," and " Felis aurea," are still " *sub judice.*" We considered them not sufficiently free of doubt to be included in our enumeration. The same remarks are applicable to the order glires.

With regard to the order cetacea, we have enumerated six species *more* than the reviewer. We certainly have *acknowledged* that number of species in the " Fauna," and though they are not all *described,* we believe that the full number exist on our coasts.

The reviewer has discussed at full length a hackneyed subject, for the purpose, we suppose, of displaying his learning ; in which he is peculiarly unfortunate. We doubt not a different inference will result from a candid perusal of his digression concerning a point which involves the question, whether or not the two great continents, (the eastern and western,) were originally inhabited by animals pecu-

liar to each :—a question, the solution of which, has
puzzled much abler heads than his. It is a problem
that can *never* be solved ; but that we do actually find
many species common to Asia and America, no *naturalist* of the present time will pretend to deny.

It is still more preposterous to assert that the animals *common* to both continents, have passed from
Asia to America ; in most instances, the reverse is
more probable. For example, in North America
there are ten species of fox, and four species of wolves;
only two of each are common to both countries. In
the instance of the fox, then, the chances are ten to
two that they passed from America to Asia. What
would be thought of a *naturalist*, did he maintain
such an absurdity, as is displayed in the following extract from the review?

" All the largest, the most clearly described, and the most
easily distinguished animals of the old world, are certainly peculiar to it ; and although there may be in the new, animals
closely resembling them, corresponding to them, and often
mistaken for them, yet they are almost always specifically,
and often generically distinct."

And again, a little further on:

" Of the celebrated ferocious animals of the feline race, we
have not one." (Vid. p. 127 of the Review.)

Had the reviewer trusted to his common sense, and
not listened to the foolish instigation of others, he
might have avoided the absurdity of rating the bear,

otter, fox, deer, sheep, &c. &c. as among those species which " are small, obscure, imperfectly observed, not easily recognized, and incapable of that precise description which may be given of the larger."

An eminent naturalist has remarked, that, though difference of country cannot be considered a proof of difference of structure, it must always be an indication of it ; and though it cannot demonstrate, should make us suspect it : and that the naturalist, without blindly following the route it points out, ought carefully to collect its indications.

In his remarks on the arrangements of the species in the "Fauna," the reviewer has pointed out an error at page 61 of the " Fauna," which we had not before noticed. We allude to the omission of the definition of tribe 2nd, " *Digitigrada*." An error somewhat similar occurs under the order Glires. All the other errors noticed and magnified by the reviewer, are comparativly, trivial in their nature, and due chiefly to oversight in the correction of proof-sheets.

Among the examples of looseness of style attributed to the " Fauna," the reviewer furnishes the following; a phrase which occurs in the description of the cranium of a fossil species of the genus Bos. (Vid. p. 278.)

" The *plane* of the occiput represents a *semicircle.*"

If this passage proves any thing, it is the imperfection of his own knowledge. We recommend him to examine the " plane of the occiput" in many graminivorous quadrupeds, when he may learn how nearly it can resemble a semicircle, &c.

The observations of the reviewer on *fossil animals* are extremely puerile, and beneath the dignity of the subject. He should have recollected that ridicule is not argument, and when applied to the pursuits of science, betrays littleness of mind. His *wit*, besides, is not original; as we have read observations similar to his own in the Edinburgh Review, applied to the researches of *Blainville* on fossil fish.

The science of oryctology has called forth the greatest efforts of genius, and has already resulted in the most splendid discoveries.

In place of misspending his time in fruitless anticipations "of imperfect and crude speculations upon fossil bones," he should have pointed out the errors in this department of the work before him, could any such be proved to exist.

The remainder of his observations on classification are above our comprehension. He appears very angry with the "*fascinating pronoun, nobis,*" and yet offers no substitute, though he can hardly be ignorant, that some word of the kind is indispensable to correct writing in Natural History.

In conclusion, the reviewer expresses "strong disapprobation at the *manner* in which are written two long notes in the 'Fauna.'" (pp. 140, 143.) This proves nothing but his prejudices in favour of our opponents. As to the *manner* in which they are written, we need only repeat, that we have made a plain statement of the facts as they occurred ; and to the *facts* we shall continue to adhere, the *disappro-bation* of reviewers notwithstanding.*

In taking our leave of the writer in the "North American," we must do him the justice to say, that, we do not accuse him of ignorance of his trade. On the contrary, he appears perfectly well versed in all the technical slang of the " Edinburgh" and " Quarter-ly." It is not in reviewing that he has failed, but in grasping at objects beyond his comprehension. We would advise him, seriously, to confine his future la-bours to the praise of such objects as Wordsworth's Works, School Geographies, and Spelling Books, &c. &c. especially when *published at Boston.*

* We intended to make a variety of other observations, on the blunders and absurdities of which the ▪ ▪ ▪wer has been guilty ; but in considera-tion that these were errors u. ▪▪▪ head, rather than of his heart, they are omitted on the present occasion. We believe that we possess the means, and may find the time, to repay his compliments " *in kind.*"

TO

DR. THOMAS P. JONES,

EDITOR OF THE FRANKLIN JOURNAL.

——— " Oftentimes, excusing of a fault,
Doth make the *fault* WORSE by TH'EXCUSE :
As patches set upon a little breach
Discredit more in hiding of the fault,
Than did the fault before it was so patched."
SHAKSPEARE : *King John.*

DEAR SIR,

As I understood before publishing my
" *Note on an article in the North American Re-*
view," in your first number, that your paper
was subscribed for by a very large number of
scientific and literary individuals, and was, moreover, intended to be a SCIENTIFIC JOURNAL, it
has amused me to find that Dr. RICHARD W.
HARLAN, with peculiar modesty, has stated in a
pamphlet recently published, that your work is
not scientific, and, by consequence, your readers
not proper judges of scientific subjects. Yet,
notwithstanding this, he has taken great pains
to furnish your readers with his pamphlet, entitled " *Refutation of certain Misrepresentations*
issued against the Author of the ' *Fauna Ameri-*
cana,' " and would fain have this " Refutation"
received as a " plain and candid" as well as a
scientific production !

In your first number I published a note,
making known one of the most singular attempts

which has yet occurred in this country, to impose on the public *translated* for original matter. In consequence of that note, the author of the Fauna has appealed to the public, and, giving loose to the violence of his passion, has plunged still deeper in the offence of which he was accused, by a more deliberate and sustained attempt to deceive. His harsh speeches, abuse, and dark insinuations, are unworthy the notice of any upright man; more especially when proceeding from a person who stands in the predicament in which we shall now prove him to be placed.

That " truth is great and will prevail" is not more certain, than that he who writes under the influence of passion is more apt to injure than to benefit his cause. The matter in question, however, is not how much Dr. HARLAN can outstep the bounds of decorum, or the dignified deportment which is characteristic of justice and truth. It is with the public that he has a heavy account to settle, for delinquencies heretofore but little known in this country. If it were in his power to blacken the robes of the angels of light, it would not remove from his own vestments, one atom of their stain.

Before making a more full and formal statement of the extent to which the plagiarism of Dr. Harlan has been carried, I beg leave to premise, that I did *not*, as he would have it understood, publish my first statement of his conduct from motives of *personal* pique. That Dr. Harlan's anger was excited a long time ago, is most true; and this was in consequence of my discharging a duty, as one of a committee of the Academy of Natural Sciences, which placed the fairness of Dr. Harlan in a very ambiguous light, and inspired many others, besides myself, with deep disgust at his disingenuous conduct. But so far from hastening to do him an injury, although I had the facts now to be proved, then in my possession and was repeatedly urged to make them public, it was not done; because I was engaged in preparing a work on the same subject, and did not wish to be charged with the desire of injuring the reputation of any man:—a feeling which I never have experienced, and assuredly I could not be under its influence as regards one, who never did, nor can injure mine. To those who urged me to publish the facts, I uniformly replied, that so long as no notice was taken of the book in this country, I should remain silent; but, as soon as any one treated it as an *original* work, the facts should be stated, and the proofs adduced.

My first statement was made as an act of justice to the cause of science, and of duty to the public: the present letter is dictated by a similar feeling, and shall be directed towards the same end; without reference to any of the asperities of language or indecorous assertions which are so abundantly scattered by Dr. Harlan in his *" Refutation."* Nothing that is here said is directed to HIM. He stands charged with an unjustifiable, and, in this country, an unprecedented *plagiarism*, or the appropriation of the intellectual property of another to his own use. He has not only done this, but has come for-

6

ward to justify his conduct, and place himself under public protection as an ill-treated and injured man. Finally he criminates all within his reach, to show that he is not singular in his want of judgment, nor standing alone in disrespect for that sacred law of right, which considers the infringement of the literary property of another as dishonest.

The proofs of this statement are immediately to follow, and although it is a disagreeable office to act in such a case, yet, in this, as in all other instances where connivance at incorrect conduct is an injury to the character and wellbeing of society, the unpleasant duty should be unshrinkingly discharged. The individual is to me nothing; his success could not in the least interfere with mine; his degradation can in no possible way yield me satisfaction or service.

In the first page of his introduction, Dr. Harlan makes the following remarks :

" A work having for its object the illustration of the natural history of our country, cannot fail to prove interesting, and has long been a desideratum to naturalists. However unqualified for the task, I have nevertheless found *ample room* for *additions*, *alterations* and *improvements*. On the *utility* of the undertaking it will be unnecessary to insist, when, on referring to the latest authorities who have treated of this subject, we are struck with the *confusion*, the *errors* and the *deficiencies* which prevail. In the very latest work, Desmarest's Mammalogie, published in the year 1820, which professes to describe all the species of Mammalia, hitherto known, the number inhabiting North America is limited to one hundred *species*. Of these many are described as uncertain, and his *accounts* of the *manners* and *habits* of *most* of them, are at best *deficient*."—*Fauna Am.*

Would not every man infer from this, that Dr. Harlan had made improvements; that he would supply those deficiencies; and study from nature the habits and manners of the animals of his own country? Would any one suppose it possible, after such observations as the above, that Dr. Harlan would be content *to copy* from this same DESMAREST, those very habits and manners, just as they stand in the original—and that too without acknowledgment? Could you, Sir, have imagined such a thing? Yet, *you have seen it;* and *all* may see it who will refer to the work of DESMAREST.

In my note on the article in the North American Review, (which was intended to show cause why the " Fauna Americana" should *not* have been reviewed as an *original* work—not to review it,) I gave Dr. Harlan full credit for ALL he *acknowledged,* after stating the probable amount of his plagiarism. In his " Refutation," after declaring the charge to be " false," " gratuitous," " a *wilful* misrepresentation," &c. he says: *Ref.* page 8.

" In the above extract, he offers an UNWARRANTABLE contradiction to the PLAIN and CANDID statement we have made in our introduction to the " Fauna " (vid. p. 4, note) to the following effect:

" Mr. Desmarest, in his advertisement to the second part of his " Mammalogie," p. 7, *limits* the number of mammalia inhabiting North America to *fifty-four* species : as this statement does not *in any degree correspond* with his descriptions, we presume he has *permitted a typographical error* OF GREAT IMPORTANCE, to escape his notice. We have *enumerated* from his work one hundred species, as inhabiting North America; the *descriptions* of *about fifty* of these having been found very accurate, are accordingly translated with very little alteration. "

The " *candid* statement," in the note above quoted from the preface, is entirely opposite to fact, besides being injuriously incorrect relative to Mr. Desmarest. The following are the words of the original :

" Relativement á leur distribution sur le Globe, les mamiféres peuvent être ainsi partagés : 54 dans l'Amerique Septentrionale : 10 *communs aux deux continens de l'Asie et de lAmerique* : 41 propres à l'Asie septentrionale : 88 á l'Europe ; 107 á l'Afrique, 29 á l'île de Madagascar, et á celle de Mascareigne : 78 á l'Afrique Meridionale et à Ceylan : 51 aux îles de l'Archipel Indien : 33 á la Nouvelle Hollande et la Terre de Van Diemen. *Trente Cétacés, ou Phoques habitent les mers du Nord,* 14 celles du Sud, et á peu prés 28 se trouvent dans les latitudes moyennes. "

(Mammalogie, partie 2*de. Avertissement, p* .vii.)

His reason for leaving out the parts of the paragraph italicised, will be obvious enough to the members of the Philosophical Society, who recollect what occurred on this subject between another member and Dr. Harlan He had a particular interest at the time of publishing his book to lessen the number given by the French author. In this paragraph, (inserted entire,) Desmarest has most explicitly and fairly stated, that North America has FIFTY FOUR species, peculiarly her own, and TEN others America; besides which, there are THIRTY cetaceous animals and seals found in the northwhich are found in Asia, as well as in North ern seas, of which Dr. Harlan has *translated* from Desmarest, TWENTY Cetacea, SIX Seals, and ONE Morse, making the whole amount of American species NINETY ONE !! as given in the above quoted sentence, by the maltreated French naturalist. Yet with this before his eyes, he had at first, the hardihood, not only to misrepresent Desmarest, but even to charge him

with allowing " a _typographical error of great
importance_ to escape his notice," and to repeat
this charge in his recent pamphlet as a plain
and candid statement!! This is the author of
the " Fauna Americana." who talks of being
" calumniated," and of " _wilful_ misrepresentations." and "_false_" and "_gratuitous assertions_"!

In his " Refutation," page 8, immediately after
the note quoted from the preface to the " Fauna,"
Dr. Harlan has the following unparalleled attack upon common decency and common sense:

" Having thus given credit to Desmarest for FIFTY SPE-
CIES, WE HONESTLY THOUGHT that we had attributed to him MORE than was justly his due"!!

This could scarcely have been anticipated,
even from DR. HARLAN, if no more than fifty
species had been copied; look at the logic of
it, supposing but fifty had been borrowed:—a
man borrows fifty dollars from another—he acknowledges it by note of hand,—he pays back
fifty; no more; and then " _honestly_" thinks he
has " attributed to him MORE than was justly his
due"!!—As a naturalist, this author is exceedingly fond of establishing and naming _new species;_ here is a _new species_ of HONESTY doubly
his, by right of discovery and by being exem-
plified in himself: one too, for the honour of
which no one will be likely to contend with
him. We would, therefore, suggest the propriety of calling it " HONESTAS HARLANICA,"
and let its " _essential characters_" be found in the
above " _acknowledgment._"

But, Mr. Editor, can you inform us, by what
magic the _characters of the orders;_ of the

B

families; tribes, and *genera*, to say nothing of
the *essential characters*, (which Dr. Harlan always translates " *characters essential*,") *synonomy* and *habitudes* of the animals, verbally and
servilely translated from Desmarest, are to be
brought within this acknowledgment of " fifty
species"? Can you show me in what way the
acknowledgment of " the descriptions of fifty
species" can be made to signify the greater part of
the whole volume entitled " Fauna Americana"?
For my own part, I am utterly at a loss to see
how it can be so significant, unless it be possible that a receipt for " fifty" could be considered a receipt for five thousand pounds.

" If copying from any author *the descriptions* of such species as have been well known, and accurately described
since the days of Linnæus, can be construed into plagiarism,
then *all* modern naturalists are plagiarists. " *Ref.* page 9.

Is this statement true?—if it be true, will any
man pretend that the great naturalists succeeding Linnæus, have *copied* Linnæus, in the sense
which Dr. Harlan *has copied* Desmarest? The
books themselves may answer. Has Illiger thus
copied Linnæus?— as Cuvier copied Illiger?—
Has Desmarest copied Cuvier? No. If they have
copied " species" they have not *transcribed* ALL
the characters of the *orders, families, tribes*,
and *genera*. word for word, letter by letter. It
was left for " RICHARD W. HARLAN, M. D." to
do this, and then to attempt to sustain himself on
that poor bundle of. reeds, the acknowledgment
of the " descriptions of about fifty species"!!

But not content with this utterly untenable
position, and as if struck by a sort of " judicial

11

blindness,' he utters the following words after the quotation last given: page 10.

" If such a construction be admissible, what must necessarily be the fate of that beautiful volume recently published by Mr. C. Bonaparte, (" American Ornithology,") which contains the description of but one single species of bird not previously *known, named* and *described.* Yet, our "technical critic" does not hesitate, on all occasions " to elevate to the rank of an *original* work," this production of his patron. "

Does he not imply by this, that Mr. Charles Bonaparte has *copied* those species of Birds which were " previously *known, named,* and *described*"? Is it not evident that such an inference is what he *wishes* to be drawn, and thus to insinuate that *he* has done no more? What is the fact? *The descriptions* in CHARLES BO-NAPARTE's truly splendid and valuable " American Ornithology," of previously known species, are more entirely *original* than any which have ever yet been published, with the exception of those by WILSON ; and they are *as original* as his. There is not a description of a bird, in the book above named, that is not wholly and solely drawn up from observing the birds themselves without reference to any previous *descriptions,* except in cases where previous descriptions are quoted in comparing species together. So much for this additional attempt to wrong another man of the fruits of his intellect and industry.

" We confess that we never enumerated the precise number of *pages* occupied in the ' Fauna,' by the descriptions of the *fifty species* attributed to Desmarest, nor do we possess the means at present of obtaining accurate information on that subject, supposing it in the least important ; but as the whole number of *species* described in the ' Fauna,' amounts to rather more than one hundred and fifty, occupying three hundred and fourteen pages, by the fairest mathematical computation, *the fifty pecies attributed to Desmarest* cannot occupy more than one third, that is to say, *one hundred* pages, in place of *two hundred* and *fifty*, agreeably to the unqualified assertion of Dr. G." *Ref.* page 10.

By this limping and inadequate confession this "*Refuter*" still endeavours to throw dust into the eyes of those who read his defence, and again would centre the whole matter upon the "fifty species." He states he has no copy of Desmarest to refer to; ' fortunately, have one; and, moreover, it shall be at the service of all citizens of Philadelphia who read French, and feel interested to know the truth of this matter: it shall be accompanied by a marked copy of the "Fauna," referring to every passage in Desmarest copied without an *acknowledgment*.

The WHOLE of the matter contained under the following heads, (with the exception, in some cases, of "*Dental Formulæ*," copied from F. Cuvier,) is literally and servilely translated from Desmarest's "Mammalogie," and introduced into the "FAUNA AMERICANA" without the slightest acknowledgment, expressed or implied, either in the *Fauna* or in the pamphlet entitled "*Refutation*," &c. but is offered as ORIGINAL "By RICHARD W. HARLAN, M. D." &c. &c.

Fauna Americana.	Beginning	Ending	From *Desmarest.*	
ORDER Carnivora; and *Genus*				
Rhinopoma, -	p. 15	p. 17	p. 107	
Genus Vespertilio, (and Genus				
Taphozous, p. 22,) -	17	19	120	132
FAMILY Insectivora, -	24	25	149	
Genus Scalops -	30	32	155	
Condylura, -	34	36	157	
Talpa, - -	41	42	159	

13

Fauna Americana.	Beginning	Ending	From *Desmarest*.
FAM. Carnivora and *Genus* Ursus,	45	46	163
Genus Procyon, -	53	54	167
Taxus, -	56	57	172
Gulo, -	59	59	174
Mustela, -	61	61	176
Mephitis, -	68	69	184
Lutra, -	70	71	187
Canis, -	74	76	190
Felis, -	93	94	216
TRIBE, Carnivorous amphibia and genus Phoca,	102	105	237-38
Genus Trichecus, -	113	114	253
FAMILY Marsupialia,	116	116	254
Genus Didelphis, -	116	118	254-5
ORDER Glires, -	121	121	277
Genus Castor, -	122	122	277
Fiber, -	131	132	279
Arvicola, -	134	134	280
Lemmus, -	145	146	286-87
Mus, -	147	148	297-98
Gerbillus, -	155	155	319
Arctomys, -	157	158	326
Sciurus, -	172	173	330
Pteromys, -	186	187	341
Genus Hystrix, -	189	190	344
Lepus, -	192	193	346
ORDER, Edentata and Genus Megatherium, -	199	200	362-65
Pachydermata, FAMILY Proboscidea and *Genus* Elephas, -	203	207	381-82
Genus Mastodon, -	210	210	384*
2d FAMILY Pachydermata, &c.	217	218	389
GENUS " Pecari or Dicotyles,"	219	220	393
Tapirus, -	222	223	409
ORDER, Pecora and *Genus* Cervus, -	226	229	422-29-30
Genus Antilope, -	248	249	450-51
Capra, -	252	253	480
Ovis, -	258	259	486
Ovibos, -	264	264	492
Bos, -	267	268	496

* Beginning at " molars rectangular."

Fauna Americana. ORDER, Ceta—FAM. Cetacea	Beginning	Ending	From *Desmarest.*
herbivora. *Genus* Manatus,	274	277	506-7
Genus R\tina, - -	278	279	510
FAMILY, Ceta; *Genus Delphi-* *nus*, *Subgenus* Delphynor- hynchus, - -	281	283	511-12
Genus Monodon, -	289	290	522
Cachalot, -	292	293	524
Balæna, -	295	296	526-27

The following *" fifty species,"* taken from
Desmarest, occur in the *Fauna Americana* between the 1st and 149th pages. These may be
considered as the species which are acknowledged to have been copied :

1. Rhinopoma Carolinien-
sis.
2. Vespertilio Caroliniensis.
3. Sorex constrictus.
4. S. Araneus.
5. Scalops Canadensis.
6 Condylura Cristata.
7. C. Longicaudata.
8. Talpa Europea.
9. Ursus Arctos.
10. U. Americanus.
11. U. Maritimus.
12. Procyon Lotor.
13. Gulo Arcticus.
14. M. Vison.
15. M. Martes.
16. M. Canadensis.
17. Lutra Brasiliensis.
18. L. Marina.
19. Canis Lupus.
20. C. Lycaon.
21. C. Vulpes.
22. C. Argentatus.
23. C. Decussatus.
24. C. Virginianus.

25. C. Fulvus.
26. C. Cinereo-argentatus.
27. C. Lagopus.
28. Felis Concolor.
29. F. Onca.
30. F. Pardalis.
31. F. Canadensis.
32. F. Rufa.
33. F. Fasciata.
34. F. Montana.
35. F. Aurea.
36. Phoca Cristata.
37. P. Vitulina.
38. P. Groenlandica.
39. P. Fetida.
40. P. Barbata.
41. Otaria Ursina.
42. Trichecus Rosmarus.
43. Didelphis Virginiana.
44. Castor fiber.
45. Fiber Zibethicus.
46. Arvicola amphibius.
47. Lemmus Hudsonius.
48. Mus Rattus.
49. Mus Sylvaticus.
50. Arctomys Monax.

The following FORTY FOUR SPECIES, occurring between the 150th and 301st page of the *Fauna Americana*, are taken verbally from Desmarest (with the exceptions specified) without any acknowledgment :

1. Arctomys Empetra.
2. Sciurus Cinereus.
3. S. Capistratus.
4. S. Niger.*
5. S. Hudsonius.
6. P. Striatus.
7. S. Hudsonius.
8. Pteromys Volucella.
9. Hystrix dorsata.†
10. Lepus Americanus.
11. Megatherium Cuvieri.
12. Megalonyx Jeffersonii.
13. Elephas Primogenius.‡
14. Mastodon Angustidens.
15. Sus Scrofa.§
16. Dicotyles Torquatus.‖
17. Cervus Alces.
18. C. Tarandus.
19. C. Canadensis ¶
20. C. Virginianus.**

* The concluding paragraph of the article on this squirrel, has the appearance of being intended for *original* matter, and consists of scientific discriminations. It is merely a verbal transfer of Desmarest's foot note (marked (1.) right side of page 334) to the text of the Fauna.

† Ending with the description.

‡ *Two paragraphs* of this article are *original;* beginning with the word " LOCALITY," page 208, and ending at " Rhinoceros," second line of page 209.

§ Ending at " beneath the eyes."

‖ *Three sentences* of the article on this species are *original,* beginning at " when attacked by the panther," &c. page 221, and ending with the article, page 222, fourth line from the top.

¶ Five paragraphs and two sentences of this article, making about *half a page* are *original;* (that is, not copied from Desmarest.) Beginning at " *cervus major*, Ord," &c.—down to " same species," page 236. The sentences are, " cast their horns, for the most part, in the month of March, the leanest Elk retain their horns the longest," and " a fine specimen," &c. at the end of the article.

** The only *original* sentence in this article, is the following, page 239, " Weight from 90 to 100 lbs." From the beginning of this article, page 238, to the middle of page 241, ending at " extensive range," is, without acknowledgment, verbally from Desmarest : the whole of the rest of the article, extending to two-thirds of page 243, is quoted from SAY, as acknowledged.

21. Antilope Americana.	33. Monodon Monoceros.
22. Ovis Ammon.*	34. M. Microcephalus.
23. Ovibos Moschatus.	35. M. Andersonianus.
24. Bos Americanus.	36. Physeter Microcephalus.
25. Stellerus Borealis.	37. P. Trumpo.
26. Delphinus Delphis.	38. Balæna Mysticetus.
27. D. Coronatus.	39. B. Glacialis.
28. D. Canadensis.	40. B. Nodosa.
29. D. Gladiator.	41. B. Gibbosa.
30. D. Grampus.	42. B. Gibbar.
31. D. Leucas.	43. B. Boops.
32. D. Anarnachus.	44. B. Rostrata.

The following species are acknowledged to
be copied from SAY; they are inserted to aid
the reader in estimating the full amount of Dr.
Harlan's *originality:*

1 Vespertilio Pruinosus.	9 Arctomys Lndoviciana.
2 V. Arquatus.	10 Sciurus Magnicaudatus.
3 Sorex Parvus.	11 S. Quadrivittatus.
4 S. Brevicaudus.	12 S. Lateralis.
5 Canis Latrans.	13 S. Grammurus.
6 C. Nubilus.	14 Cervus Virginianus.†
7 C. Velox.	15. C. Macrotis.
8 Pseudostoma Bursarius.	

The following are from SABINE:

1 Arctomys Franklinii.	3 Lepus Glacialis.‡
2 A. Richardsonii.	

The Arctomys Parryii, is from Richardson.

A few days after the publication in the first
number of the Franklin Journal, a friend convinced me that I was mistaken in relation to
" Bonnaterre's Cetologie," which is not a *distinct work,* but forms an article in the " *Encyclo-*

---

* The greater part of the synonomy, and the whole of
the " essential character."
 † Beginning from page 241; ending 245.
 ‡ Excepting the two last paragraphs which are from Desmarest, and *unacknowledged.*

pedie Methodique," and had been for some time
in this city. I was in error as to its *not* being
in Philadelphia. Nevertheless, it is true, that
although Dr. Harlan had the *opportunity* of
quoting *the original,* yet has he been content
to transcribe *Desmarest's* citations of *Bonnaterre,* as if he had never seen the work of the
latter.

But Dr. Harlan has had recourse to another
uncommon and disingenuous manœuvre in relation to Desmarest; which is, that of frequently
transfering Desmarest's scientific, critical, mar-
ginal, and foot notes, into the text of the
" *Fauna,*" as *original* matter, in such a manner
as to deceive any one who has not the French
book before him; and what is worse, even
those which relate to such authors as Catesby
and Bartram, and as to facts which have occurred in *this* state. For proof of this refer
to, and compare his " NOTE," page 172, with
Desmarest's " *nota,*" page 336; his observations, contained in the two last paragraphs of
the article " sciurus niger," and Desmarest's
foot-note, (1.) page 334; *his* facts relative
to the gray squirrel, pages 174-5, and *Desmarest's,* page 332: as well as various others,
which will be seen in the marked copy of the
" Fauna." After having made this comparison,
the reader, in admiration of the ingenuity displayed, will be tempted to exclaim, " Oh, shame!
where is thy blush?" How he is to bring this
ingenuity (" NEW SPECIES" ?) under his acknowledgment of the " descriptions of fifty species,"

C

he may settle with the public, by "*mathematical computation*"—if he can.

He talks much and loudly of the number of species he has *established;*—If to *assert* be to *establish*, he has *just as solidly* thus established. that the "Brown Bear," (*U. Arctos,*) the European Mole,* (*Talpa Europea,*) the *Rhinopoma Caroliniensis* of Geoff. the common Eu-

---

* The authority upon which this genus was introduced into North America, is not a little laughable. In the Museum, the European specimens have their numbers placed within a *red* square : these specimens having been frequently removed for the sake of cleaning, &c. a European Mole was inadvertently placed behind a label having no *red* mark. On this authority, together with the assertion of the Museum profile-cutter, who depended on the same infallible guide, this European Mole was introduced as a North American animal, and figures as such in the " Fauna." In his synonymy of the species, the author supports himself, by quoting " *Talpa Americana*, black mole, Bartram's manuscript notes, " which is not of the slightest avail, because the genus Scalops was not established when Bartram wrote ; granting, however, that it had been, there is no proof that the *Talpa Americana* above stated, is the European Mole.

This is not the only instance in which the local knowledge of Mr. Moses Williams has been of service to this *original* writer. An importation of a few living European Moles, would not be a bad mode of supporting the assertion that Talpa Europea is found native in North America. It is a new mode of *establishing* animals in any country, merely to *assert* their existence. Neither of the Messrs. PEALE, of the Philadelphia Museum, has ever found this animal in this country ; and certainly their ample experience and opportunities of so doing will not be denied. Who, amongst those that have devoted themselves to the research, can say, that he has ever seen the species called European Mole, inhabiting the soil of North America? It is no more an inhabitant of this country than the Kangorou, or the Cameleopard.

ropean Weazel *(Mustela Vulgaris,)* the Fetid shrew, *(sorex araneus,)* &c. are all inhabitants of North America. We are yet to learn which of his species will stand *"established;"* judging by the number of those which he has attempted to establish in other departments, and which have been overthrown, but little hope remains of *one* in twenty escaping the same fate.

It has now, I believe, been shown, that the Fauna Americana is *not* what it pretends to be. The numerous deviations of its Author from rectitude, having been distinctly and dispassionately pointed out, I take leave of the work with sincere regret that an American Naturalist should have acted in such a manner as to render the exposure of his conduct an indispensable though an unpleasant act of duty to the community at large. Before this letter is closed, a few words may be said on one or two topics, which, however, stand only in collateral relation to the principal object of this publication.

In a note to page 9, of his *Refutation,* Dr. Harlan has the following remarks:

"What renders the charges of the " critic " still more presumptuous, is the fact, that he himself stands publicly convicted of plagiarism ; for the proofs of which we need only refer to an able review by Dr. N. R. Smith, in the Philadel. Medical and Surgical Review, No. 2, vol. 2d, of a work entitled " Anatomical Investigations, by John D. Godman, M. D. " In this paper are examined certain claims set forth in the "Investigations " to a few of those raræ aves, Anatomical discoveries. See further proofs in the Medical Recorder, vol. 8, p. 825. It is not to be presumed that he will attempt to escape from this stigma, by pleading ignorance of Anatomical works so well known, and so justly esteemed as those of Bell and Bichat."

One thing only is wanting to make this note a " palpable hit." That one is truth : Dr. Smith *did* write a keen and flippant article in relation to my " Anatomical Investigations." The editor of the Medical Recorder *did* bring forward some sentences which he thought proved that my ideas were not original. Dr. Smith was uncandid and unjust, for in the preface to my " Anatomical Investigations," stands the following sentence, which he took no note of, but made his attack as if no such thing were there :

" Among the most interesting parts of these researches, is the demonstration of the *manner* in which the capsular ligaments of the great joints are formed. I am by no means anxious to claim great merit for *proving* the continuity of fasciæ, and the connexions thus produced between different parts—although Bichat contented himself with *asserting* that the fibrous membrane may be traced into the *periosteum*. But I do expect the thanks of Anatomists and physiologists for pointing out the *mode* in which the capsular ligaments are made up from the coverings of the muscles, and thus rendering their natural conditions more intelligible and opening the way to new views of their possible situations resulting from disease or accident. I am sure of receiving the grateful applause of every unprejudiced student for having in this part of the science substituted simplicity for complexity and regularity for confusion. "

Anat. Invest. Introd. p. xi.

Moreover, neither of these writers took the trouble to give a correct view of my observations, which (as explicitly stated in more than one part of my preface) were intended to show the *mode* or *manner* in which certain structures existed— not that the structures had never before been seen; to show the various points at which some textures were continuous, and not that their

continuity had never before been *asserted*. Br
CHAT made some general enunciations, that the
fibrous membranes were continuous, by running
into the periosteum or membrane surrounding
the bone. Bell stated in equally general terms,
that all the fibrous texture might be viewed as
one system. My researches showed, not only
the truth of these assertions in detail, but led
to many interesting views of fibrous membranes and peculiar modifications of continuity,
never pointed out by either of the above named
celebrated anatomists.* The truth of these conclusions I have repeatedly demonstrated before
some of the most respectable of the surgeons
and physicians of this city, and am ready at
any time to convince any gentleman by reference to the knife alone, and not to argument.

To conclude with Dr HARLAN; he has taken
pains to sneer at my " forthcoming work on
Natural History," and I am happy to state it is
much nearer being laid before the public than
he has any idea of, and when it is placed at
their disposal, I am perfectly sure that it will give
evidence of my "progressive improvement."
His own book he talks of reprinting, and asserts

---

* A year subsequent to the publication of my researches
Dr. Gerdy of Paris, published a paper containing almost
precisely the same views as I had offered in relation to the
muscular sheaths. Clarus of Holland, according to Meck-
el, has taken a view of the extension of the fascia superfi-
cialis, very similar to that given by me. Gerdy's observations were published as novel and interesting, in 1824, nor
does he any where think it necessary to attribute the fruits
of his observations to Bichat, because the latter has said in
general terms, that the fibrous membranes are continuous.

that the first edition was not DEAD-BORN. No later than yesterday, (31st March,) the printer who owns the remainder of the first edition, and the bookseller whose shelves still groan under them, stated, that with the exception of those furnished to the subscribers, which barely defrayed the expense of printing, but TWO COPIES had been *sold*, *one* of which was purchased by myself. He may publish the second edition when he pleases; the *first* is restored to its rightful owner, and Dr. HARLAN has acquired a notoriety, which few men, except himself, in this community, could desire or deserve.*

He has brought forward some *errors* of mine in the Journal of the Academy of Natural Sciences, in a way which is also peculiarly illustrative of his character. His remarks relative to the structure of the ear of the scalops and condylura are, in an especial manner, worthy of attention. I spent as many weeks in the fields studying the habits and manners of these two animals as Dr. Harlan was employed in getting out his whole work, and as I was very anxious to learn as far as possible from living nature, in but one instance did I kill either of

---

* His introduction of Cuvier's mere acknowledgment of having received the copy of the Fauna presented to him, strongly reminds us of Sheridan's formula, which he employed in answer to the authors who teased him with presents of their works, in order to win from him a commendatory letter: it ran thus—

Dear Sir—I have received your very interesting [*book*, *essay*, *poem*, *farce*, or whatever it might be,] and shall, no doubt, be very much delighted with it—when I have read it. With the highest respect, &c. *R. B. Sheridan.*

the animals for dissection. My remarks on them were read to the Academy on the 8th of June, 1825, and on the 9th of August, 1825, having in the interim procured another specimen for dissection, and discovered my mistake, I read a note correcting it, to the Academy, and this note is published in the Academy's Journal.* Dr. Harlan was present, heard that correction read—even made some remarks about its not being necessary to refer it to a committee, as it was a correction of a paper already published. On *the Tuesday following*, Dr. Harlan had the *candour* to come forward and read *the correction now published* in his pamphlet, as if I had never corrected my own error!

What was his plea for so doing? He had *read a paper* on the scalops six years ago, before I was a member of the Academy. The paper itself, is not on the files of the Academy. *What* was in *that paper?* All rests on Dr. Harlan's own *assertion:* and who, after knowing the facts which are here stated, can receive any thing on *the assertion* of one capable of thus acting?

He may produce *his papers*, and make them show *what he pleases;* let any man of honour refer to the minutes of the Academy of Natural Sciences, and, finding the above statements confirmed, then put faith in Dr. Harlan *if he can.*

As to any errors into which I may have fallen while engaged in pursuing my studies, I have not the slightest objection to acknowledge, and

---

* Page 135, Vol. V. Part I.

am always sincerely desirous to correct them. That I am *infallible*, I never pretended : that I am *honest*, I feel well assured. For proof of this, let the consistency of my conduct speak; let those who have been concerned in business with me answer; let the voice of public approbation, which has, in the short space of *five* years, given to a young, unknown, and friendless stranger, a standing seldom conferred under similar circumstances, testify whether or not I have been an ardent and undeviating votary of truth, an industrious and faithful discharger of the trusts confided to me : or whether I have ever been known to shrink from any peril of life or health, when duty bade me jeopard either? I say not this boastingly, nor in the belief that my merits have been equal to the degree of public favour which I have enjoyed : I can truly say, that my supreme desire is to become more and more worthy of it, by the correction of my errors and the improvement of my mind.

Most respectfully,

I remain your friend, &c.

JOHN D. GODMAN.

Philadelphia, April, 10th, 1826.

P. S. I have deposited Desmarest's work, in company with a marked copy of the Fauna, in a situation where they may be fairly compared by the curious. For the benefit of those who have not an opportunity of examining the books, a specimen is subjoined.

SPECIMEN OF THE FAUNA

Contrasted with the work of A. G. Desmarest.

N. B. All the articles referred to in pages 12, 13, 14, 15 and 16 are as servilely and as inaccurately translated as the subjoined, which are all selected from the *unacknowledged* matter.

It has been industriously urged to the public that naturalists are in the habit of appropriating to themselves the property of others without acknowledgment. To disprove this entirely, refer to Desmarest's work, and it will be seen that he gives credit with scrupulous exactness, for all that he borrows.

SECONDE FAMILLE. INSECTIVORES, *insectivora.* *Car. Essent.* **Pieds** courts, armés d'ongles robustes ; ceux de derriére toujours á cinq doigts, ayant leur plante entiérement appuyèe sur le sol ; ceux de devant le plus ordinairement á cinq doigts. (Point de membranes pour voler.) Dents molaires ayant leur couronne hérissée de tubercules aigus ; Canines tantôt fort longues, tantôt fort courtes.

Incisives en nombre variable. Corps couvert de poils ou de piquans ; nourriture, des insectes, des racines tendres, des fruits.

Patrie, les contrées temperées des deux continens.

1*re Division.* Deux longues incisives en avant, suivies d'autres incisives et de petites canines, plus courtes que les mâcheliéres. p. 147

Family INSECTIVORA. *Char. Essen.* Feet short, armed with robust nails; hind feet always five-toed, resting *on the anterior part of the sole* ; fore feet most generally five-toed; crowns of the molar teeth elevated into sharp tubercles ; canine teeth sometimes very long, sometimes very short.

Number of incisors variable. Body covered with hair, or spines ; feeding on insects, roots, and fruits.

Inhabit the temperate climates of both continents.

1*st Division.* Two long incisors before, followed by others, and by small canines shorter than the molars. P. 24.

D

XLIIe *Genre.*
Sorex, Linn. Erxl. Schreb.
Cuv. Lacép. Illig.
Musaraneus, Brisson.

Incisives supérieures intermédiaires à double crochet, ayant un fort éperon situé á leur talon ; incisives inférieures alongées,sortant droites de l'alveole, et ne se recourbant qu'á l'extremité. Fausses canines, surtout les superieures, beaucoup plus petites que les incisives intermédiaires Molaires á couronne large hérissée de pointes, les supérieures étant les plus grandes et ayant leur tranchant oblique ; tête trés alongée ; nez prolongé et mobile; oreilles courtes, arrondies ; yeux petits, mais visibles.

Queue plus ou moins longue tantôt tetragone, tantôt comprimée dans une partie de sa longueur, quelquefois téretile. Corps couvert de poils fins et courts ; pieds á doigts foibles, séparés, munis d'ongles crochus non propres á fouir la terre; mammelles au nombre de six ou de huit, tant pectorales que ventrales; une glande sébacée sur chaque flanc, entourée des soies roides et serrées, laissant suinter une humeur grasse.

HABIT. En été se tiennent dans des trous ; en hiver pénétrent dans les grenier á foin ; vivent de vers et d'insectes ; ont une démarche lente ; répandent dans le temps du rut, une odeur as-

Genus.
Sorex,Linn. Erxleb.Schreb.
Cuv. Lacep. Illig.
Musaraneus, Brisson.

Superior intermediate incisors in form of a double hook, having a *short* spur situate at their base ; inferior incisors elongated, proceeding straight from the alveoles, and are recurved only at their extremity. False canine, particularly the superior, much smaller than the intermediate incisors. Molars with broad crowns, having sharp tubercles, the superior are largest and have the cutting surface oblique ; head very long ; nose elongated and moveable ; ears short and rounded ; eyes small but visible.

Tail more or less long, sometimes quadrangular, sometimes partly compressed, at others teretile. Body covered with fine short hair; feet terminated by feeble toes, separate, furnished with hooked nails, not proper for digging the earth ; mammæ, both pectoral and ventral, to the number of six or eight ; a sebaceous gland on each flank, surrounded by stiff and compact hairs, secreting an oily liquor.

HABIT. In summer, living in holes ; in winter, penetrating hay-mows ; feeding on worms and insects ; of slow progression ; during the rutting season they diffuse a strong odour ; [hence their

sez forte, &c.

Patrie les contrées tempérées et chaudes de l'ancien continen. P. 149.

Nota. Quelques individus ont du blanc au bout de la queue, au nez, sur les pattes et, comme celui de Catesby, copié dans l'Encyclopédie autour du cou.
(1) Cette espéce nous parait différer de la variété noire de l'écureil capistrate, par la taille plus petite, par la douceur du poil, et parce que le nez et les oreilles ne sont pas réguliérement blancs.— Elle s'éloigne de la variété noire de l'écureil gris par la brièveté de la queue. p. 334

HABIT. Les élans vivent en petites troupes dans les forêts marécageuses. Ils ont des allures beaucoup moins lègéres que celles des autres cerfs et courent ordinairement au trot. Ils vivent de bourgeons d'arbres et d'herbes. Pour paître, ils sont obligés, à cause de la brièveté de leur cou, de se mettre à genoux ou d'écarter les jambes de devant. Le rut, pour cette, espèce, commence à la fin du mois d'août et dure tout le mois de septembre. Les femelles mettent bas depuis la mi mai jusqu'à la mi-juin ; la première fois, elles ne font qu'un seul petit, ensuite constamment deux et rarement trois. Les vieux élans per-

vulgar name, " pole-cat shrew."]
Inhabit temperate climates of both continents. P. 25.

Some individuals have white at the end of the tail, nose and feet, also like those of Catesby's (copied in the Encyclopædia) around the neck.

This species differs from the black variety of the *S. Capistratus* in its small size, the softness of its hair, & because its nose and ears are not regularly white. It is separated from the black variety of the Gray Squirrel by the shortness of its tail.   p. 178

HABIT. The moose live in small troops in swampy places. Their gait, which is commonly a trot, is much less active than that of other deer. They feed on the buds of trees and on herbs. When they attempt to eat from the ground, they are obliged, from the shortness of their neck, either to kneel or to separate their fore-legs. The rutting season commences with them about the end of August and continues during the month of September. The females bring forth from the middle of May, to the middle of June ; the first time they produce only one young one, afterwards two, rarely three. The old moose loose

dent leurs bois en janvier et février, et les jeunes en avril et en mai. Les premiers ont leur bois nouveau à la fin de juin, et les autres au mois d'août. Durée de la vie, quinze à vingt ans.

PATRIE. L'élan appelé *Elk*, *Elg*, *Elend*, *Ælg*, *Los*, *Loos*, etc., par les peuples du nord de l'ancien Continent, se trouve en Europe, depuis le 53e degré de latitude, dans une partie de la Prusse, de la Pologne, de la Suède ; en Finlande, en Russie, et surtout en Livonie et en Ingrie. En Asie il descend plus bas, depuis le 45e degré jusqu' au 51e, surtout en Tartarie.

En Amerique, ou il est nommé *mousou* par les Algonquins, *moose* ou *moose deer* par les Anglais, et *original* par les Français, on le rencontre depuis le 44e degré jusqu'au 53e, autour des grands lacs, &c. p. 430

(1.) Le Lièvre du Groenland ou *rekalek*, qui reste entièrement blanc, même en été, avec du noir au bout des oreilles, le jeune étant d'un gris-blanchâtre. Sa femelle met bas huit petits à la fois. La nourriture de cet animal se compose principalement des herbes tendres qui croissent le long des ruisseaux dans les gorges des montagnes du Groënland.

their horns in January and February, and the young in April and May. The first have their new horns by the end of June, and the others in the month of August. Duration of life, fifteen or twenty years.

COUNTRY. The Moose Deer called Elk, Elg, Œlg, Los, Loos, &c. by the northern inhabitants of the ancient continent, ranges in Europe from the fifty-third to the sixty-third degree of latitude through part of Prussia Poland, Sweden, Finland, Russia, and particularly in Livonia, and in *Jugrie*. In Asia it descends lower, from the forty-fifth to the fifty-first degree of latitude, particularly in Tartary.

In America, where it is named *Monsoll* by the Algonquins, *Moose* or *Moose deer* by the English, and *Original* by the French, it is met with in the more northern parts of the United States, and beyond the Great Lakes. p. 331-2.

NOTE.—Perhaps may be referred to this species also the Greenland hare, or Rekalek, which remains entirely white, even in summer, with black at the ends of the ears ; the young being whitish-gray ; the female bringing forth eight young at a time. The food of this animal consists principally of the tender herbs, which grow along the brooks on the slopes of the Greenland mountains. p. 196.

NATURAL SCIENCES IN AMERICA

An Arno Press Collection

Allen, J[oel] A[saph]. **The American Bisons, Living and Extinct.** 1876

Allen, Joel Asaph. **History of the North American Pinnipeds:** A Monograph of the Walruses, Sea-Lions, Sea-Bears and Seals of North America. 1880

American Natural History Studies: The Bairdian Period. 1974

American Ornithological Bibliography. 1974

Anker, Jean. **Bird Books and Bird Art.** 1938

Audubon, John James and John Bachman. **The Quadrupeds of North America.** Three vols. 1854

Baird, Spencer F[ullerton]. **Mammals of North America.** 1859

Baird, S[pencer] F[ullerton], T[homas] M. Brewer and R[obert] Ridgway. **A History of North American Birds:** Land Birds. Three vols., 1874

Baird, Spencer F[ullerton], John Cassin and George N. Lawrence. **The Birds of North America.** 1860. Two vols. in one.

Baird, S[pencer] F[ullerton], T[homas] M. Brewer, and R[obert] Ridgway. **The Water Birds of North America.** 1884. Two vols. in one.

Barton, Benjamin Smith. **Notes on the Animals of North America.** Edited, with an Introduction by Keir B. Sterling. 1792

Bendire, Charles [Emil]. **Life Histories of North American Birds** With Special Reference to Their Breeding Habits and Eggs. 1892/1895. Two vols. in one.

Bonaparte, Charles Lucian [Jules Laurent]. **American Ornithology:** Or The Natural History of Birds Inhabiting the United States, Not Given by Wilson. 1825/1828/1833. Four vols. in one.

Cameron, Jenks. **The Bureau of Biological Survey:** Its History, Activities, and Organization. 1929

Caton, John Dean. **The Antelope and Deer of America:** A Comprehensive Scientific Treatise Upon the Natural History, Including the Characteristics, Habits, Affinities, and Capacity for Domestication of the Antilocapra and Cervidae of North America. 1877

Contributions to American Systematics. 1974

Contributions to the Bibliographical Literature of American Mammals. 1974

Contributions to the History of American Natural History. 1974

Contributions to the History of American Ornithology. 1974

Cooper, J[ames] G[raham]. Ornithology. Volume I, Land Birds. 1870

Cope, E[dward] D[rinker]. The Origin of the Fittest: Essays on Evolution and The Primary Factors of Organic Evolution. 1887/1896. Two vols. in one.

Coues, Elliott. Birds of the Colorado Valley. 1878

Coues, Elliott. Birds of the Northwest. 1874

Coues, Elliott. Key To North American Birds. Two vols. 1903

Early Nineteenth-Century Studies and Surveys. 1974

Emmons, Ebenezer. American Geology: Containing a Statement of the Principles of the Science. 1855. Two vols. in one.

Fauna Americana. 1825-1826

Fisher, A[lbert] K[enrick]. The Hawks and Owls of the United States in Their Relation to Agriculture. 1893

Godman, John D. American Natural History: Part I — Mastology and Rambles of a Naturalist. 1826-28/1833. Three vols. in one.

Gregory, William King. Evolution Emerging: A Survey of Changing Patterns from Primeval Life to Man. Two vols. 1951

Hay, Oliver Perry. Bibliography and Catalogue of the Fossil Vertebrata of North America. 1902

Heilprin, Angelo. The Geographical and Geological Distribution of Animals. 1887

Hitchcock, Edward. A Report on the Sandstone of the Connecticut Valley, Especially Its Fossil Footmarks. 1858

Hubbs, Carl L., editor. Zoogeography. 1958

[Kessel, Edward L., editor]. A Century of Progress in the Natural Sciences: 1853-1953. 1955

Leidy, Joseph. The Extinct Mammalian Fauna of Dakota and Nebraska, Including an Account of Some Allied Forms from Other Localities, Together with a Synopsis of the Mammalian Remains of North America. 1869

Lyon, Marcus Ward, Jr. Mammals of Indiana. 1936

Matthew, W[illiam] D[iller]. Climate and Evolution. 1915

Mayr, Ernst, editor. The Species Problem. 1957

Mearns, Edgar Alexander. Mammals of the Mexican Boundary of the United States. Part I: Families Didelphiidae to Muridae. 1907